The Barrakee M

Other Titles by Arthur W. Upfield in ETT Imprint:

ARTHUR W. UPFIELD

The Barrakee Mystery

ETT IMPRINT, EXILE BAY

ETT IMPRINT & www.arthurupfield.com
PO Box R1906, Royal Exchange NSW 1225 Australia

First published 1929 by Hutchinson & Company

This edition published by ETT imprint 2016

Copyright William Upfield 2013

ISBN 978-1-925416-40-4

Chapter One

The Sundowner

WITH EYES fixed thoughtfully on the slow-moving muddy stream of the River Darling, William Clair lounged in the golden light of the setting sun. His frame was gaunt, his complexion burnt-umber, his eyes were blue and unflickering, his moustache drooping like that of a Chinese mandarin was jet-black, despite his fifty-eight years.

It was the beginning of March, and the river was low. The birds, perched on the up-thrusting snags, were taking their evening drink; the galah, the cockatoo, and the kookaburra mingling their screeches, chatterings, and maniacal laughter with the funeral caw-cawing of the sinister crows. Not a breath of wind stirred the light-reflecting leaves of the giant gums bordering the river. From gold the sunlight turned to crimson.

Just below Clair were moored three small boats. Behind him was the homestead of Barrakee Station, set amid the paradisaic oasis of cool green lawns edged by orange trees. A little down the river, above a deep hole at a bend, were the men's quarters, the kitchen garden, the engine that raised necessary water into the two great receiving tanks set upon thirty-foot staging. Further down was the huge corrugated-iron shearing-shed, adjoined by the shearers' quarters—all now empty. In the shearing-shed were Clair's swag and ration-bags.

Half a mile upstream the river took a sharp turn to Clair's left, and above the angle of the opposite bank a pillar of blue-gum smoke marked a camp-site. It was a camp of blacks, and interested the gaunt man mightily.

Beneath the gums the shadows darkened. The glory of the dying day laid over the surface of the river a cloth of crimson, patterned with shimmering silver rings where the small perch leapt for flies. The colour of the cloth dimmed magically to that of glinting steel. A kookaburra broke off his laughter and slept.

Clair waited, motionless, until the last glimmer of day had faded from the sky. Then, without noise, without haste, he slithered down the steep bank to where the boats were moored, pulled out the iron spike at the end of one of the mooring chains, softly coiled the chain in the bow, got in, and silently swung out the oars. The operation was so noiseless that a fox, drinking on the opposite side, never raised its head.

The "sundowner", for Clair at that time was carrying his swag with no intention of accepting work, sat facing the bow and propelled the boat forward by pushing at the oars. There was no suspicion of the sound of water being dug into by oars, nor was there any noise of moving oars in the row-locks. Boat and man slid upstream but a darker shadow in the gloom beneath the overhanging gums.

At the bend, half a mile above, a dozen ill-clad figures lounged about a small fire, not for warmth, but for the sake of spirit-defying light. Clair pushed on silently for a further two hundred yards, when he slanted across the stream and landed.

It is the law of New South Wales that no white man shall enter a camp of blacks. Of this Clair was not ignorant. Nor was he ignorant, being well read, that laws are made for men, and not men for laws.

Avoiding fallen branches and water gutters with the ease of a born bushman, he passed through the darkness to the camp, where he halted some twenty feet from the fire.

"Ahoy! Pontius Pilate!" he called.

Lolling figures about the fire sprang up, tense, frightened at the suddenness of the voice in the night.

"I want to speak to you, Pontius Pilate," called Clair.

A grizzled, thick-set aboriginal stared suspiciously in Clair's direction. He gave a low-spoken order, and three gins hastened to the seclusion of a bough-constructed humpy. Then, striking an attitude of indifference, Pontius Pilate said:

"You want-it talk me; come to fire."

When Clair entered the firelight the grizzled one and a youth of nineteen or twenty regarded him with unfriendly eyes. After a swift appraising glance, Clair sat on his heels before the fire and casually cut chips off a tobacco-plug for a smoke. The two aborigines watched him, and when he did not speak they edged close and squatted opposite the law-defying guest.

"Have a smoke?" said Clair, in a tone that held command. The elderly black caught the tossed plug, bit a piece out of it and handed it to his companion. The young man wore nothing but a pair of moleskin trousers; the elder nothing but a blue shirt.

"Only got one suit between you," observed Clair unsmilingly. "Well, I reckon you can't get sunburnt, so what's the odds? You fellers belong to this part?"

"We come up from Wilcannia las' week," came the literally chewed response. "Where you camped, boss?"

"Up river a bit. Is old Mokie down river, anyway?"

"Yaas—old Mokie, he married Sarah Wanting. You bin know Sarah?"

"I reckon so. Sarah must be getting old," Clair replied, though as a matter of fact he had no idea to which of the many Sarahs Pontius Pilate referred. Blacks marry and get divorced with a facility somewhat bewildering to the white mind. "I come down from Dunlop," he went on. "Ted Rogers breaking-in horses up there."

"He's still there?" was the young man's first speech.

"I think," said Clair dreamily, "that I said it."

The conversation was carried on disjointedly, punctuated by meditative smoking and tobacco-chewing. Then Clair put the question he had asked at countless camps in the course of many wandering years. No one present, not even the suspicious gossiping blacks, would have thought that his visit was solely for the purpose of asking this question:

"I knew an abo once, a terrible good horseman, feller called Prince Henry—no, not Prince Henry, some other

3

name—tall big feller, old feller now. You know an abo called Prince Henry?"

"No Prince Henry," demurred Pontius Pilate, the gravity of a great chief having settled over his ebony features. "You no mean King Henry?"

Not a muscle of Clair's face moved. Not a sign betrayed more than ordinary interest.

"Maybe he was King Henry," he said slowly. "Worked one time here at Barrakee, I think."

"That's him, boss," agreed the elderly black. "King Henry, Ned's father. This here is Ned—King Henry's son."

"Oh," drawled Clair, glancing from one to the other. "And what's your mother called, Ned?"

"Sarah Wanting."

"Humph! Sarah believes in change."

"Oh, but Sarah she leave old Mokie now King Henry come back," chimed in Pontius Pilate, pride of knowledge shining in his eyes.

"Ah!" The exclamation came like a sigh from the gaunt man. "Then your father isn't far away, Ned?"

"Nope. He come down from Nor' Queensland."

"What's he been doing up there? Thought he was a Darling abo."

"Dunno," interjected the elder, and then innocently contradicted himself. "Him bin do a get from white feller wanta killum. White feller him dead now."

"Oh! So the coast is clear at last, eh?" And then came Clair's momentous question:

"Where's King Henry now?"

"Him down Menindee. King Henry him bin come up alonga river with Sarah. Going to camp with us."

The puffs of tobacco-smoke came with unbroken regularity from the gaunt man's lips. The gleam of satisfaction, of triumph, was hidden by narrowed eyelids. After a moment's silence, abruptly he turned the conversation, and ten minutes later rose and left the camp.

4

Back at the boat, without sound, he unmoored it and stepped in. Without a splash, he pushed it across to the further tree-shadows, and, merely keeping it on its course, allowed the current to drift him gently by the camp, down to the station mooring-place.

He was at the open fireplace outside the shearing-shed half an hour later, drinking jet-black tea, and eating a slice of brownie. Between mouthfuls he hummed a tune—not a white man's tune, but the blood-stirring chant of some war-crazed tribe.

"Well, well, well!" he murmured. "My years of tracking have brought me in sight of the quarry at last. William, my lad, you must go first thing in the morning to the prosperous Mr Thornton, abase yourself before him, and ask for a job."

Chapter Two

The Sin of Silence

MRS THORNTON was a small woman whose fragility of figure was somewhat deceptive. Her age was forty-three, and, although it is not generally politic to state a woman's precise age, it has here to be done to prove that hardship, constant battling against odds, and self-denial, do not necessarily impair the bloom and vigour of youth. Vitality, both physical and mental, radiated from her plain yet delicately-moulded features.

On the morning following the visit of William Clair to the blacks' camp she sat sewing on the wide veranda of the Barrakee homestead. The weather was warm, Nature drowsed in the shade, and the only sound came from the big steam-engine operating the pumps.

Now and then Mrs Thornton glanced between the leaves of the morning glory creeper shading the veranda to observe a tall, blue-shirted man digging the earth above the roots of the orange-trees beyond the lawn. Which of the men it was she could not make out, and uncertainty made her irritable.

At the sound of a heavy iron triangle being beaten by the men's cook, announcing the morning lunch, the worker disappeared. For a moment the mistress of Barrakee allowed the sewing to fall to her lap, and a look of balked remembrance to cloud her brown eyes.

A moment later the house gong was struck, and the little woman went on with her task with a sigh. Came then the sound of ponderous steps on the veranda boards, and round an angle of the house there appeared, carrying a tray, an enormously fat aboriginal woman. Like a tank going into action the gin rolled towards Mrs Thornton, near whom she placed the tray of tea-things on a small table.

Mrs Thornton gazed up at the beaming face with disapproving eyes. Without an answering smile she noted the woman's flame-coloured cotton blouse, some six times wider at the waist than at the neck, then at the dark blue print skirt, and finally at the bare flat feet. At first the feet were stolid, immobile. Then at the continued steady gaze the toes began to twitch, and at last under the pitiless silent stare one foot began lightly to rub the other.

When Mrs Thornton again looked up, the gin's eyes were rolling in their sockets, whilst the beaming smile had vanished.

"Martha, where are your slippers?" asked her mistress severely.

"Missy, I dunno," Martha gasped. "Them slippers got bushed."

"For twenty years, Martha, have I tried to encase your feet in footwear," Mrs Thornton said softly, but with a peculiar grimness of tone. "I have bought you boots, shoes and slippers. I shall be very angry with you, Martha, if you do not at once find your slippers and put them on. If they are bushed, go and track them."

"Suttinly, missy. Me track um to hell," came the solemn assurance. Then, bending over her mistress with surprising quickness in one of her avoirdupois, she added in a thrilling whisper:

"King Henry! He come back to Barrakee. You 'member King Henry?"

For fully thirty seconds brown eyes bored into black without a blink. The white woman was about to say something when the sound of a wicket-gate being closed announced the approach of her husband. The gin straightened herself and rumbled back to her kitchen.

Almost subconsciously the mistress of Barrakee heard her husband banteringly reprove Martha for the nakedness of her understandings, heard the woman's mumbled excuses, and with an effort of will regained her composure. She was pouring tea when Mr Thornton seated himself beside her.

"Martha lost her shoes again?" he asked with a soft chuckle.

He was a big man, about fifty years of age. Clean-shaven, his features, burned almost brown, denoted the outdoor man and dweller under a sub-tropical sun. He had clear, deep-grey, observant eyes.

"Wasn't it Napoleon who, after restoring order in France, tried all he could to make her one of the Great Powers, if not the greatest?" she asked, with apparent irrelevance.

"I believe it was," agreed the squatter, accepting tea and cake.

"Wasn't it his ambition, when he had brought chaos to order, to maintain order by a European peace?"

"Well, what of it?" counter-queried Mr Thornton, reminded of his wife's hero-worship of the great soldier of France.

"Only, that every time he enforced peace on the continent of Europe, to allow his governmental machine to run smoothly, it was constantly being put out of action by the grit of a fresh coalition formed by England. England was his bugbear. Martha's naked feet are my bugbear."

"Well, well, we must remember that Martha once was a semi-wild thing," Thornton urged indulgently. "Doesn't it ever surprise you that Martha, who has been with us for twenty years, has never wanted to return to her tribe?"

"It does sometimes."

"It's the one exception to the rule," he said. "And that's that. I suppose you're now counting the hours?"

"I am. Ralph's train reaches Bourke at eleven, doesn't it?"

"Yes. They should be here about three."

"I quite expect he will have grown enormously," she said with wistful eyes.

"He will certainly be a man. Nineteen years old yesterday. Even five months makes a big difference to a lad of that age."

For a while they were silent. Having finished his morning tea, the man lit a cigarette and the woman pensively picked up her sewing. Her boy was coming home from college, and she ached for the feel of his strong arms around her. To her it had been a sacrifice to agree to his spending the last Christmas vacation with friends in New Zealand. She had not seen the boy, whom she passionately loved, for five long months, and was as tremulous as a woman standing on a jetty watching the arrival of her sailor husband's ship.

"More than once it's occurred to me," drawled her life-partner, "that as Ralph is almost of age it would be a wise thing to tell him the truth regarding his birth."

"No, John ... No!"

And before he started the fight Thornton knew he had lost it, seeing the iron will reflected in his wife's face. That Mrs Thornton was strong-willed, a woman who invariably had her own way, he had known long before marriage. It was that trait of dominance in her character which had attracted him. He had been comparatively poor when the need of a partner was felt first; and, like a wise man, knowing the trials and hardships of the Australian bush, he did not select a weak, clinging woman, doubtless an ornament to a city drawing-room. His choice was reflected by his poise as well as his bank balance.

"But what we have to remember, Ann, is that Ralph one day may find out," he argued. "Would it not be better for us to tell him gently, than for someone to tell him roughly that he is not your son, but the son of a woman who was our cook?"

"I see neither the reason nor the necessity," she said, her eyes on the darting needle. "Mary, his mother, is dead. The doctor who brought him into the world is dead. Don't you remember how ill I was when Ralph was born, ill and nearly mad with grief because my baby died? In her last moments Mary gave him to me. She saw me take the baby with a cry of joy, and cover it with hungry kisses. And when Mary died she was smiling."

"But—"

"No, no, John. Don't argue," she pleaded. "I made him mine, and mine he must be always. If he knows I am not his real mother there will be a difference, there will arise a barrier between him and me, no matter how we try to keep it down."

The woman's passionate desire for a baby, and subsequently her sublime love for another woman's child, had always been a matter of wonder to John Thornton. He, no less than his wife, had been deeply grieved at the death of his day-old heir, and he, with her, had opened his heart to the adopted boy. But he was a man who hated secrets, or subterfuge. His mind would have been relieved of the one burden in his life had his wife agreed to their adopted son being informed of his real parentage. Still he struggled:

"Ralph is too fine a lad to allow the knowledge to make any difference," he said. "We know that Mary would not name her betrayer to us, but the man, likely enough, is alive and knows our secret. We can never be safe from him. He may come forward any day, probably try to blackmail us. If such a thing should happen, we should be obliged to tell Ralph, and the boy would then be perfectly justified in blaming us for our silence."

"Mary's betrayer would have come forward long ago if he intended to get money by blackmail," she countered.

"But the possibility remains. Again, one day Ralph will marry. It might be Kate, or Sir Walter Thorley's daughter. Think of the recriminations that would occur then. Can't you see that absolute frankness now would be better for the lad, and better for us?"

"The past lies buried twenty years deep, John. Ralph is safe. I made him my baby. Do not ask me to put him from me."

The man gave the sigh of the vanquished. Rising to his feet, he said:

"All right! Have it your own way. I hope it may be for the best."

"I am sure it will, John," she murmured. And then, by way of final dismissal of the subject, she changed it. "Who is it working among the orange-trees? Is he a new hand?"

The squatter paused in his walk along the veranda to say:

"Yes. I put him on this morning. I thought I knew him at first, but he says he has been all his life in Queensland. He answers to the name of William Clair."

Mrs Thornton leaned back in her chair, her eyes closed as though relieved from great strain. And about her firm mouth was the ghost of a smile.

Chapter Three

The Homecoming

THE HOMESTEAD of Barrakee Station was set, white-walled and red-roofed, in an oasis of brilliant green lawns and orange groves, the whole surrounded by a thick windbreak of ten-foot waving bamboo. The bottom extremity of the gardens was separated from the river by a dry billabong, some fifty-odd yards in width.

At that point of the river were moored the station boats used chiefly to transport travellers to the farther side, as well as to provide anyone belonging to the station with recreation on the river.

To the south of the homestead, and close to it, were the offices, the barracks used by the bookkeeper and the jacke-roos, the store, and the shops. Facing the offices and divided from them by a large clear space were the tennis-courts and the croquet-lawn.

The essential factor, which made Barrakee homestead one of the show places in the western division of New South Wales, was the limitless supply of water from the river. Mrs Thornton ruled the homestead; her husband reigned over the vast run, the thirty or forty employees, and the fifty to sixty thousand sheep. Neither interfered, by a single suggestion, in the domain of the other. Both were united in the one purpose of leaving Ralph Thornton a great inheritance.

At a quarter past three, one of the junior hands, who had been stationed on the staging supporting the great receiving tanks, observed through field-glasses the approach of the Barrakee high-powered car. He signalled its appearance by firing a shotgun.

Thornton and his wife were outside the garden gates which opened to the clear ground in front of the offices to receive their son. The car drew up close by with a noiseless application of brakes, and from it sprang a dark handsome boy dressed in grey tweed of most fashionable cut. He was followed more circumspectly by a young woman dressed in white.

"Mother!" ejaculated Ralph Thornton, clasping the small mistress of the homestead in his arms.

"Ralph! Oh, Ralph, I am glad you are here," she said, looking up with proud, wistful eyes.

For a moment he held her, more like a lover than a son and, during that moment, it flashed into her mind that if he had known his maternal parentage he would not have held her thus. How glad she was that she had been firm in her insistence that the knowledge must be withheld.

"You must be tired, Katie," the squatter said gently to the girl. "It's been a hot day."

"Has it, Uncle?" Her voice was sweetly allied to her fresh beauty. "I've been too excited meeting Ralph to notice it. Don't you think he has grown?"

"I haven't had much chance to notice anything yet," he replied, with twinkling eyes.

"Notice now, Dad," the young man commanded, his face flushed with happiness, reaching for his foster-father's hand. "I declare, both you and the Little Lady look younger than ever. And as for Kate—she just takes a fellow's breath away!" Then, seeing the bookkeeper hovering behind, he exclaimed, going to him: "Hallo, Mortimore, how are you?"

"I do not look nor do I feel any younger, Mr Ralph," the bookkeeper countered. "When I first saw you, ten years ago, you were make-believing you were playing the piano on the office typewriter. And now! It seems but yesterday."

"That is all it is, too. You are mistaken about the ten years," the young man said, with a happy smile. Then, returning to his mother, he took her on his right arm and caught the squatter on his left, the last, in turn attaching Kate Flinders; and so aligned, the reunited family slowly returned to the house.

From Brewarrina to Wentworth and from Ivanhoe to Tibooburra the two women of Barrakee were famous. From the squatter and his manager to the boundary-rider and the sundowner, Mrs Thornton was known as the "Little Lady". Her unvarying kindness to all travellers, from swagman to Governor-General, was a by-word. The example on which she patterned herself was Napoleon Bonaparte. Her gifts were bestowed with discretion, and her judgements were scrupulously just, but always tempered with mercy.

Katherine Flinders, her orphan niece, was about Ralph's age. Her lithe, graceful figure was the admiration of all, and once seen on a horse was a picture to live in memory. The easiest way to purchase a ticket to the nearest hospital was to speak slightingly of either—together referred to as the "Women of Barrakee".

A combined light lunch and afternoon tea was set out on the broad veranda, where they found Martha applying the final touches. Her great face was irradiated, though not beautified, by a gigantic smile. She stood beside the table while the small party mounted the veranda steps, her figure encased by a voluminous blue dressing-gown belted at the waist by a leather strap stolen from a bridle. Her poor feet were concealed by highly polished elastic-sided brown riding-boots. Truly on this occasion she was superb.

The whites of her eyes were conspicuous. The wide grin of genuine welcome revealed many gaps in the yellowing teeth. Her greying hair was scanty. She was nearly overcome with excitement.

"Well, Martha! Not dead yet?" greeted Ralph gravely, holding out his hand. She took it in her left, her right being pressed to her vast bosom.

"Oh, Misther Ralph!" she articulated with difficulty, "Poor Martha no die till she look on you once more."

"That's right," he said with a friendly smile. "I shall be very much annoyed," he added, "if you die now."

The squatter and his wife were content with a cup of tea, whilst their "children" ate a long-delayed lunch. Anticipating the boy's lightest wish, the Little Lady hovered at his side, her eyes sparkling with happiness, her small finely-moulded features flushed. She and her husband were content to listen to his description of the holiday spent in New Zealand and of his last term at college.

As a collegiate product he was perfect. His speech and manners were without reproach. There was, however, inherent in him a grace of movement which no school or university could have given him. Of medium height and weight, he sat his chair with the ease of one born on the back of a horse. His dark, almost beautiful face was animated by a keen and receptive mind; the fervid enthusiasm of the mystic rather than the unveiled frankness of the practically-minded man was reflected from his eyes.

He was to both his adopted parents a revelation. Six months previously he had left them, still a college boy, to return to college. He had come back to them a man, frankly adult. The youthful boastfulness had given place to grave self-assurance—too grave, perhaps, in one still in the years of youth. Never once did he mention football, cricket, or rowing, his previous enthusiasms. If superficial, his knowledge of politics, of the arts, and of the lives of the great, was extensive. The heart of the Little Lady overflowed with pride and exultation: her husband was admittedly astonished by the lad's mental and physical growth in six short months.

"Well, Dad, and now that I've finished with college, what do you want me to do?" he asked suddenly.

"Why, dear, you must know what we want you to do, surely?" interposed Mrs Thornton.

"I was thinking," the squatter remarked quietly, "that your education and your address indicate the Church."

The Little Lady's eyes widened with amazement. The young man's face clouded. Kate alone saw the suppressed twinkle in her uncle's eyes.

"Would you like to be a parson, Ralph?" she inquired, with a laugh.

"Surely, Dad, you cannot mean what you say?"

"What do you want to do?" he asked kindly. "The choice is yours. Whatever path through life you choose, Law, the Church, the Services, or any of the professions—your mother and I will accept."

The young man's sigh of relief was audible.

"I thought you meant that about the Church," he said slowly. "I would rather—and I mean no reflection on the Church—I would rather carry my swag up and down the Darling all my life than be a bishop. I would rather be a boundary-rider than an army general, or a bullock-driver than an Under-Secretary. If there is one thing I've learned in this last half-year, it is that I cannot be happy away from Barrakee. Down in the city I feel like a caged bird, or an old sailor living out his last days away from the sea. I want to stay here with you three. I want to learn to be a pastoralist, to breed better sheep and grow finer wool. I hope you approve?"

"Oh, Ralph, dear, of course we approve!" declared Mrs Thornton, leaning towards him with shining countenance. "I should have been heartbroken had you chosen otherwise."

Chapter Four

Dugdale Goes Fishing

FRANK DUGDALE, not quite twenty-eight years of age, held the position of sub-overseer on Barrakee Station. Ten years before he had found himself almost penniless and practically without friends. He had no recollection of his mother, and when, on the verge of bankruptcy, his father killed himself, the loss left him dazed and helpless.

Mr Dugdale senior was the sole representative of Dugdale & Co., Wool Brokers and General Station Agents, and at the time of the crash the son was about to enter the firm. From their schooldays his father and Thornton had been friends, and, whilst lamenting the fact that his friend failed to apply to him for financial assistance, the squatter had offered the youth the opportunities of a jackeroo.

The offer was eagerly accepted. Dugdale came to Barrakee and resided with the bookkeeper in the barracks. In ten years he had proved his worth. At the time that Ralph Thornton left college Dugdale was renowned for his horsemanship, his knowledge of wool, and his handling of sheep.

Of average height and build, his complexion was fair and the colour of his eyes hazel. Ralph and Kate were playing tennis when Dugdale passed, smoking his pipe and in his hand a fishing-line. For a moment he watched the flying figures in the golden light of the setting sun, and his pulse leapt as it never failed to do when he beheld Kate Flinders.

"Hallo, Dug! Are you going fishing?" asked the flushed girl, energetically gathering the balls to serve.

"No—oh no!" he drawled, with a smile. "I am going kite-flying."

"Now, now, Dug! No sarcasm, please," she reproved, half-mockingly.

Pausing in his walk he faced her, holding out the line for inspection, saying:

"I cannot tell a lie, as Shakespeare remarked to Stephen. Here is the kite-line."

"Quite so," she observed sweetly. "But you should conceal the spinner. Also your quotation is hideously mixed. It was Washington who boasted he never told a fib."

"And Stephen lived a few centuries before Shakespeare," Ralph contributed.

"Did he?" replied Dugdale innocently. "I fear my education is fading out. And what year did the lamented Stephen arrive upon the throne?"

"In the year eleven hundred."

"BC or AD?"

"AD, of course, you ass."

"Then I am constrained to marvel at your poor arguments. I distinctly said—"

"Goodbye, Dug, and good luck! Service!" cried Kate joyously. She was not sure of herself regarding Frank Dugdale. He said nice things, quaint and unexpected things. He was efficient, neat, and self-assured, but ...

Reaching the river-bank, he descended to the boats, and just then the sun faded. This being unexpected for another half-hour caused him to look westward, when he saw a dense bank of clouds behind which the sun had disappeared. Selecting the lightest of the boats, he pulled out into the stream, proceeding to attach the shining spoon-spinner to the line, and then, pulling slowly again, he allowed it to run out over the stern. His end of the line he fastened to the top of the springer-stick lashed to the side of the boat, so that when a fish "struck" the "springer" would hold it without the line snapping. The springer took the place of a second fisherman.

The line set, Dugdale slowly pulled up the sluggish stream,

keeping to one side when the absence of snags allowed, pulling out and round the snags when he reached them.

Although the evening was brilliant the air was still and humid. The softest bird-cry, the faintest splash of a fish, was an accentuated sound. When a kookaburra chuckled, the devilish mockery in its voice struck upon the heart and mind of the fisherman as a portent.

Now, for several years, Dugdale had loved Kate Flinders. It was the white passion of pure love which seeks not possession but reciprocity, the acme of love which strives to keep the adored object on a pedestal; not to reach upward to bring it down.

Dugdale regarded the fulfilment of his love as hopeless. He knew himself a penniless nobody, the son of a bankrupt suicide. The highest point to which he could rise in the pastoral industry was a station managership. To attain such a position would be the result of influence far more than of ability. There was no certainty in that dream. It was more probable that he might obtain an overseership; but he had decided that he could never ask Kate Flinders to accept an overseer for husband.

Whilst the Thorntons always treated him as an equal, he realized that his position, social or financial, would never reach theirs. There was, however, one way in which his dreams could be realized, and that was to be lucky enough to win a prize in the great New South Wales Land Lottery.

If he were sufficiently lucky to win one of the prizes—and to be so he would have to be lucky enough to draw a placed horse in a lottery—he would possess an excellent foundation on which to build, with his knowledge of sheep and wool, a moderate fortune in a few years. About this, as about the managership, was no certainty.

He had reached the bend at which Pontius Pilate and his people were camped. His boat was well over the hole gouged out by countless floods, but the spoon bait, many yards astern, was at the edge of the hole when the great cod struck.

The spring-stick bent over and down to the water. Leaving the oars, he jumped for the line, taut as a wire. The boat began to move stern-first, drawn by the fish, and Dugdale waited tensely for the moment when the fish would turn and give him the chance to gain line with which to play it.

The boat was travelling faster than when he had been pulling. Rigid with excitement, oblivious to the excited cries of the blacks on the bank, Dugdale waited. Thirty seconds after the fish had struck it turned, and dashed up-stream beneath the boat.

He gained a dozen yards of line before the fish reached the shortened length of its tether, and then began a thrilling fight. The dusk of day fell and deepened the shadows beneath the gums. The cloud bank, racing from the west, was at the zenith. It was almost dark before the fish gave up and sulked. Slowly he hauled it to the boat, a weight listless and lifeless, as though he had caught a bag of shingle.

That it was a huge fish he knew by its dead weight. Slowly he brought it alongside. The boat unaccountably rocked. For a moment he caught the outline of the broad green back, and then searched aimlessly with a foot for the crooked lifting-stick.

"Let me, boss," someone said. "Bring him back alongside. Aye—a little more."

Not daring to remove his gaze from the sulking cod, at any time likely to renew the fight, Dugdale saw a powerful black arm come into his vision holding the short stick crooked like a gaff.

The arm and stick suddenly moved with lightning swiftness. The small end of the gaff slid up into the gills, there was a heave that nearly upset the boat, and the great fish—which eventually scaled at forty-one pounds odd ounces—lay shimmering greenly in the gloom.

From the fish Frank Dugdale looked up at his timely helper, and beheld the very finest specimen of an aboriginal he had ever seen. The man was naked but for a pair of khaki shorts. The width of his chest, the narrowness of his hips, his powerful legs and arms now glistening with water, were magnificent. The colour of his skin was ebony-black, the colour of his thick curly hair snow-white.

He was old—Dugdale thought him to be near sixty—but the vices of white civilization had not touched him. When he spoke his accent was Australian. In his voice there was no trace of the tribe:

"That's a bonzer fish," he said. "I thought by the way he fought that he was a walloper and that you'd want a hand to land him."

"Thanks for your help. I don't think I would have landed him without it," the fisherman conceded. "If you care to send someone along to the station in the morning for a part of it, you may."

"Goodo! I'll send my son, Ned. Any idea what the time is?" he asked.

"Must be about half past eight."

"Thanks. I'll get going. I got a meet on."

And, without a splash, the aboriginal dived into the river, and disappeared in the gloom, now so profound that Dugdale only guessed he swam to the station side of the river.

The remainder of the tribe having gone back to their camp-fire, Dugdale disentangled the line and slowly wound it on the small length of board.

The boat was then in the gentle back-current of the bend, being imperceptibly taken up-river. Some few minutes were occupied in removing the spoon-spinner from the line: a few more in pensively cutting chips of tobacco for his pipe. Then, with it satisfactorily alight, he manned the sculls and slowly pushed himself forward into the main stream, and let himself drift down to the homestead.

He was a hundred yards from the landing-place when the first drop of rain, splashing the water near him, coincided with the sound of a thin whine abruptly culminating in a dull report similar to that made by a small boy hitting a paling with a cane.

It was a sound the like of which Dugdale had never before heard. It made him curious, but by no means alarmed. Without hurry he approached the landing-place, got out, and moored the boat.

It was while driving in the iron peg to fasten the boat that he was astonished to hear above him the gasp of human agony; and now, alarmed, he straightened up to listen further. There came a low thud; then silence.

For a moment he was paralysed, but only for a moment. In the pitchy darkness he clambered up the steep bank. At the summit the deluge fell on him. Again he listened. In the distance, towards the bottom fence of the garden, a dry stick cracked with a sound like a pistol-shot.

Immediately Dugdale stood there listening. Lightning flickered far away, but by its reflection he saw the narrow embankment on which he stood, he saw the dry billabong between it and the garden, and he saw dimly the white-clad figure of a woman before the garden gate.

Thunder rumbled in the distance. Slowly he went down into the billabong, feeling his way in the utter darkness. The lightning came again, flickering and brilliant. His gaze, directed on the garden gate, saw no white-clad figure. But the gate gave him direction in the darkness.

Still slowly he moved towards it. So dark was it that he almost ran into a gum-tree, his hands alone saving him from a nasty collision. Rounding the bole, he again took direction, and had just left when a glare of bluish light almost blinded him, and the instant following, thunder dazed him.

But, revealed by the flash, he saw right at his feet the form of the aboriginal who a short while before had helped him to land the great fish.

Calm suddenly settled upon the world and upon his mind as well. Producing a match-box, he struck a light and bent low. The whites of the staring eyes, fixed and glassy in the light of the match, and the terrible wound at the crown of the man's head, left no room for doubt that the man was dead.

Yet the appalling discovery was not so acutely registered on Frank Dugdale's brain as was the vision of a white-clad figure dimly seen at the garden gate not thirty yards distant.

Chapter Five

A Wet Night

FROM THE river to the west boundary of Barrakee Station was about eighty-three miles. The area that comprised the run was roughly oblong in shape.

For administrative purposes it was divided into two un-equal portions, the longer and western division being gover-ned by George Watts, the overseer, who resided at the outstation at Thurlow Lake. The river end of the run was managed by the sub-overseer, Frank Dugdale.

But while Thornton overseered Frank Dugdale, he rarely instructed George Watts, who deserved, and had, his em-ployer's implicit faith. Every evening at eight the squatter repaired to his office, where he telephoned in turn to each of the boundary-riders in his division, obtaining their reports and outlining the work for the succeeding day. Even on Sat-urdays and days preceding holidays he rang up at the same time; for these men lived alone in their huts, and in the event of no reply being received to his ring it could be assumed that some accident had happened and that the man lay injured out in the bush. In the squatter's time it had been necessary to send out search-parties on three occasions.

When he had finished with his riders, he habitually rang up Thurlow Lake to discuss with the overseer the conditions of the stock and kindred topics, and advise on, or sanction, any matter that might be submitted to him.

He was in high fettle because George Watts had reported steady rain when communicated with on the evening Dugdale caught the forty-one-pound cod. And, since no rain had fallen for nine months, a good rain at this time meant green feed for the coming lambs, as well as an abundance of surface water, which would prevent heavy ewes having to travel miles to the wells to drink and back again to feed.

Whilst he still talked to the overseer, the rain reached the river, pouring in a continuous roar on the office roof of corrugated iron. From the telephone he turned to the task of writing several personal letters. He was so engaged when the door opened, and the dripping sub-overseer almost bounded in.

"Good rain, Dug, eh?" Mr Thornton said cheerfully.

He could not distinctly see Dugdale's face until the latter entered the circle of light cast by the electric bulb over the desk. When he did observe the unusual expression on his subordinate's face, he added: "What's gone wrong?"

Dugdale recounted the landing of the fish, with the help of the strange black fellow, his return to the mooring-place, what he heard or fancied he heard, and his discovery of the dead man.

"Are you sure the man's dead?" pressed Thornton.

"Quite."

"We'll go and examine him. Better get an overcoat."

"Not for me. I can't get wetter than I am."

"Well, I am not going to get wet for all the dead abos in the Commonwealth," announced Thornton. "Wait till I get a waterproof and a torch."

He was back in a minute, and together, with the brilliant circle of the torch lighting them, they made their way past the tennis-court and down into the billabong to where the corpse lay.

A first glance settled the question of death.

"The rain coming just now will make things difficult for the police, Dug," remarked Mr Thornton gravely. "Already most of the tracks have been washed out. But from those that are left it is evident that there was a struggle. Even those tracks will be gone by morning."

"It is a terrible thing," Dugdale said, and thankfulness filled his heart that the rain had come.

"It is. But we can do nothing for him. Go along to the men's quarters and ask some of them to come and carry the body to the carpenter's shop. Lay it on one of the benches and cover it. Think you can feel your way in this damned darkness?"

"Yes, I believe so. But stay a minute with your light on till I get to the pumping-engine, will you?"

"All right."

Guided by the ray from the squatter's torch, Dugdale at last reached the engine, where the going became easy, since he was then on a beaten path. He shouted that he was all right; and Thornton, satisfied that his sub was beyond danger of slipping down the now dangerously greasy bank of the river, made his way back to his office.

There he telephoned to the police at Wilcannia.

"Good evening, Sergeant," he said, when the senior officer answered his call. "Great rain we're having."

"What! Raining up your way?" ejaculated the gruff-voiced sergeant. "Quite fine here, Mr Thornton."

"I am sorry to hear that. I was hoping it was a general rain. Must be only a local storm. In any case, we have had a murder."

"Excuse me! A what?"

"A m-u-r-d-e-r," Thornton spelled slowly.

"Oh, is that all?"

"Isn't it enough for you? I'm not joking."

"You're not? When did it happen? How did it happen?" came the rapid and now seriously-asked questions.

The squatter answered them in sequence, and reported that he had ordered the body to be removed to the carpenter's shop.

"I don't think there's anything more for me to do, is there?" he inquired.

"No, I think not," agreed the policeman, adding: "I'll ring up later to find out if it is still raining your way. If it is, I'll be obliged to ride a horse. I've got so used to a motor that I don't fancy sixty miles on horseback. Damn the rain!"

"Now, now!" Mr Thornton reproved. "Remember that I'm a Justice of the Peace."

"Sorry, Mr Thornton," the sergeant chuckled. "But why the devil couldn't the black get himself murdered some night that was fine?"

"I couldn't say. Ask him when you get here tomorrow." And, chuckling, the station-owner rang off—to ring up George Watts and transmit an item of news to news-hungry people.

Later, Frank Dugdale entered. "We shifted the body," he reported.

"Good!" The squatter nodded to a vacant chair. "It would be as well," he said, "as you are—or will be—the most important witness, for me to take down in writing the incidents which led to your discovery. Tell it slowly, and try to miss nothing, Dug."

Frank Dugdale retold his story of the significant sounds he had heard when in the boat and when mooring it. When he had finished, Thornton leaned back in his chair, selected a cigarette, and pushed the box across the desk.

"It seems," he said thoughtfully, "that the killing was just at the time you were mooring the boat."

"Yes. It's my belief that the sickening thud I heard was the striking of the blow."

"You saw nothing?"

The two were looking straight at each other. Dugdale said, without hesitation:

"I saw nothing, nor did I see anyone."

"It is surprising that the murderer could have got away in the time. What space of time do you think it was between the sound of that blow and the moment you saw the corpse in the lightning?"

Dugdale pondered for a moment or two. He felt elated at having told one of the few lies in his life. His gaze, however, was centred on the brass inkstand.

"Difficult to estimate," he said slowly. "It might have been only a minute, or it might have been three minutes. Certainly not more than three."

"Humph!" The older man added something to the written details. "The police-sergeant wanted to know why the black couldn't get himself murdered on a fine night. I would like to know, too, why that black selected my station, and close to my homestead, to get himself murdered. It will cause a lot of inconvenience. It's one of my unlucky days. Even the rain is stopping."

Chapter Six

The Inquiry

"Now, MR THORNTON, after that very excellent lunch we will examine the men." The khaki-breeched, blue-tunicked sergeant of the New South Wales Mounted Police paused with the squatter outside the office. Near by, in waiting, was a group of seven men, while on the barracks veranda stood Dugdale, Ralph, and a jackeroo named Edwin Black.

The sergeant was conducted to the office, where the two men seated themselves on the far side of the wide desk. The uniformed man filled his pipe, and, seeing that he did not intend to open his examination at once, Thornton took a cigarette, saying meanwhile:

"Thought you'd want to examine the scene of the murder first."

"I might have done, had the rain not fallen last night and wiped out tracks," the dapper, grey-moustached official rejoined. "As it is, we will start to get the story ship-shape, beginning with you."

"With me!"

"With you."

"What do I know about it?"

The sergeant smiled. "Don't know yet. I'll soon find out. What time did Dugdale tell you of his discovery?"

"At nineteen minutes to nine," was the unhesitating answer.

"You are sure of the time?"

"Positive."

"What sort of condition was Dugdale in?"

"He was drenched to the skin and, I think, a little upset."

"Yes, yes. Of course. But was he out of breath? Were his clothes disarranged, torn?"

"No, to both questions."

"Very good. Now, how many men do you employ here?"

"There are seven at present working about the homestead or riding the near paddocks."

"Is this the list of their names?"

"Yes. Added to it are the inmates of the barracks and the name of my son."

"Then I think we will first see Dugdale."

"Call Dug, Mortimore, please," the squatter said to his bookkeeper.

When the sub-overseer appeared the sergeant appraised him with a fixed stare, motioning with his hand to a vacant chair.

"I am told that you found the body of an aboriginal last night between the garden and the river," he said in his most official manner. "You made the discovery on your return from a fishing expedition. Tell me just what happened from the moment you entered the boat to go fishing. Take your time, and miss nothing."

When Dugdale paused at the end of his narrative, he was asked:

"Do you know the native?"

"No, I have never seen him before," Dugdale replied quietly.

"You say that as you were nearing the bank on your return you heard a peculiar whining sound that ended in a sharp report. Why a peculiar sound?"

"Because never before had I heard such a sound, unless it reminded me of the whirr of ducks flying close overhead."

"Ah! That's something." For a moment the interrogator gazed pensively out of the window. Then:

"After the sound, when you were ashore and mooring the boat, you heard someone gasp for breath. Was that gasping sound caused by a man being out of breath from struggling?"

"I think not," the sub replied slowly. "It was like that of a man who had dived deep into water and, having been down some time, filled his lungs with air on reaching the surface."

"And you saw no one?"

"It was dark."

"I know that. But did the lightning reveal anyone?"

"No."

"Sure?" suddenly barked the sergeant, for his penetrating eyes observed a slight flush about Dugdale's cheekbones.

"Quite sure."

"Very well. That will do for the present. Send Mr Ralph Thornton in, please."

When Ralph entered the office the sergeant was writing on a slip of paper. Pushing it across to the squatter, he nodded affably to Ralph to be seated. On the slip of paper which Thornton read was the sentence:

"The lightning revealed someone to Dugdale."

"How did you put in the evening last night, Mr Ralph?" the young man was asked in a much kinder spirit.

"I played cribbage with Black in the barracks after dinner."

"What time did you start playing? Any idea?"

"A little after eight, I think. We played till ten o'clock."

"That lets you out. Ask Mr Black to step in for a moment, please."

Edwin Black corroborated Ralph's statement, and in turn sent in Johnston, the carpenter. Johnston was not asked to be seated.

"Where were you, Johnston, between the hours of seven and nine o'clock last night?" asked the sergeant, resuming his official poise.

"In the men's hut."

"Doing what?"

"Reading a blood about a bloke wot arsenicked his three wives."

"Oh! You mean you were reading a novel?"

"Something like that," Johnston, tall, angular, and red-haired replied. "In my young days we called 'em 'blood and thunders'. I remember—"

"Precisely. Who was in the hut with you at the time you were reading this blood?"

"Bob Smiles, Bert Simmonds, and Jack O'Grady."

"That's four of you. Where were the others—Clair, McIntosh, and Fred Blair?"

"How the devil do I know?"

"Now, now! Were those three absent between half past eight and nine o'clock?"

"Look here, Sergeant! I'll answer any question about me," murmured the carpenter, with studied calmness.

"All right, Johnston," came the unruffled dismissal. "Send in Bob Smiles."

Smiles, Simmonds, and O'Grady briefly corroborated Johnston's replies, and at last William Clair came in. He wore a six-day growth of whiskers.

"I don't know you, Clair. Where do you come from?" was the first question put to the gaunt man.

"Can't say as I come from anywhere," Clair replied in a hoarse voice.

"Got a sore throat?"

"I have," Clair said calmly. "I wish you had it instead of me."

"I don't. Where is your home address?"

"I haven't no address. I've been carrying my swag most of my life. The last place I worked on was Humpy-Humpy Station, out of Winton, Queensland, in nineteen-twenty."

"Right. Now how did you spend last evening?"

"I was away down the river most of the time setting half a dozen dog-traps," Clair replied.

"Must have got wet."

"If I hadn't, I wouldn't have got this blasted cold."

"You're unlucky. When did you start out on your trap-setting?"

"About sundown."

"And you got home?"

"Just after they had lugged the corpse up here to the carpenter's shop."

"All right, Clair. Send in McIntosh."

To the sergeant's questions, McIntosh, a youth of eighteen, admitted that he was "courting" the housemaid, and that they had sheltered in the shearing-shed during the rain.

Blair, the last man, then entered.

He was a little wiry man, under five foot six inches, a man more than fifty years old, but with the spring and suppleness of a youth. A blistered complexion accentuated the greyness of his hair and the goatee beard that jutted forth from his chin.

He was employed as bullock-driver. To the people of Wilcannia he was known as the fierce little man whom it required the combined energies of the entire police force to put into the lock-up. This occurred every time Blair visited Wilcannia, which was every quarter.

Now, Sergeant Knowles was a pearl among policemen in that he possessed a keen sense of humour. He never bore Blair any malice for sundry bruises received whilst helping his subordinates to lock him up. He had for Blair a profound admiration, owing to his courage and fighting qualities, drunk or sober. With perfect gravity, he said:

"Is your name Frederick Blair?"

Blair, knowing this inquisition had nothing to do with his employer, and wishing to make sure that the sergeant should not think he was nervous in any way, seated himself in the vacant chair with studied insolence, elegantly crossed his legs, and as elegantly placed his thumbs in the arm-holes of his much-greased waistcoat.

"Is my name Frederick Blair?" he remarked, to the ceiling. "Now I wonder!"

"I am asking you," the sergeant said gently.

"How many demons 'ave you got with you?" Blair inquired, with equal gentleness.

"Trooper Dowling is outside."

"Only two of you? I can manage you with one 'and." Blair's goatee raised itself towards his nose. "Now look 'ere, Sergeant, the last time I was in Wilcannia you wanted the bleeding jail whitewashed, so you goes and grabs me and two other blokes on the d. and d. charge, and gets us fourteen days without the op, so's you can get the jail whitewashed without paying the award rates. Wot I wants to know is, when your flamin' jail wants whitewashing again?"

"Not for another three months, Blair. But what I want to know is, where—"

"Never mind what you want to know," interjected the little fury. "What I want to know is whether the next time I come to Wilcannia, and the jail don't want whitewashing, you'll let me alone to have a quiet drink in peace."

"We'll have to wait till the next time. Where were you last evening?"

"Like to know, wouldn't you?"

"I want to know," the policeman said at last impatiently.

Blair suddenly leaned forward with twinkling blue eyes.

"As a matter of fact, Sergeant, I met the black fellow last night and asked him for a match. He cursed me for a police pimp. Me! Me, Sergeant, a police pimp! So I ran up to the house, grabbed the maids' step-ladder, took it down to the black, made him stand still beside it, climbed to the top to get level with his head, and then hit him with a cucumber I pinched from the garden." Then, turning to the squatter, he added: "You see, Mr Thornton, being a small bloke, I couldn't reach the nig's head without them steps. But I took 'em back and put 'em where I got 'em."

Both men were obliged to laugh. Blair, however, remained perfectly serious.

"But, look here, Blair. Honestly, now, where were you about eight-thirty last night?" persisted the sergeant.

"I told you," Blair returned. "I murdered the nig by 'itting 'im on the 'ead with a rotten cucumber. I own to it. You arrest me, Sergeant—and see 'ow you get on. Two of yous! Why, I could crawl over you."

"Not in the office, Blair. You'd smash the furniture," Thornton murmured.

"All right, Blair. You had better go," the policeman said resignedly.

Blair rose slowly to his feet, the goatee now at its normal right-angle with the bottom of his chin. Slowly he walked to the door, as though reluctant. At the door he turned, a man bursting with some hidden withheld information. The sergeant was at once hopeful; Blair slowly returned to the desk and, leaning forward, whispered:

"Say, are you quite sure you don't want to arrest me, Sergeant?"

"Quite sure. When I do, I'll arrest you."

"My oath! You, with your bloomin' speelers to lend a hand." Blair almost cried with disappointment. Then, appealingly: "But 'ave a 'eart, Sergeant! Don't bung me in next time to whitewash the jail. I goes to Wilcannia and gets drunk like a respectable wowzer, not to whitewash jails. That's a bit thick."

With a regretful nod, Blair left them.

"What do you make of Blair?" asked the squatter, chuckling.

"Blair is a fighter, not a murderer," replied Sergeant Knowles, grinning. "The two don't mix outside a drunken brawl, and this murder was not the result of a drunken brawl. How many house servants have you got?"

"Three. Martha the cook, Alice the maid, and Mabel the laundry girl."

"Humph!" the sergeant re-read his notes carefully. Then, looking up, he added: "I'll have a look at the corpse. Then we'll look at the scene of the killing. Then I'll examine the blacks in that camp up-river. As far as your people are concerned, I am not satisfied with Clair. I'll send Trooper Dowling with him to see if he did set traps last night. Also, Mr Thornton, Frank Dugdale did see someone in the lightning."

Chapter Seven

The Only Clue

"DAMN THE rain!" rasped Sergeant Knowles, staring down at four wooden pegs set at the points of a cross to mark where the body had been found. "There is not a track left for a black tracker to see, let alone a white man."

"What seems significant to me is that the abo stood six feet four inches in height, and yet, as you say, the blow at the crown of his head was delivered downwards," murmured the squatter. "Such a combination rules out any man of medium height, unless he adopted Blair's plan and used a pair of step-ladders."

"Just so," the sergeant agreed absently. He stood on the river side of the four wooden pegs and consequently faced the garden fence. "Is Dugdale in love with any of the maids, or with Miss Flinders, do you know?"

"I don't know. I've no evidence of any love-affair. Why do you ask?"

"For no real reason," came the absent response. "Let us go along to the camp. Hallo! Who is this?"

Along the bank of the river, walking towards them and the homestead, came a young lubra. The two men watched her approach, the sergeant at least noting the springing gait and the beautiful contours of her limbs. Her age might have been twenty, but her figure was unusually lovely for a lubra, for somehow the angular awkwardness of the aboriginal girl changes with startling rapidity to the obesity of the gin.

She was dressed in a white muslin blouse, a neat navy-blue skirt, black stockings and shoes. She wore her cheap but well-fitting clothes with the unconscious grace of a white woman. When close, she looked at them fearlessly.

36

According to the white man's standards it cannot be said that the Australian lubra is anything but ugly. This girl, however, was a rare exception. Her face was oval and flat. Her forehead neither receded nor bulged, but was high and broad. Her nose, for an aboriginal, was not spread, and the nostrils were finely chiselled; whilst her lips, thicker than those of the white woman, were by no means as thick and coarse as those of the average black. For an aboriginal she was remarkably good-looking.

"Good-day, Nellie! You going up to the house?" Thornton asked kindly.

She smiled, and the sergeant noted that her smile was restrained and not the customary broad beam.

"Yeth, Mithter Thornton," she said. "Mithess Thornton sent for me to give Mabel a hand. She wash tomollow."

"Ah, yes! Tomorrow is Monday, isn't it?"

"What is your name, young lady?" Sergeant Knowles put in.

"I'm Nellie Wanting." She regarded the blue tunic with awe, the man with native dignity.

"Who is your mother?"

"Sarah Wanting."

"And your father?"

"I dunno," she replied, with utter simplicity.

"Well, well! We won't keep you."

They watched her move across the billabong and climb the farther bank to the garden gate.

"A fine-looking lass, that," essayed the sergeant thoughtfully. "I wonder who she's married to, or who she's living with. It's all the same to them."

"Heartwhole, I think. Anyway, she's a good girl, and comes up to give the maids a hand two or three times a week. What now?"

"I think we'll go along to the camp."

The policeman rowed the boat upstream, and during the short trip did not speak. He was a man who, whilst making an excellent officer and an efficient administrator of a police-controlled bush town, would never make a good detective. Detectives are necessary in centres of population. In the Australian bush a good policeman must combine the qualifications of soldier, scout, and administrator.

Simple murder, with the murderer defined and at large, he could have dealt with. The apprehension of a known criminal would have been a matter of tracking, even across the continent. But, whilst his inquiries were not yet complete, the rain had obliterated all tracks made prior to nine-thirty the night before.

At the camp they were greeted by Pontius Pilate, engaged in the somnolent variety of fishing, which is to say, fishing in the mood of caring little if the fish bite or not. He moored the boat for them, and with deep seriousness escorted them up the bank to the fire near the humpies.

"Who is here, Pilate? Wake your people up and tell them I want to see them," ordered the sergeant.

The buck growled a few unintelligible words, and, as spirits raised by incantation, there appeared an enormously fat gin, another only a shade less fat, two thins laths of girls about sixteen, and five younger children. The young fellow, Ned, rose from the ground beneath a gum, yawned, and stretched himself. He still wore the moleskin trousers; Pontius Pilate was still barely half-covered by the simple blue shirt.

"Where are your trousers?" Sergeant Knowles demanded severely.

"Well, boss, you see Ned, he ride-it outlaw, and him pants all busted. So I loan him mine. By im by, ole Sarah she fix Ned's pants, and I git mine back."

"Which is Sarah?"

"That Sarah. She Sarah Wanting," answered Pontius Pilate, seating himself tailor-fashion with extraordinary dexterity; and pointing out the huger of the two huge gins.

"Well, you mend Ned's trousers quick and lively, Sarah," she was ordered. "We can't have Pontius Pilate wandering about like an angel."

Sarah said nothing. Her eyes widened and protruded.

"Now, Pilate, who is your friend that got himself murdered last night?"

The black fellow's countenance assumed tremendous gravity.

"He got one hell of a bash, eh, boss?" he said.

"How do you know?"

"I went alonga and seed 'im this morning. Poor ole King Henry! Good feller, King Henry."

"Was that his name? He's not a river black, is he?"

"Yaas, boss. He belonga river long time ago. One time broke-in horses for Mithter Thornton. He—" His eyes widened hungrily at the cigarette-case from which the squatter was abstracting a smoke. Slowly he said: "Anyway, boss, it's a plurry dry argument."

John Thornton smiled, and tossed him a cigarette. Instantly, the less fat gin was at Pilate's side when he caught it. Breaking it neatly in halves, he gave her one, and then, stripping off the paper from the other half crammed the tobacco into his mouth and began chewing.

"Now, Pontius Pilate," the sergeant said. "King Henry you say, was once breaking-in horses on Barrakee. When was that?"

"Long time ago."

"When? How many years?"

"Dunno. He went away when Ned was a li'l baby."

Turning to the young man, Knowles said:

"How old are you, Ned?"

"Twenty last January," he replied in excellent English.

"What did he go away for, and why was he away for years?" the elder black was asked.

"Ah! You see, boss, King Henry he was a no-fear man, but he was feared of some white man," Pontius explained. "This 'ere white feller he tell King Henry he get him quick, and so King Henry he go walkabout."

"And who was the white fellow?"

"I dunno."

"Sure?"

"Yaas, boss."

"And where's King Henry been all this time?"

"Up Nor' Queensland."

"Oh! And why did he come back?" pressed the sergeant.

"Well, you see, boss, it was orl like this." Pontius Pilate seized a short stick and drew fantastic figures on the soft damp earth. "Ole King Henry he married Sarah Wanting. That old Sarah. Tellible fat. Ned's mother. Nellie's mother, I don't believe it, though. She mother to a lot of fellers and lot of gins. Well, you see, ole King Henry, he find out that white feller who was tracking him got busted, killed, or something, so he come back and took Sarah away from ole Mokie, and then he bring Sarah up here to my camp. Course, Sarah didn't know he was gona git murdered like that."

"But why was the white man tracking him?"

"I dunno."

For half an hour the sergeant fruitlessly questioned him and Sarah Wanting on that point. They did not know, and appeared to take no interest in the matter. Nor did they know or appear interested in the reason prompting King Henry's visit to the station after dark.

That the dead man had held a certain power over these people was quite evident, and the sergeant surmised that he was a kind of king, as his name implied.

But any useful information he did not obtain. If these people knew anything about the crime, they kept the secret so well hidden that Sergeant Knowles was convinced that so far as the actual killing was concerned they were none of them implicated.

At the oars once more, with the squatter facing him from the stern seat, he growled:

"I'm hanged if I can see any light. Here is a man who left the district eighteen or nineteen years ago because his life was threatened by a white man. For years he wanders, pursued by the tracking white. The white gets killed, and King Henry at once comes back and takes his wife away from old Mokie. He leaves the camp here about dark, helps Dugdale with his fish, dives overboard again, and swims the river on the way to the station, where he is killed.

"Why does he go to the station after dark? And why is he killed at his first appearance at the station for nigh twenty years? The man who hunted him died, or was killed, and he had no one to fear. Yet someone—and a white man—killed him. Why? Did he kill him for the same reason that that other white had tracked him for years?

"I can make out only one clue, or coincidence. Pontius Pilate said that King Henry had come down from North Queensland, and William Clair admitted that the last job he had had was near Winton, in Central Queensland. When did you give Clair employment?"

"Last Friday week," the squatter answered. "But Clair said he was away setting dog-traps."

"He may, and he may not, have been."

"Anyway, Trooper Dowling has gone to find out."

"I'm betting that Clair will show him the traps all right. The moving finger points to Clair, and then to Dugdale, and then back again to Clair."

"I cannot agree with you about Dugdale," was Thornton's emphatic response. "I've known Dug intimately for ten years. What he says he heard I'm sure he did hear. And, as he said he saw no one, I'm sure, too, that he saw no one."

"Maybe," Knowles conceded. "I am not quite so positive that he lied when he denied seeing anyone in the lightning. Still, when I pressed him on that point, he flushed under his skin. If he's a liar, he's a darned good liar."

"Knowing him as I do, I can guarantee that he's not a liar. I've never yet found him out in a lie."

"Well, I don't know." The sergeant sighed. "Straight-out murder I don't mind, when I know the killer. But these Mysteries of the Rue Morgue are beyond me. Anyway, Dow-

41

ling and I will get on back. I must send in my report, and then try and work out the puzzle. We might be able to learn something of Clair from the Winton police. Time, too, is always on our side. I'll keep in touch with you, night and morning, by phone. Oh, here's Dowling waiting for us."

The trooper was standing at the edge of the water at the mooring-place.

"Were the traps there, Dowling?"

"Yes, Sergeant. Clair set them some three miles down the river in a bend."

"Humph!" The senior man got out of the boat and climbed up the steep bank, followed by the others. "We'll examine the scenery," he said. "Take a line from this tree to the garden gate. You quarter the right side and I'll do the left."

The squatter, taking yet another cigarette from his case, watched the two uniformed men examining the soft dark-grey soil from the high bank or natural ramp dividing the billabong from the river. He experienced not a little irritability at the whole wretched affair. That such a to-do should be made over the killing of an ordinary abo was ridiculous. He heard the sergeant say:

"Don't expect to discover anything. If the murderer re-members dropping anything, he had plenty of time to recover it before we arrived this morning. See any fresh tracks your side?"

"Several," Dowling answered. "But all making from the boats to the homestead via the tennis-court. Hallo! Here are small shoe-prints going to the garden gate."

"They'll have been made by Nellie Wanting, the black girl who's working at the homestead this afternoon," stated the sergeant.

Thornton was absent-mindedly examining, on the trunk of the gum near which he stood, a deep incision some nine to ten inches in length. The tree-wound was fresh and still bleeding sap. He noticed two raised bumps in the centre of the gash, at equal distance from the ends. He took no further notice of it. He did not even mention it to the two policemen.

Had he known, this was the one and only clue to the murderer of King Henry.

Chapter Eight

A Round of Inspection

THE POLICE returned to Wilcannia without having secured a clue to the murder of King Henry. By the sergeant's orders the body was interred in the tiny cemetery near the homestead, which already contained five graves.

There was one point that occurred to Sergeant Knowles two days later, and, ringing up the station, he said to the squatter:

"That girl, Nellie Wanting—does she live in the blacks' camp?"

"Yes."

"Then how did she cross the river the afternoon she met us on her way to the homestead? I noticed no boat at the camp."

"I'm afraid I have no information on that point," the station-owner replied. "I'll see her and find out. You'll agree that she didn't swim the river like her alleged father."

"No. She didn't swim."

The explanation, when forthcoming, was simple enough. As has been said, the level of the river was very low, and at a point about half a mile above the blacks' camp an outcrop of rock formed the bed of the river at the lower rim of a deep hole. Most of the rocks were now uncovered and provided easy and safe stepping stones.

Although Thornton was in daily communication with the police-sergeant at Wilcannia, nothing occurred to help forward a solution of the mystery. The week's work went on, that of Barrakee with its usual orderliness and regularity. The squatter prayed for rain.

Blair, with McIntosh for his offsider, was sent out to the back of the run with the bullock team to clean out a dry surface tank with a scoop. Clair went about his odd jobs, gaunt and taciturn. The only person for whom the murder still had a painful interest was Frank Dugdale.

At the time he denied having seen anyone revealed by the lightning, he could almost have sworn that the white-clad figure hurrying through the garden was Kate Flinders. This was his reason for suppressing that fact.

Whilst scouting the possibility of Kate having killed the black fellow, he could not but conclude that she was implicated. The why and the wherefore of this worried him to distraction.

And then one evening he saw Alice, the maid, and Mabel, the laundress, leave the house to stroll up the river, and experienced an unaccountable sense of relief when he noted that both girls were dressed in white. Upon that came instant recollection of having seen the young lubra, Nellie Wanting, dressed all in white, on more than one occasion. Mrs Thornton, too, generally wore a white costume. So that, instead of the hurrying figure at the garden gate being definitely Kate Flinders, it might, with equal plausibility or otherwise, have been that of one of four other women.

On realizing this, Dugdale felt immeasurable relief. His conviction that he had seen Kate Flinders in the lightning flash was now replaced by the conviction that he had not. And so indifferent did he become, as did Thornton and the other men, that this murder of a mere semi-civilized aboriginal was very quickly relegated to the sphere of forgotten crimes. Had King Henry been a white man, this indifference would have been impossible.

One morning in early April, when the sun was rapidly losing its summer intensity, Thornton ordered Dugdale to get out the big car for a run to Thurlow Lake.

The squatter never had taken to car-driving and usually delegated the job to the sub-overseer. Dugdale had the car outside the double garden-gates that morning about ten o'clock, when Ralph appeared carrying the last of three hampers and a moment later was followed by the squatter and Kate. Dugdale's heart missed a beat, and he could have groaned and shouted at one and the same moment in anticipation of the bitter sweetness of being in her society most of that day.

Thornton and his niece occupied the rear seat and Ralph sat beside the driver. After an assurance from the book-keeper that the out-back mail was all in the bag in the boot, they glided away over the grey river flats.

Once out of the home paddocks and off the flats, they had a straight run of twelve miles over a good hard track, across a blue-bush plain. It was the finest piece of road on the run, and the great car leapt into its stride like an unleashed kangaroo-dog. On the elderly man the speed made no emotional impression but the girl it almost thrilled.

Looking between the two in front, she watched the speedometer register forty, forty-five, fifty five, sixty-two miles an hour. From the indicator her eyes went to the small powerful hands caressing the wheel, iron hands that could handle equally well a spirited or vicious horse.

"My! That was lovely," she gasped when they pulled up before the first gate. "It's not so quick as you have done it, Dug. But better luck next time."

"And what is the quickest time we have done it in?" he asked, without turning his head. Ralph opened the gate and they moved slowly beyond it.

"Sixty-four, the time before last," she replied at once.

"That's nothing," Thornton remarked. "One time last February, when I had an important appointment, and we were late, Dug hit her up to seventy-eight."

"No, really! Oh Dug, you've been cheating me of fourteen miles an hour."

Ralph having shut the gate and got in, the sub-overseer let in the clutch. He said gently:

"The back country is rather proud of the Women of Barra-kee. If it were known that I ever endangered the life of one of them I would be due for a rough time."

46

"Oh, Dug, but it's quite safe," she said reproachfully.

"Quite," he agreed. "Unless a wheel comes off, or a tyre blows out, or the steering-gear fails, or I want to sneeze."

"Well, if you keep me down to only sixty-four, I shall never forgive you."

"I would do anything in reason to avoid that," he said gravely. "But not to avoid it will I risk your life."

Eighteen miles from the homestead they pulled up at a boundary-rider's hut, near a great earth dam. The stockman was out in one of his paddocks, so his mail was left on the table, the door shut again, and they went on, stopping sometimes to open the few gates dividing the eight- and twelve-mile-square paddocks, once to take a survey of a flock of three thousand sheep.

"They're not looking bad, Dug, considering the dry time," their owner decided.

"No, they look quite all right, so far. Pity we can't have a good rain to bring on the feed for the lambs," came from the sub-overseer.

"We might get it yet. How much water left at the Basin Tank?"

"About two feet."

"Humph! Remind me that we send O'Grady out there to get the bore and engine in order next Monday. Right! We'll get on."

The stockman at Cattle Tank had just come home when they arrived there. He was a lank, bow-legged man about forty, and when they pulled up he lounged beside the car, after removing his felt to Kate Flinders, who said:

"Good morning, David."

"Morning, Miss Flinders," he returned with conscious awkwardness.

"How's the sheep, David?" inquired the squatter.

"The weaners are losing a bit, but the wethers in top pad-dock are holdin' their own."

They conversed for ten minutes about sheep. At one time Kate, who often accompanied her uncle on these journeys of inspection, asked the squatter why he tarried so long at these places, talking over matters of which the evening telephone reports must have fully advised him. And this was his reply:

"My dear, if you led the life these men lead, you would not like to see your boss flash past in his car. You would enjoy a short chat with him, or with any other human being."

When Thornton decided to go on, she had ready a large square basket, which she offered to David.

"Auntie sent this out to you, David," she said. "Leave the basket on the table, and we'll get it on our way home if you are out."

David smiled, a genuinely grateful smile. No wonder Mrs Thornton was known affectionately far and wide as the "Little Lady". She always gave her husband baskets of eggs and fruit for the riders, adding butter in the winter.

"Now we forgot Alec's basket, Uncle," she said when they moved off. "Don't let me forget to give it him on our way back. Has David got his mail?"

"I gave it to him, Kate," Ralph informed her.

"What, Ralph, have you just awoken? That is the first time you've spoken since we started."

"The wise are always silent," he said, with a smile, looking back at her. "As a matter of fact, I have been thinking."

"Oh—of what, if I am not rude?"

"You are, but I'll tell you," he said. "Peculiarly enough I was thinking of Nellie Wanting, and I arrived at the stupendous conclusion that she would be a really pretty girl if she was white."

Kate Flinders laughed deliriously. Dugdale suddenly smiled. Thornton was absorbed in watching the country, i.e. the state of the sheep feed.

"I believe, Ralph," she said, "that you are falling in love with little Nellie Wanting, the lady of colour."

"You would, doubtless," he replied dryly, "be much astonished if I did."

Chapter Nine

The Washaways

TEN MILES west of Cattle Tank they reached the Washaways. It had been a standing joke for years that Thornton repeatedly stated he would have a bridge, or series of bridges across this maze of creeks, winding in and out among themselves like the strands of a rope. The bridges, however, never materialized.

On Barrakee these creeks, divided by steep box-lined banks, ran from north to south, and in flood-time carried water from the Paroo to the Darling, a kind of overflow. The Paroo itself, when it does run water, empties it into the Darling, just above Wilcannia.

The Barrakee road to Thurlow Lake crossed five creeks, forming the Washaways at that point, in three-quarters of a mile, and it was on the west bank of the last of them that Thornton directed Dugdale to pull into the shade of a great box-tree for lunch.

Kate Flinders always enjoyed these alfresco lunches. While she set out the food on the car's running-board to baffle the myriads of ants, Dugdale gathered the wood for a fire, and Ralph filled the billy from one of the two canvas water-bags hanging from the side of the car.

Dugdale invariably arrogated to himself the task of boiling the billy, and whilst he was thus engaged the squatter announced that that morning the annual Land Lottery was opened.

As a sop to the insatiable hunger for land in the western half of New South Wales, the Government "resumes" a dozen or so small areas of land every year from the big pastoral leases, and these areas, commonly known as "blocks", are offered to the public. For every block thus thrown open there are up to a hundred applicants. A Land Board, consisting of two or three highly-salaried gentlemen, eventually visits the bush towns and hears the applicant's qualifications. Since no special qualifications are demanded and since the qualifications of past successful applicants are by no means uniform, the necessary qualifications for success are purely a matter of guesswork to the bush public.

Hence this annual allotment of blocks is humorously called, in many places, the "Great Land Lottery". To Frank Dugdale, any one of these blocks would enable him, in a few years, to ask Kate to marry him. Success in the Lottery would be infinitely quicker than waiting weary years for a manager-ship.

"Do you know any of the blocks, Mr Thornton?" he asked promptly.

"Yes. One of them is Daly's Yards paddock."

Dugdale's eyes gleamed.

Daly's Yards was a large paddock on Tindale Station, and joined the west boundary of Barrakee. In area it was some 25,000 acres, and, whilst this does not constitute a large area for Australia, everyone knew that Daly's Yards was well scrubbed, and that there was a very fine surface dam in the west, and a good well in the east. The rent would be about thirty pounds per annum, and the value of the water supply—to be paid by arrangement to the owners of Tindale—would be something like six hundred pounds. Ownership of such a lease meant independence in less than ten years.

"There will be a lot in for that block," murmured Dugdale.

"Are you going to put in for it, Dug?"

The sub-overseer tossed a handful of tea into the boiling water, and allowed it to boil for half a minute, before taking the billy off the fire.

"I am, Ralph," he replied grimly. "It will be the fifth time I've put in for the Lottery, and I might win a block. What other blocks are out, Mr Thornton?"

The squatter mentioned a few he had memorized from the *Government Gazette* announcement.

"You'd find it fairly lonely living on a block by yourself, Dug," he suggested.

"For a start, yes," Dugdale agreed, stirring the tea to induce the leaves to sink. "But if I got Daly's Yards it wouldn't be long before I had a house built. And with a house I might induce a woman to marry me."

"There is that possibility, I admit," agreed the squatter dryly.

"If I were extra special nice, would you propose to me, Dug?"

He looked up into the smiling face. He, too, was smiling, but his eyes did not smile. She remembered his eyes long afterwards.

"If I were lucky enough to win a block, I would not be lucky enough to win you," he told her, laughing. "It would be most improbable that one would win two such prizes in a lifetime."

"But isn't it considered the thing to do, if one wins a block, to appreciate one's stupendous luck by heading a syndicate of one's friends to invest in Tattersall's Melbourne Cup Sweep?" asked Ralph.

"It is the custom."

"Then that shows belief in a run of luck," the young man pointed out. "You'd better not be extra special nice, Katie, or you'll find yourself married."

"If you come trying to steal my niece, Dug, you and I will engage in debate," said the squatter with assumed gravity. "When you become a pastoralist, you'll have no time for anything but to keep paying the taxes."

"I'll pay them all right."

"I know you will. The tax-gatherers will see to that. But you'll be kept busy, I assure you. Australia, with a population less than that of London, can't keep up European appearances on the lavish scale of a sixty-million people without taxing us, our children, and our children's children, to the bone."

"Bother politics," interrupted Kate irreverently. "Here, help yourselves to these sandwiches, and let's talk about Sir Walter Thorley."

"That scoundrel," the squatter shouted.

"That absent owner of half Australia!" ejaculated Dugdale.

The effect of that name on the two sheepmen was astonishing.

"You have poured petrol on the fire now, Kate," laughed Ralph.

"I think he is a lovely man," added Kate daringly, finishing her petrol.

Thornton choked. Dugdale bit savagely into his sandwich. Distaste for Sir Walter Thorley was common to both, but their reasons were different.

Dugdale, a member of the great homeless, land-hungry army, detested not so much the person as the combine whose head Sir Walter was. This combine had bought up station after station, so that now it owned hundreds and hundreds of miles of Government landed property. It dismissed the employees, sold the sheep, allowed the buildings and fences to rot, and stocked each station that successively fell under what was called the "Blight", with cattle, in charge of one poorly paid white man and half a dozen blacks.

Mr Thornton and his associate squatters, the majority of whom elected to reside anywhere but on their properties, were incensed against the Birthday Knight, because he cynically ignored the clause in each of his leases which specified that the holder must do all possible to keep down the wild dogs. Sir Walter's cattle stations were notoriously among the finest breeding grounds of the sheepman's deadliest enemy.

By no stretch of imagination could Kate Flinders be accused of hoydenishness. She was, however, the kind of girl who regards all men as wilful boys, and sometimes she took keen delight in rousing them. Once she had told the Little Lady:

"I love teasing Uncle and Dug. When roused, Uncle looks just like Mr Pickwick scolding Mr Snodgrass, and Dug grits his teeth as though he would like to bite me."

But, once having roused them, she did all she could to reduce them speedily again to normal.

"Well, if you don't like my mentioning Sir Walter, I won't," she said placidly. "Let's talk about the Land Lottery."

So, until the end of lunch, they discussed the advantages of the various blocks, and the chances their personal friends had of obtaining one of them.

After leaving the Washaways, the road ran over undulating grass country, bearing here and there clumps of belar. Six miles west of the maze of creeks they came to yet another hut, called One Tree Hut, with its well. Here lived two boundary-riders, and to one of these Kate gave a hamper packed by the Little Lady.

These men, being under the administration of the overseer, Thornton did not engage long in conversation. The last lap of the journey, twenty miles, was covered in leisurely fashion.

Approaching Thurlow Lake the road takes one up a slight rise to a belt of oak-trees, and, when through these, the lake of brilliant blue and the white-walled, red-roofed buildings of the out-station burst suddenly into view.

At midday Thurlow Lake is a glittering blue diamond, lying on an immense expanse of dark green velvet. Roughly circular in shape, with a diameter of two miles, the blue water is edged by a ring of brilliant green box-trees with an outer border of radiant red sand-hills, the whole surrounded by the omnipresent dark green bush.

To emerge from the high belt of oaks is like meeting the sea after a weary, dusty, interminable country tramp.

"Oh, why don't we live here instead of by the old river?" exclaimed the girl when they dropped down towards the cluster of neat buildings.

"It is beautiful, Kate, isn't it?" replied the squatter. "It is unfortunate, though, that the lake is filled so rarely.

Remember Thurlow Lake when it is dry and wind-blown, Kate?"

"Yes, it is horrid then. Here is Mrs Watts waiting for us. I've never seen her yet without a small child hanging to her skirts."

A large, pleasant-faced woman, a little more than thirty, opened the gate leading into the miniature garden, when they pulled up before it. Mrs Watts was a bushwoman, one of the small band of heroic women who live cheerfully and happily in the semi-wilds of Australia. The Women of Barrakee were her nearest female neighbours, and Barrakee was seventy-nine miles east. She loved her husband and adored her six children. She cooked for him and them, she gave her children their primary education, and she incessantly struggled with the elements to make the garden a tiny paradise.

"Come in, come in," she exclaimed in a low, sweet voice. "The tea is made and the scones are just out of the oven. Kate—Oh Kate, my dear, what are the young men doing to leave you still heartwhole? But there," with a sharp glance at Dugdale, "as George says, the young men today haven't got much backbone."

"I don't know so much about that," Kate rejoined. "Ralph hasn't said anything yet, but he'll be a whirlwind when he starts."

Mrs Watts' blue eyes, set wide in her big face, beamed upon the young man. Ralph smiled in his quiet way and said:

"It will be Desdemona and Othello, or the Sheik and the lovely white girl, darkness matched to fairness, black opal against a white diamond."

"Now, now, we'll have no Romeo and Juliet just at present," interrupted the squatter genially. "Wait till we get our wool to Sydney and the advance cheque in the bank. I'll be richer then than I am now—till the tax-gatherers hunt me up. Where's George, Mrs Watts?"

"He went out to the Five Mile, Mr Thornton. I'm expecting him back any minute," she said. "But what are we doing standing here? Come in—come in."

54

The child clinging to her voluminous skirt was swept off its feet by the turn she made to lead them into the house liked loved relatives she had not seen for years. Her happiness was infectious. Even Dugdale's heartache was banished for the time being.

Chapter Ten

Sonny's Hundredth Case

GEORGE WATTS, returning in time to join them in an early afternoon cup of tea, went off on a tour of the back paddocks with the squatter and Dugdale, leaving Ralph the pleasant task of talking to the two women. He did this till the conversation veered to babies and dress fashions, when, these subjects not being in his line, he drifted across the stockyards, in which he had seen a bunch of horses.

At that time there was engaged at Thurlow Lake a horse-breaker. The popular conception of breaking-in horses appears to be to rope the animal in cowboy style, fling a saddle across its back, mount and ride till either bucked off or crowned with the laurels of victory. As a matter of cold fact, such procedure would not merely break-in a horse, but break it up, too, into a dispirited, abject, miserable animal.

Some of the best horse-breakers in Australia are the worst horse-riders. Such a one was Sonny. No one knew his surname; it is doubtful if he knew it himself. He was no rider, but he had no equal in handling a colt or a spirited filly, mouthing it, training it to lead, to stay rooted to the ground when the reins were dropped, and to step up immediately to a man, if that man wanted to ride it, when commanded by the lifting of an arm. Vicious horses, bucking horses, bolting horses, are in ninety-nine cases out of a hundred the result of bad breaking-in. But that afternoon Sonny was in despair with the hundredth case—the born vicious, unbreakable beast.

"I can't handle him and I can't ride him," Sonny wailed when Ralph had perched himself on the top-most rail of the round yard.

The horse was a beautiful, jet-black, three-year-old gelding. Sonny had got the bridle on him with great difficulty, and had been fruitlessly trying to give him his first lesson. With forefeet planted like sticks in the ground, the gelding refused obstinately to move one inch. The short length of rope attached to the bit-rings was taut. The animal's head was thrust out and down under the breaker's pull, ears flattened, eyes sloe-coloured in a sea of chalk.

Sonny relaxed the strain on the rope by edging towards the horse, which remained immobile. He gained its side and gave its rump a cut with the light switch. The gelding swung its hind-quarters round away from the breaker, its forefeet pivoting slightly, but still as straight as sticks. The relative positions of horse and man were precisely the same.

"I wish I could ride, you black devil," Sonny cried. "I'd break you or bust your big, damned heart."

"I can ride a bit, Sonny," came Ralph's musical drawl. "Let me have a go, will you?"

"Well, Mr Ralph, I've never let anyone ride my hosses till I say they're broke-in," replied the short, powerful-armed Sonny. "But this 'ere beast will never, never be any mortal use. Don't you ride him, now. He'll kill you."

"Not he. Take the bridle off him and hand it to me."

Ralph Thornton was not exactly a fool. He had learned to ride at a very early age, and had since never ridden an easy horse if a spirited animal was to be had. He was an excellent rider in that he possessed instinctive balance. There are many, many good riders, but few, very few, riders of good balance.

Sonny knew this. And, though he thought he knew that the young man was an inexperienced buck-jump rider, he was aware that a super buck-jumping horse is so after successfully unseating many riders. Sonny reckoned that once Ralph was on its back the gelding would hardly know what to do. Even so he took no chances.

His slim hands quickly undid the neck-strap, the stodgy yet infinitely gentle fingers deftly removed the bridle. Instantly, when free, the horse whipped round and lashed out with both hind hoofs; but Sonny was on the top rail alongside Ralph.

"I didn't oughter let yer, Mr Ralph," he said, "and I'm going to only on the condition that you square off the boss if I've got to shoot that black swine."

"Why would you have to shoot him?"

"Why! 'Cos when he throws you, if he does, he is going to kill you if I don't drop him with a bullet," Sonny replied shortly. "Don't you tackle him, now, till I gits my gun."

Ralph waited confidently. He had no doubt of his ability to stick, once he had his legs across that gleaming black back. As for the horse, he knew that, should Sonny give it up, Mr Thornton would have it shot, for the squatter believed in having not one useless animal on his run.

When Sonny returned he carried a .32 Winchester rifle and a saddle. The saddle he handed up to the young man. The rifle he examined before taking a clear view of all parts of the yard. Ralph, still on the twelve-foot fence, adjusted the stirrup leathers to his length.

"Don't you shoot, now, unless he gets me down," he said to the breaker.

"You leave the shooting to me," replied Sonny gruffly. "I'm going to git the sack for letting you ride him. I'll git hanged if I let him kill you."

Smiling, the young man dropped into the yard, swiftly leaning the saddle against the inside of the fence. The horse on the farther side watched him with flattened ears and wicked eyes. Without looking at what he was doing, Ralph adjusted the bridle over his left forearm, so that when the time came there would be no fumbling.

Nothing escaped the blue eyes of Sonny, knowing and poignantly regretting his limitations as a rider.

Ralph made no hurry. For fully a minute he stared into the eyes of the horse, who at first seemed inclined to rush him with white, rending teeth. But, whilst the seconds passed,

58

Sonny saw first uneasiness, then the first hint of fear flicker in the white-rimmed, blazing orbs.

It was then that slowly, arms and head motionless, eyes holding those of the horse in remorseless stare, Ralph walked across to it, till he stood directly in front of the shining satin muzzle.

"My Gawd, 'e mesmerizes 'im like a black fellow," Sonny grunted, the rifle held to his shoulder as though in a vice, his right eye glued to the foresight.

Now Ralph was gently patting the sleek velvet neck; his left hand, on whose wrist hung the bridle, rose with the slow inexorability of fate to the animal's nostrils, rose higher and higher up its face, between its amazed eyes, fondled its ears. The bit seemed to rise into the horse's mouth without guidance. Five seconds later, the bridle was fixed behind the still flattened ears, and in three more the neck-strap was buckled. And the horse neither moved nor flinched.

The horse had utterly refused to be led by Sonny. Holding the reins, Ralph slipped backward towards the saddle till brought up by the obstinate gelding. Once more he stared into the black eyes. It was not mesmerism, as Sonny thought, it was not overmastering will-power that compelled the horse to follow, step by reluctant step, the slowly-backing Ralph. In the young man's fixed eyes the animal saw that which made it shiver, made the delicate nostrils expand to show the red, made its halting walk similar to the rigid action of a sleepwalker.

Saddling was a prolonged operation, for Ralph could not then hold the animal with his eyes. But the impression of his stare remained sufficiently long to enable the saddle finally to be slid over the animal's back, the girth tightened cruelly; the surcingle followed, then the crupper and the martingale. For the first time in its life the gelding found itself saddled. It was astounded, and, before the stunning surprise could give place to fiendish anger, Ralph vaulted lightly on its back.

Sonny gasped. The horse became a statue. For a full minute it hardly breathed. It was galvanized into a living volcano by the sharp digging of Ralph's heels.

The gelding seemed to sink. Then it screamed with rage. Swiftly as light it whirled in a half-circle, its forefeet turning within an arc of not more than twenty inches. The perfectly balanced figure glued to its back had not moved the breadth of a hair out of the saddle.

Then came a succession of routes round the circular yard. First away from the fence, then towards it, out again, in again, always kept from the rails by a narrow margin.

The dust rose in a cloud. Again came the demoniac scream of rage, this time attracting the two women from the house. Now in the centre of the yard, the horse paused for two seconds. Again it appeared to sink, again it pivoted on its forefeet, rose again directly its hind hoofs touched the ground, came down on all fours, its legs like sticks.

Ralph was jarred by that springless drop. His knees were grazed, though he did not realize it, by the terrific unyielding pressure against the saddle-flaps. Between the rails Kate and Mrs Watts followed every movement with wide eyes and beating hearts. Kate even then wondered why Sonny held a rifle at the ready.

For the third and last time the horse screamed. Then it went mad. Rearing, it walked on its hind legs. Ralph, lying along its neck, tried to stop it, but it reared over and backwards to crush the demon, the unshakeable demon on its back.

Mrs Watts cried out. Kate's heart stopped. Sonny swore, for horse and man were invisible in the rising dust-cloud. In its centre writhing figures moved. The watchers did not see that Ralph had leapt clear, that before the horse regained its feet he was once more in the saddle.

Horse and man came charging out of the dust. Sonny determined to shoot the mad thing at the first chance presented. Buck! The horse behaved like an old hand.

It tried to get its head round to tear at one of Ralph's legs. It rushed the fence to roll against it and sweep its rider off. Failing, it entered into so terrific a buck that it somersaulted heels over head. Ralph flung himself sideways out of the saddle, landing lightly on his feet, the end of the reins still in his hands.

The horse was on its back. It was Sonny's chance, but he did not shoot. His love of horses overcame his common sense. Besides, Ralph was on his feet. A wriggle, a heave, and the gelding was kneeling like a camel. A feather dropped on its back. Ralph was again in the saddle.

Lathered with sweat, the horse was caked, every inch of it, with mud. When it scrambled to its feet the wind whistled through its distended nostrils like escaping steam.

And then it stood quietly for a spell. Not beaten. This was only the end of the first round, which it had lost on points.

But the strength of the horse was greater than that of the lad. Ralph could not afford to give his mount any time to regain its wind. He snatched off his felt and slapped the gelding's ears.

It seemed that in the first round the black fiend had gained the experience of years. There followed a succession of lightning bucks and spins, lasting second by second beyond a minute. The terrific motion told on Ralph. He began to feel the muscles of his legs grow laggard to respond to his will. A tearing, ripping pain in his side made breathing intensely difficult. He could have cried from the agony of impending defeat when he had been so sure he had the battle won.

The horse suddenly changed its tactics. It flung itself to the ground. Ralph never knew how his feet got out of the irons. But he was standing at the horse's head whilst it rolled over and back again, in a frenzied effort to free itself from the galling saddle. The deep loose sand prevented damage to the harness.

Sonny had his second chance to end the battle, but, though he sighted the horse's chest several times, his finger refused to press the trigger. Mrs Watts clung to the rails, her face like marble, her breathing checked. Kate, had she been able, would have screamed out idolatrous praise of the dauntless lad.

Once more the horse hunched its legs to rise. Once more Ralph leapt a full yard to the saddle. In it, he was shot up by the springing horse.

And then again came the eternal succession of whirling spins, high-flung rear-hoofs, back-rearing with fore-hoofs clawing the sky, humped arched back, gathered bunched feet, then up, up, to be suspended between earth and Heaven and down with terrific force on four stiffened legs. Buck, spin, rear; rear, spin, buck. On and on and on, without cease.

Horse and man were covered with bloody foam. Lethargy stole over the weaker. Less and less grew the pressure of knees against heaving flanks. Every bone in Ralph's body felt as though crushed to dust.

Buck, buck, buck. Spin and spin again. Buck, rear on fore-feet, rear on hind-legs, fore-feet thrashing the dust-thickened air. Rear, spin, buck, and buck again. In and out of the dust-cloud maddened beast and puny human charged in sickening lurches, whirls, and undulating rushes.

Mrs Watts did not see the end. She slumped down against the rails in a faint. Kate clung to the great fence as though all strength had ebbed from her limbs. Nothing of her moved but her eyes. Sonny was stunned.

Horse and man were enveloped in the dust, invisible. It seemed to Kate that something awful had happened. The world ceased to be. Movement stopped. Everything—time, her heart—stood still. Slowly the dust was wafted aside by a zephyr wind. Like the picture on the developing plate there came into her vision the still, mud-caked form of a horse lying stretched out, stiffened in death, its heart broken. And standing, regarding it pitifully, Ralph Thornton, the reins yet in his hands.

She saw him raise his head slowly. She saw his handsome face disfigured by dust, and the dust on his cheeks was furrowed by great, slow-falling tears. From a far distance she heard him say, plaintively:

"Katie, Katie! Oh, Katie, I've killed him!"

She saw him close his eyes and fall as if shot across the body of the great horse.

Chapter Eleven

Poor Old Bony

DUGDALE DROVE Kate Flinders and her uncle back to Barrakee the next afternoon. Ralph had been left behind, enthroned in the hearts of the overseer and his wife, and occupying the position of a god to the worshipping Sonny.

He had recovered from the faint of exhaustion to find himself in the horse-breaker's arms, whilst that alarmed man was carrying him to the house, followed by the two women, Mrs Watts having been revived by Kate. But the next morning, though he was quite uninjured, the young man could hardly walk.

He was wearing a pair of the overseer's trousers—his own having been frayed to ribbons—but the inner sides of his legs were red raw from the friction of the saddle, and walking was extremely painful. Kate and the squatter agreed that Mrs Thornton must not see him like that, or even know of his strenuous ride, for of late the Little Lady had complained of her heart.

"I think, Kate, we were wise to leave Ralph behind for a day or two," the squatter remarked, after an unusually long silence. "We must tell your aunt that Watts required additional help. What have you been thinking about?"

"Ralph."

The squatter waited, but Kate did not continue. He fell to wondering if his niece had discovered that she loved Ralph. Sincerely he hoped so, for her marriage to his and his wife's adopted son had been their joint dream. The girl had come to them at the death of her mother ten years earlier, her father having died but one month before. She occupied a place in his heart similar to that occupied by Ralph in the heart of his wife. After an interval, she said:

"What did you say to Sonny, Uncle?"

"Quite a lot," he replied grimly. "But, after all, he was not much to blame. He knew Ralph could ride, and like all of us who know horses, he didn't dream that the gelding would fight like that, certainly not that the brute would go mad. No, he wasn't much to blame, and he had the sense to get his rifle ready for use if the horse had thrown the lad and gone for him." For a moment he hesitated. "By gum, I'd have given a thousand pounds to see that ride."

"I would never have believed that a horse could have bucked so," she said with shining eyes. "And never would I have believed that any man could have ridden him. Ralph was just wonderful."

"He's got sand all right, Kate. He's altered a lot during his last school term. He is quieter, and I have the idea that he is thinking a great deal."

"Worrying about something?" she asked.

"No, not worrying. Just thinking—thinking out some problem. I may be quite wrong. Do you love him, Kate?"

"Of course I do," she flashed back.

Mr Thornton sighed. He knew that her unhesitating answer indicated one thing only. She went on:

"Why do you ask that, Uncle?"

"I was wondering," was his answer. "I should like to know in plenty of time, so that I could see about the wedding."

The car was travelling over the fine last stretch of road at fifty-five miles an hour. But Kate was insensible to the speed. A soft blush suffused her cheeks when she met the direct gaze of her companion.

"I don't love him that way, Uncle," she said. "Or at least I don't think I do." She added reproachfully: "You really should not have drawn that confession from me."

He saw her embarrassment, took her nearest hand in his two and pressed it. His voice was only a whisper when he said:

"Perhaps not, Katie. But never keep any secrets from your old uncle. Some day you will love. Some day Ralph will fall in

64

love. Your aunt and I would be happy if you were to fall in love with each—But no matter, my dear. Whoever is Mr Right—and the man you choose will be Mr Right—be assured, Katie, that you and he have in me a lovers' friend and confidant. I only want you to be gloriously happy."

Looking into the beautiful face, he wondered as he always did at the purity written upon it. Just then her eyes were moist and her lips a little parted. She was about to speak, but refrained. Her eyelids fell and the blue liquid pools were hidden. Putting her other hand over his two, she clasped them with a tight, affectionate squeeze.

When they reached the homestead dusk was falling. Their explanation of Ralph's absence given, they saw a momentary flash of disappointment in the Little Lady's face.

"Well, well, don't keep him out there long, John," she said, putting her arm through his. "You see, he will always ride the most outrageous horses, and sometimes I am afraid."

"Afraid you needn't be. Ralph can ride anything," replied her husband with conviction.

After dinner he left his wife reading in the long drawing room, and Kate playing soft airs on the piano, and proceeded to his office to read the mail arriving that day, and to ring up his riders. For an hour he lounged in the swivel chair behind his desk and was thinking of rejoining the ladies when someone knocked on the door.

"Come in," he answered, and reached for a cigarette.

A man entered, closing the door again softly. Striding to the desk, he came into the light from the low-hung bulb, and proved to be a stranger.

"Mr Thornton?" he asked in faintly drawling tones.

"Yes. What can I do for you?"

The squatter saw before him a man, whose age he guessed to be between thirty-five and forty. His features were those of the white man; his complexion was a ruddy black, not the jet-black of the thoroughbred aboriginal. He was dressed as a bushman.

"I have a letter for you, Mr Thornton, which will explain my presence."

The station-owner noted the accent and the grammar, which spoke of constant association with whites from an early age. He accepted a long blue envelope. It contained a sheet of foolscap, headed, "Police Station, Wilcannia", and read:

Dear Mr Thornton,

The case of the recent murder near your house presents a problem, now no nearer solution. Murders of, or by, aboriginals generally are difficult to investigate, for as you well know the mind of the aboriginal baffles the intelligence of the white.

The baptismal names of the bearer are Napoleon Bonaparte, but he may be persuaded to adopt a nom de plume. In any case, he is entitled to admiration for his powers of observation and deduction, as proved by many past successes in the solving of mysteries concerning aboriginals. In short, he is the finest bush detective in the Commonwealth.

HQ have loaned his services from Queensland, and I have been instructed to ask the favour of your assistance, which is necessary. He himself suggests that you give him employment about the homestead, such as painting your two boats, which I observed required paint. Although he stands much higher in the Force than I do, he will want to dine and live with your hands.

The letter was signed by Sergeant Knowles, and was marked "Strictly Confidential". Thornton glanced up and regarded his visitor with interest.

"Sit down, Mr Bonaparte," he said, indicating the chair on the far side of his desk.

The man smiled, revealing gleaming teeth. His blue eyes—the only other indication of the white in him—were twinkling when he said:

"My name, Mr Thornton, is Bony, without any 'Mister'. Everyone calls me Bony, from my chief to my wife and children in Brisbane."

"Then I, too, will call you Bony," agreed the station-owner pleasantly. "How did you come by your startling name?"

"I can assure you it was no wish of mine to insult the illustrious Emperor," explained the stranger. He accepted a cigarette with grace, and lighting it, went on, "I was discovered at the tender age of two weeks with my dead mother under a sandalwood tree in the far north of Queensland, and I was taken to the nearest mission station. There, a little later, the necessity for a name arose; and, whilst various names occupied the mind of the respected matron, she observed me trying to eat a copy of Abbott's *Life of Napoleon Bonaparte*. I have concluded since that the matron was a humorous soul."

"Sergeant Knowles says here that you have obtained not a little renown in the detection of crime. I don't think I've ever heard of you."

"I am glad to hear that, Mr Thornton." Bony blew a series of perfect smoke-rings. Then, calmly giving expression to an astounding vanity, he added: "If everyone had heard of me there would be no murders. My occupation would be gone, and I would be a most unhappy man."

"The sergeant says you want me to give you a job here," Thornton said.

"Yes. I thought I might allay suspicion by painting your boats. That occupation will give me opportunity to examine the scene of the murder. I will live with the men. Is Clair still here?"

"Yes. But I am thinking of sending him out to the back of the run. Will you want him?"

"Not just now. Are the blacks—Pontius Pilate's crowd—still camped up the river?"

"They are."

"Good! I may want them. Treat them with all kindness, Mr Thornton, for, as I said, I may want them. Should they suddenly decide to go for a walkabout, I might ask you to give them rations to keep them."

"Yes, all right. Have you formed any theories regarding the murder?"

"Plenty. However, it's certain that the crime was the conclusion of a feud lasting many years. Did you know King Henry? Did he ever work here, as Pontius Pilate stated?"

"Although at the time I did not remember him, I found on looking up my business diaries that he was employed here some twenty years ago for a period of ten weeks."

"Ah! And Clair?"

"Clair has never worked here before."

For a little while they stared at each other. Then:

"Clair's past is a mystery," Bony said thoughtfully. "However, I do not suspect Clair above others. D'you know if Clair can throw a boomerang?"

"As far as I am aware, he cannot. Why?"

Bony ignored the question.

"Have you seen at any time any of Pontius Pilate's crowd throwing a boomerang?" he asked.

"No. Why these questions?"

"If you answer my next question in the affirmative I will tell you. Sergeant Knowles informs me that there are several gum-trees about the place where King Henry was found dead. At the time of the murder, or since, you have not by any chance observed a wound on the trunk of one of them, such as would be made by being sharply struck by a sharp-edged piece of iron?"

Instantly Mr Thornton was taken back to the day following the crime. Again he saw the two policemen quartering the ground looking for clues, and the trunk of the giant gum bearing just such a wound as Bony described.

"Yes," he said, and gave the details.

"Good!" Bony announced with satisfaction. "We now know that if King Henry was not actually murdered by a boomerang one was thrown at him. How do we know? In his statement Frank Dugdale said that he heard a sound like the whirring of ducks, followed by a sharp report similar to a paling being struck by a stick. That was the flight of a boomerang and its impact against a tree. You see how sensible were the officials of New South Wales to loan from Queensland poor old Bony."

Chapter Twelve

Bony on Boomerangs

"Ah!" Bony and the squatter were standing before the great gum-tree bearing the strange wound. The clean-cut fresh injury was now distorted by gummy exudations, light amber in colour and crystal clear. After a minute inspection at a distance of two yards, the half-caste placed the packing-case he had brought against the tree and, stepping on it, proceeded to remove the gum crystals with a clasp-knife.

It was the morning following his appearance at Barrakee. Bony had been with the men at nine o'clock when they gathered outside the office to receive their orders and, taking care that he was heard, he had asked the squatter for work.

Thornton had appeared to cogitate, and then stated that the applicant could start right away and paint the two boats.

One of the boats had been hauled up on the riverbank, and lay there bottom-up on low trestles. A blow-lamp to remove the old paint and several triangular scrapers were in evidence.

No one recognized Bony, or guessed his profession, but one man. The instant he saw him, Clair's eyes narrowed; for, while the half-caste never remembered having seen the gaunt man before, Clair remembered the black trackers who had at one time left Longreach with the police to hunt down a madman. And when, from behind the pumping-engine, Clair saw the two by the gum-tree, he was sure that the newcomer was there to investigate. He wondered what Bony was doing to the bark of the tree.

It had been urgently impressed on Thornton that the ultimate success of Bony's activities depended on everyone on the station, including the women, being kept in ignorance of his profession. The squatter had given his word to remain silent on that point.

At the end of ten minutes the strange detective stepped down from the case and shut his knife.

"The examination and study of boomerangs, Mr Thornton, is of absorbing interest," he remarked.

"It must be," the other agreed, inwardly agreeing also that the study of this educated and refined half-caste, a foundling picked up from the shade of a sandalwood tree in Northern Queensland, was also of absorbing interest.

"Having always been interested in lethal weapons, my knowledge of the boomerang is unsurpassed," Bony stated, with unconscious but superb conceit. "There are three kinds of boomerang," he went on. "The Wongium, which returns in its flight to the thrower; the Kirras, which does not return; and the very heavy Murrawirrie. The Yarra blacks, now unhappily wiped out by you gentle white people, used only the first two—the Wongium for killing birds, and the Kirras as a war weapon.

"The Central Australians employ the last two—the Kirras for throwing and the Murrawirrie for use as a sword. You see, therefore, that the Kirras is, or was, in general use all over Australia; but there is a sharp difference in the carving. The eastern blacks always flattened one side; the Central Australia blacks never flattened either side, but kept the weapon round.

"Now, a Kirras made that wound. The boomerang was round, indicating that it came from Central Australia. It was thrown at a range of about thirty yards. Had it struck King Henry's head fair and square, it would have smashed it to pulp; had it reached him from a distance of a hundred and fifty yards, it would have killed him by cutting his head open. Having a description of King Henry's wound, I am inclined to reason that it was not the boomerang in flight that killed him."

"Well?" The squatter was astonished, and showed it.

"To proceed," Bony went on. "The weapon which made that mark I have proved came from Central Australia. From tip to tip it measured about thirty-three inches, and it probably weighed about two pounds. Without seeing the weapon, I can go farther. I can tell you the precise district in Central Australia from which it came, and the name of the tribe that made it. It is not a sharply-curved boomerang. On the outer edge, at equal distance from the centre, are two deep incisions cut diagonally; and those marks—which show in reverse on the tree there—were cut as a mark of respect to an ancient chief who, hugging two enemy warriors in the same embrace, crushed them to death."

For a little while Mr Thornton regarded Bony with undisguised admiration. "What else does that wound tell you?" he asked.

"That the thrower of the boomerang was not skilled in its use," replied Bony promptly. "A practised hand would never have missed at thirty yards, even in the dark. But enough of boomerangs for a while. Have you the list of names I asked for?"

"Yes. Here it is."

Bony glanced down the names written on foolscap, the occupation of each person being also given.

"Are all these people still about the homestead?" he asked.

"All but Blair and McIntosh, who are out on the run cleaning out a dam, and my son, now at Thurlow Lake."

The half-caste's expression was inscrutable; his blue eyes veiled. From a pocket in his dungarees he produced a silver pencil-holder and, kneeling beside the packing-case, used it as a desk. He added another name to the list, saying:

"John Thornton."

"Surely I am not suspect?" inquired the station-owner dryly.

Bony looked up. "I am looking for a sting-ray," he said. "I examine all the fish that come into my net to make sure if the sting-ray is there. There is a Mrs Thornton, is there not?"

The squatter laughed heartily.

"There is," he admitted.

Down went Mrs Thornton's name, and then yet another was added.

"And a Miss Kate Flinders, I believe," Bony murmured. Once more on his feet, he said: "I have here the name of every person at Barrakee homestead the night King Henry was murdered. I also have a list of the blacks up along the river. Our friend, the sergeant, definitely ascertained that there was not a single traveller on either side of the river for a distance of twelve miles up and twelve miles down on that precise night. Therefore, one of the names on my list is the name of King Henry's murderer.

"The case is one of exceptional simplicity," Bony went on, with astounding assurance. "I have to find the killer among only twenty-four people. My confreres in the city have to find a wrongdoer among hundreds of thousands, which is why they often fail and I never do.

"Adopting my original and exclusive methods of detection, I shall proceed to take a name and prove the innocence of the owner by inductive reasoning. With this process of elimination there will in the end remain one name—the name of King Henry's murderer."

"You make me nervous, my friend," Thornton said. "I shall have no peace of mind till you tell me you have erased my name."

"Then I will tell you when I do."

"Thank you! Here is my wife, curious to know why we are conspiring here."

Mrs Thornton and her niece were walking across the billabong. Bony regarded them with keen eyes. To him they were fish in his net, and either might be the sting-ray. When near, the Little Lady looked at him kindly; Kate with interest. The squatter smiled, and said:

"I am having the boats painted, dear. Not, I am afraid, before it was needed."

"You are right, John. They need it very much. Kate and I were walking in the garden, and your long conversation has made us curious."

"My dear, you should not be curious," admonished her husband. Turning to the half-caste, he said: "This is a new hand, with the exceptional name of Napoleon Bonaparte."

"Napoleon Bonaparte!" Mrs Thornton echoed.

"Madam, it is my regret that I am not the illustrious Corsican," Bony said gallantly. "It is my regret that his name has been taken in vain by those who gave it me. Alas! no man can be responsible for his parents: I certainly was, however, responsible for my name, though I was but six months of age."

Bony described his christening, following the mutilation of Abbott's famous history.

"I hope you have read that history," the Little Lady said, looking at the dark face, the blue eyes, and the sharp features of the new hand.

"If I had read the Bible through as often as I have read that history, Madam, I should today be a Doctor of Theology."

Two tiny vertical lines appeared between Mrs Thornton's eyes. Before her stood a gentleman in dungarees, an Australian half-caste with the manner and accent of a university man. Bony was something entirely new to her.

"In that case," she said, "you will always experience poignant sympathy with the Eagle of France chained to the Dreadful Rock."

"Madam," he said in return, "it was an unspeakable tragedy. My ancestors on my mother's side knew not Christ, but they were better Christians than the Emperor's jailers." For a moment the squatter's wife and the half-caste gazed steadily at each other. Then Bony bowed with instinctive grace, waited for the ladies, escorted by the squatter, to move away, and finally sat down on the upturned boat and lit a cigarette.

For several minutes he remained in deep thought, smoking pensively. Suddenly he produced a small diary and, opening it at the page marked with that date, he wrote: "Mrs Thornton, capable of strong emotion."

74

Chapter Thirteen

Mrs Thornton's Ambition

A WEEK PASSED with accustomed quietude at Barrakee. The river had almost ceased to run, and the long shallow stretches between the holes at every sharp bend were dry, with the exception of a meandering runnel. The days were brilliant and deliriously cool after the fierce heat of summer; and the nights, clear and invigorating, were lightened by the winking lamps of Heaven, so bright and big as seemingly to be affixed to the topmost branches of the gums.

Bony fell naturally into his place among the men, and with them quickly became a favourite. If at first his correct and somewhat magniloquent speech aroused comment, this single peculiarity was quickly dimmed by familiarity. His supply of stories was unfailing, and his wonderful accomplishment of eliciting haunting strains from a single gum-leaf was an inexhaustible source of pleasure.

A few days after Bony's arrival Sergeant Knowles called in for afternoon tea on his way from the little township of Louth. Ranking much higher in the social scale of the bush people than do his peers in the British police force, the sergeant was always welcomed by the Women of Barrakee.

The reason for this difference in status is no mystery. Australia's mounted police are recruited from bushmen. Whilst not attracting gentlemen adventurers, as similar organizations in other dominions may do, the force does attract sound men from a community that contains ninety-nine per cent natural gentlemen.

A farmer often lives all his life on his little farm; the city-dweller all his life in one suburb. Beyond the suburb and the farm the world is a myth. With the majority of bushmen, however, the restless nomadic habits of the blacks they have displaced have eaten into their vitals. Even the semi-civilized blacks must go on a walkabout when the call is heard; and it is the same call which urges a bushman suddenly to leave his job, break for the nearest hotel to spend his cheque, and then take his walkabout before settling again for a little while in a new job.

The walkabouts cover in many cases hundreds of miles, and in a few years make the man familiar with all the States. His mind is broadened by travel and fresh human intercourse. His philosophy is one of simple happiness. The amount of his reading is prodigious, the range of it is wide.

Such, then, is the material that goes to make an inland policeman. The class and the police-court mould the recruit's speech as the riding-master weans him from his easy seat on a horse to military stiffness. The force finishes his education, so well begun by the walkabouts.

Thornton and the sergeant were standing beside the latter's car after tea. The sergeant was in plain clothes, but there was no mistaking the soldier-policeman in his upright figure and keen face.

"What do you think of Bony?" he asked, with a smile.

"I think him the most extraordinary man I have ever met," Thornton replied. "He knows as much about the Emperor Napoleon as he does about boomerangs and playing on a gum leaf."

The sergeant chuckled.

"He asked me once who I considered the greatest man who ever lived, and when I named Jesus Christ he said solemnly: 'Jesus is the Son of God; but the first Emperor Napoleon was the God of the French nation'."

"I fully believe it," the squatter said thoughtfully. "He was giving me a lecture on boomerangs the morning after he came here and, my wife happening to join us, I introduced him to her, wholly, I think, on account of his name. She, too, is a great admirer of the Little Corporal. Yes, he's an astonishing person."

"I had a letter two days ago from a brother-in-law who is an inspector at Charleville, Queensland," said the sergeant. "He said he had heard that Bony was being sent here on this case, and gave me rather a good history of him.

"For many years he was a black tracker in the far west of that State, but before that he earned the degree of an M.A. at Brisbane University. Do you remember the case of the kidnapping of the Governor's daughter whilst the vice-regal party were touring North-West Queensland?"

"I do."

"It was Bony who got the child back from the outlaw gang, and Bony who led the police almost across the Northern Territory to West Australia after the gang, which they caught. They offered Bony membership in the police force, and Bony told them he was not a policeman but a detective. Somehow, he thinks the two quite different. The Governor saw him about it, and Bony said that his gifts and his education entitled him, at the lowest, to the position of detective-sergeant. They gave it him.

"Today he ranks as detective-inspector and, as I told you in my letter, is the very finest bush detective in the Commonwealth. He's married to a half-caste, and has three children. They, and his wife, live on a ten-acre block of dense tea-tree scrub not far out of Brisbane, and once every year the whole family roll up their swags and accompany Bony on his annual walkabout." The sergeant lit his pipe and climbed into the driving-seat, and then added: "Yes, they think a lot of Bony in Queensland. My brother-in-law told me he's never failed in a case."

"He must be a good man."

"By all accounts he is. You see, he's a specialist in bush-craft and in the black fellow's psychology, neither of which a white man will ever be expert at. Well, goodbye! You might have Bony with you some time, but he'll surely win."

The sergeant drove away on the down track, and the squatter sauntered into his office. There he rang up Thurlow Lake, and asked for Ralph.

"Well, how is it, Ralph?" he asked, when the young man spoke.

"Good as gold now, Dad."

"I am glad of that. Has Dug arrived? I sent him this morning with a load of rations on the truck."

"No, he is not here yet. What time did he leave?"

"About nine. It's three now, so he should be about due. Look here, Ralph!" The squatter's voice dropped to a whisper. "Can you walk easily now?"

"Yes, oh, yes!" murmured the young man.

"Well, you had better come in tomorrow with Dug. Your mother is getting anxious about you. Mind, not a word about that fool ride of yours."

"All right, Dad, I'll remember."

"Good lad! Bye-bye!"

The squatter rang off and turned to signing cheques made out by the bookkeeper. After that he put on his felt and walked down to the shearing-shed, more to fill in time than for any purpose.

The next morning, early, Black, the jackeroo, drove him and Kate to Wilcannia, where, his turn due, he occupied the Bench and gave judgement in a few "d. and d." cases and a matter of infringement of one of the countless motor laws.

In consequence, the Little Lady was sitting alone that afternoon on the wide veranda, waiting to give Ralph afternoon tea. She had heard the arrival of the big two-ton truck, followed by the voice of her beloved boy whilst on his way to the bathroom. Now, with eager expectation on her kindly face, and carrying the scent of garden flowers wherever she went, she made one of her sudden resolutions.

And then all at once the light went out, for two strong hands slipped round her head and covered her eyes. A face was pressed to her greying hair, and from its depths a low, harsh voice demanded:

"Guess, Madam, who I am."

"Ralph!" was her instant reply.

Over her left shoulder appeared the young man's face, his eyes dancing, his white teeth revealed by a light smile. Quickly turning, her hands went up to his head, and they kissed.

"Mother mine!" he murmured, embracing her. Then he snatched a chair close to her and, searching her face with his eyes, added:

"You are not looking so well as I would like you to look, Little Lady. I must tell Dad about it, and get him to take you to Sydney for a holiday before the lamb-marking."

"It's your imagination, dear. I feel quite well," she assured him.

"A nice restful holiday with the sea-breeze blowing in your face will bring the roses back, anyway."

"Silly! I'm too old to have roses in my cheeks."

Their conversation was interrupted by the arrival of Martha with the tea-things. When Mrs Thornton saw her huge bare feet, she sighed audibly. It was Martha who spoke first, hurriedly, as though quite prepared with a very excellent defence.

"Missy," she rolled out, "that there Bony he go plant-it my boots. I bin give him cup of tea, and now him gone."

"You get on his tracks, Martha, straight away," laughed Ralph. "Take a waddy with you and wallop him."

"Mine tinkit I knock off his plurry head," Martha replied ferociously, and thundered away—to find her best elastic-sided brown boots on a kitchen-chair. How was she to know that Bony wanted one of them for a particular purpose?

"This Bony appears to be somewhat of a character, Mother," remarked Ralph over his tea.

"He's quite a character," she said. "Kate and I saw your father talking to him near the boats he is repainting, and, like women, as we wanted to know what they were talking about for such a long time . . ." She told the lad the half-caste's explanation of his name, ending by saying softly: "Bony and I found that we had a bond of sympathy."

"Oh! In what way?"

"We both adore the Emperor Napoleon, Ralph. In fact, our first interview ended almost theatrically."

"Explain, please."

She told him, and Ralph's interest in Bony was excited.

"I must make his acquaintance," he announced. "Although I have read Mr Abbott's history, I cannot agree that the Emperor was quite the demi-god that historians would have us believe. Still, he was a great man, in that he always played the game when his opponents did not."

"Which was where he made his greatest mistake," she said swiftly. "Anyway, Ralph, let us put aside the Emperor for a little while and discuss something else—ourselves, for instance."

"The subject will be equally interesting. How shall we start?"

"I have been thinking a very great deal about you, Ralph, since you came home from school," she said, her eyes fixed on his. "I am glad, so glad, that you are learning so well and quickly to take up your burden. Sometimes I think I shall not be much longer with you, and when my call does come I should like to know that your position in the world was assured and that you were settled."

He would have spoken, but she went on hurriedly.

"No, no, dear. Don't be alarmed. I am not going to die for a long time yet. Your father and I have decided to go down to the sea directly the shearing is over, and I shall come back a new woman. We'll talk about you, and the plans I have made for you. You don't mind my making plans for you, do you? All mothers do."

"Of course not," he said gently, uneasiness about her health in his eyes, and shocked by the first hint of mortality in his young life.

"You know, dear, that when your father and I are taken, you inherit Barrakee and all your father's wealth, after sufficient has been deducted to provide Kate an annuity. But, when you become the Squatter of Barrakee, you will need a good wife. A good wife means so much to a bushman. Ralph, don't tell me unless you wish, but have you thought about Kate?"

"As a wife?" Ralph asked, with not a little surprise.

"Yes, as a wife. Do you love her, Ralph?"

"I do. I am very fond of Kate," he said warmly. "Why she is the prettiest girl in the world, and the sweetest; but I've never thought of her as a sweetheart. Honestly, it always seemed to me that we are brother and sister."

"No doubt; but you are only cousins," Mrs Thornton said softly. Then, reaching forward, she took both his hands in hers. "Never forget, Ralph, that I think only of your happiness. Had I not been so sure of Kate, I would never have mentioned her in this way. Whatever you do, never marry except for love. There is plenty of time for you, but Kate is a beautiful girl, and every man makes himself agreeable to her, courts her, and could easily fall in love with her. I would hate for you to suddenly discover that you loved her when it was too late. Think about it, will you?"

"Certainly I will." He laughed gently. "It would not, I think, be difficult to love Kate sufficiently to make me want to marry her. As a matter of fact, I never thought about it, but, now you have made me think about it, there's no knowing what may happen."

For several moments she looked into his dark, handsome eyes, searchingly, longingly, a great affection in hers. Slowly and softly, she said:

"If you were to fall in love with Kate, Ralph, and one day, not necessarily soon, you were married, I should be so happy. You see, I love you both, and I am afraid that some other boy will win her, a prize that should be yours."

Again they looked deeply each at the other. Their eyes eventually falling, a silence fell upon them, a long silence broken by Ralph pushing back his chair and standing over her, saying:

"Give me a week, Little Lady. I'll search my heart and tell you then what I find there."

Chapter Fourteen

Bony's Imagination

BONY RECLINED with his back against one of the trestles supporting the first boat to be repainted. All the old paint had been burned and scraped off, and the boat, lying keel uppermost, appeared like an old hen whose feathers have all dropped out. He sat in the sun, smoking a cigarette, and looking with vacant eyes at the border of gums on the farther bank of the river.

By his side lay a slab of cement-hard clay, dark grey in colour, and about a foot square. That morning he had cut it carefully out of hard ground near the garden gate.

To ordinary eyes there was nothing of interest about that slab of dry clay. To ordinary eyes there was no mark on it until they had gazed for a long time at its flat surface. Then might vague perception dawn of a series of opposing curves, very faint and irregular in impression.

Bony's eyes, however, were not ordinary. He saw here on the flat surface a clear impression of a man's left boot.

Over all that vast area of Australia not broken up by the plough the ground is an open book for those who can read. The history of the wild is written there. Reptiles and animals cannot live without making and leaving their mark. Even birds must alight sometimes and register themselves by their tracks.

The reader of the open book gains proficiency only by practice, and his final expertness is limited by his eyesight. The habit of observation is the first essential, knowledge of the natives of the wild the second, and reasoning power the third. Whilst the first and third essentials make a white man an efficient tracker, the second essential, combined with supervision, makes the black man an expert tracker. And, through his black mother and his white father, Bony possessed the three essentials, plus abnormal vision; which was why he was a king of trackers.

His keen eyes saw impressed on the piece of clay that which only the microscope and the camera would reveal to the white man. A freak of Nature had preserved it from the rain that had fallen after it had been made, for it was the only track left.

The depth of the curves proved that the imprint had been made after three or four points of rain had fallen and slightly moistened the surface. The succeeding rain had not been prolonged sufficiently—and the gauge at the homestead proved that the quantity had been twenty-eight points—to dissolve the surface into sufficient mud to flow into the indentations. Why that single track had been preserved was because the surface of the clay on which it had been made was absolutely level. Thus gravitation had not caused mud to flow there as it had done on all surfaces not absolutely level.

To Bony's keen vision and reasoning was due the revelation that the person wearing a No. 9 boot who made the impression stood on that spot two or four minutes after the thudding sound that evidently killed King Henry reached Dugdale. And, allowing half a minute for the killer to make sure of his work, two minutes and three seconds were necessary for him to walk rapidly away from the corpse, across the billabong, to the place where he left the solitary track. Bony had walked it, and timed the walk.

The wearer of a No. 9 boot, therefore, was in the vicinity of the murder at the precise moment the deed was done. If the wearer had not actually struck the blow, he had been within seventy-three yards from the place where the blow had fallen.

It was a clue, certainly, towards the elucidation of the crime. Bony was intensely happy. For a whole week he had searched when opportunity offered for that possible track. And, knowing that a No. 9 boot is generally worn by a person of twelve stone and over, by a quick process of elimination the finger of fate pointed to three persons—Clair, John Thornton and Martha the gin.

Within twenty-four hours of his arrival Bony had noted the boot size of every person on his list, other than Martha. He knew that John Thornton's boot size was No. 8, and he knew, too, that Clair's was No. 9. That afternoon he had ascertained that Martha's elastic-sided riding boots also were the man's size No. 9.

Clair or Martha had made that track, and Clair or Martha was within seventy-three yards of King Henry when he met his death.

Bony had become great friends with the black cook, and had watched his chance to borrow her boots, with which he made an impression on a prepared piece of clay. The Research Department at Headquarters would tell what even Bony's hawk eyes could not see. With camera and microscope the original track and the rough cast would be examined to discover if there were identical marks or not on both. If there were, proof that one and the same boot made them would be established. If not, then it would be necessary to apply the same process to Clair's footwear, and on some pretext or other Clair must be brought in from his pumping job, since it was not advisable for Bony to go out to the Basin.

Regarding Clair, too, the half-caste had sent a letter to a friend of his living in the district where roamed that tribe of blacks whose bygone chief, a super-wrestler, had hugged two men at once to death.

To Bony the case afforded mental exhilaration. Because the rain had wiped out the letters and words stamped on the ground, Bony cried blessings on the rain. It was not now a humdrum case where good tracking only was required. To clear up the case successfully demanded inductive reasoning of a high order, and this mental activity was infinitely preferable to the physical labour of moving about. Moreover, it was beautifully restful to sit there in the sun and merely think. One need not even think if one did not wish. There was tomorrow, and there were the days following tomorrow when one could think. Yes, to the devil with thinking! So Bony slept.

How long he did sleep he never would say, although he knew precisely by the position of the sun when he fell asleep and its position when he awoke. He was awakened by a masculine cough, but the process of his awakening was confined to the quiet opening of his eyes. Before him, sitting on an oil-drum, was the smiling Ralph Thornton.

"Had a good nap?" he asked.

"I was thinking out a problem," Bony lied. "It has ever been my misfortune that I cannot sleep in daylight."

Ralph laughed at the glibly-spoken double falsehood.

"Is your name Napoleon Bonaparte?" was his second question.

"Those were my baptismal names. But"—solemnly—"I call myself Bony."

"Well, Bony, are you acquainted with a lady named Martha?"

"I have that pleasure."

"Then it will interest you to know that Martha is looking for you with a waddy in her hand," said the grinning youth. "She says you stole her No. 9's."

"The human mind is always liable to delusions," Bony murmured. And then, seeing Ralph look curiously at his clue, he added blandly: "That piece of clay contains my problem."

"Ah! And the problem is—"

"The problem is a difficult one, because it requires imagination to study it and to find a solution," explained the half-caste, picking up the slab of clay and holding it carelessly, knowing the unlikeliness of the young man's observing the bootprint. "In this lump of matter," he went on, "we hold a universe. Let us in imagination crush it to fragments and separate a fragment from the mass.

"Here we fall back on facts, for on examining our fragment we find that it is composed of atoms. Separating one of the atoms, we see before us a solar system—sun, moon and planets.

"Behold, then, established facts, reality, truth. Behold now Bony's sublime imagination. The ordinary human mind is limited. It clings to facts, measurements, and scales. My mind rises above all three. At the bottom of the scale—the human scale made by the human mind—we have the atom, a miniature solar system, invariably in close proximity to countless other solar systems. At the top end of the scale we have our vast far-off solar system and our immeasurable universe. But perhaps you are not interested."

"I am. Please go on."

"Well, then, listen attentively," commanded Bony, a re-incarnation of Plato talking to his students. "You may deride imagination, but imagination rules the world, the universe. I have shown you the bottom and the top of our scale—our average human scale. I will now show you that Bony's mind recognizes no scale, no limit. My imagination invents a super-super-microscope, and with super-instruments takes up one of the planets in the atom and sees a world composed of yet smaller atoms—atoms from a world within an atom which forms part of our world.

"My sublime imagination invents a telescope which ranges beyond and out of our universe, and I see that our solar systems are but neighbouring atoms, the whole comprising, let us say, a stick of wood on a greater world. I see, too, a man walking towards the inert stick of wood, and the time he takes to move each of his feet is a million of our years, our little whizzing years. The man lays down his swag. He is thirsty. He wishes to boil his billy. And, casting around for fuel, he picks up the stick of wood wherein is our world, our solar system, our universe, and with other sticks of wood starts a fire. Time to him is eternity to us; time to us is eternity to the atoms in this lump of clay. Half a million of our years expire whilst he draws a match across his match-box. The fire catches the wood, our universe; and soon we are gone, turned into floating gas.

"The Bible says: 'In the beginning.' We think it means the beginning of our world. Even Bony's imagination cannot conceive the Beginning, or the End."

The lad was gazing at the half-caste with rapt interest. Bony noted his intelligent face, and smiled; and when Bony smiled one lost sight of his colour and saw only a calm, dignified countenance lighted by dark-blue eyes, whose far-seeking gaze bespoke, at times, the visionary. The man's egotism was simple, almost unconscious. His mind was high above the average human standard, and he was honest enough to take pride in the fact.

"Where did you learn all this?" Ralph asked.

"In books, in men, and animals, in sticks of wood and lumps of clay, in the sun, moon, and stars," Bony told him. "My imagination, as I have said, is without limit; but there are very severe limits to my knowledge. Still, should I live another thirty years, those limits may be widened a little."

"My mother tells me you are keen on Napoleon," Ralph said.

"Your mother, sir, is a good woman. She sees goodness where goodness is found. Naturally, she would find it in the Emperor. 'Honour thy father that thy days may be long, but honour thy mother that thy soul may live for ever!' I honour neither my father nor my mother."

"And why not?"

"Because they did not honour me. My mother was black, my father white. They were below the animals. A fox does not mate with a dingo, or a cat with a rabbit. They disobeyed the law of the wild. In me, you see neither black nor white, you see a hybrid."

"Oh, I think you are too hard on yourself," Ralph objected.

"Not a bit," Bony replied. "I am what I am. I am not ashamed of it, because it is not my fault. But I feel sometimes as if black and white are at war in me, and will never be reconciled."

They looked at each other silently for a while. Then Ralph said, in his frank way:

"I think I can imagine your feelings, Bony. But, though you bear marks of your people's guilt, they have at least bequeathed you a fine brain, and I think that a great brain is the greatest gift a man can have."

Bony smiled once again. Then he said, in a lighter tone:

"Plenty of grey matter is an asset, isn't it?"

Chapter Fifteen

Chasing a 'Killer'

RALPH THORNTON had fallen under the spell of a half-caste detective. The quiet, thoughtful young heir to Barrakee felt strangely drawn to this link uniting the worlds of black and white, with his imaginative flights, quaint philosophy, and colossal vanity withal.

Bony's headquarters had written to say that the imprint he had made of Martha's boot did not correspond in important details with the one upon the slab of clay he had dug out of the ground near the garden gate. A simple yet effective plan was then carried out, with the cooperation of John Thornton, to obtain the bootprints of Clair.

A pretext was found to get Clair away from the Basin one morning. Ralph had been directed to call for him with the light truck, and to take the gaunt man to another part of the run to help repair a windmill. An hour after the two had left the Basin, the squatter and Bony arrived there, and the latter took plaster impressions of several of Clair's tracks.

April continued dry, brilliant, and warm, and ended in a burst of unusual heat. At ten o'clock on the morning of the last day the sun was powerful in spite of its growing swing to the north.

That really hot morning of the last day of April saw Ralph and Kate Flinders riding in what was known as the North Paddock. The young man had been ordered to ride the thirty-odd miles of fence which formed its boundary, and turn in from it any sheep that might be 'hanging on it'—a sheepman's phrase meaning sheep that are hugging the fence instead of moving towards the great water-tank in the centre of the paddock.

Kate having elected to accompany him, much to his delight, Ralph had supervised the placing of her light lunch in the saddlebag and, in addition, the strapping of a quart pot to her saddle. The two were young, light-hearted, and rode mettlesome hacks that would prefer a galloping race to alternate walking and cantering.

They were cantering across a wide flat side by side, when suddenly the young man pulled up and went back a dozen yards, his eyes searching the ground. When the girl turned, Ralph was off his horse and walking in small circles with the earnest downward scrutiny of a Scotsman looking for a lost sixpence. Dismounting also, Kate joined her companion in searching for tracks.

"There's nothing here, Ralph," she said presently. "What did you think you saw?"

"I didn't 'think' I saw anything, Katie," he told her, still moving in circles, his horse's reins over his arm. "No, I didn't 'think' anything. Here, quite plainly, we have the tracks of three ewes and two lambs. Do you see them?"

"I see sheep-tracks," was her reply.

"Yes, and they are travelling our way along the fence, and they are not walking. In fact, Katie, they are being chased by a dingo."

"A dingo! Are you sure?"

"Quite. Here and there are his tracks. We'll follow them for a while. They are quite fresh."

Copying him, she mounted her horse and followed just behind, watching with a curious sense of proprietorial pride the way he unerringly rode his horse over the tracks. Only occasionally did she see a sheep-track on the hard ground of the flat, never once that of the dog.

Across the flat they came to a line of low sand-hills, and here she saw distinctly the tracks of three sheep and two lambs, as well as those of the pursuing dog. But her knowledge of tracks did not indicate to her which way the sheep were travelling, how many there were of them, and if they were walking or running.

Once off the sand-hills, the tracks on the hard surface were again invisible to her, but Ralph led the way, twisting first to the left and then again to the right close to the five-wire fence. In and out of timber belts, across another flat, and to yet another line of low sand-hills Ralph urged his horse, never once removing his gaze from the ground a yard or two beyond his animal's head. And on the summit of the sand-hills, he yelled: "Come on, Kate!" Seeing his horse leap into a gallop, her own mount was eager to follow. The wind whistled in her ears and the pace became hard. Beyond the figure of her companion, a quarter of a mile distant, she saw the white mass of a dead sheep, saw beside it the red tawny shape of a wild dog. The dog, seeing them, stared at their oncoming rush for some six seconds, and then, turning, became a red streak flying northward, parallel with the fence.

The horses were wild for a gallop. Seeing the fleeing dog in the lead, the excitement of the chase gripped them no less than it did their riders.

Through the fence was the dog's one salvation, but it did not realize it. At first increasing the distance between itself and its pursuers in a tremendous burst of speed, the horses' greater stamina soon outstayed the increase and, for some two miles, dog and horses kept their relative positions. But the speed of both horses and dog began rapidly to lessen.

Immediately the dog showed signs of fatigue, Ralph gently pulled back his horse whilst keeping close to the fence, with the purpose of edging the dog away from it. Once it got beyond the fence it would have won the race, for the fence would have balked the riders, who were not mad enough to put untrained mounts at it.

Slowly but inevitably they drew near the sheep murderer, who led them across flat and sand-hill, and through belts and clumps of dense mulga. Quite suddenly the dog turned to the left, running along a narrow margin of clay-pan between flat and sand-hill.

When the dog turned, Kate immediately did likewise, but Ralph took a greater curve, bringing their positions relatively parallel, then about four hundred yards behind the quickly-tiring dog.

Sometimes it looked back at them, ears flattened, tongue lolling and dripping foam. Every hundred yards now its speed slackened, and slowly Ralph reined back his mount to an easy canter. There was plenty of time, the dog was well away from the fence, and two riders were behind him wide apart and able to head him off the fence, should he turn that way. There was nothing that could save the dog from imminent vengeance.

From a long lope the dog's gait dropped into a laboured trot. The tender flesh between the cushions of its foot-pads was full of torturing burrs, and with a pitiful whimper it essayed to sit for a moment to extract them with its teeth.

But Ralph was upon him, and with a fresh burst of speed the wild dog increased its lead. Keeping his horse to its easy canter, all his actions closely followed by the girl, the young man pressed forward and, when he saw that the dog was almost done, he unbuckled his right stirrup-leather and, drawing it out of the saddle, gathered buckle and end together and swung the stirrup-iron like a sling in a circular motion, the iron forming a ring of burnished light.

The wild dog was now done up. Kate's heart was sick with pity for its condition, but Ralph's eyes were blazing with hate, his mind being filled with the picture of the torn, dead sheep.

Then followed a spell of sharp dodging, the dog allowing the rider to keep constantly at its heels. Dog and horse whirled and doubled back, circled and angled for half an hour. Never for a moment could the dog shake off Nemesis. Every second its actions were slower.

Finally it stopped suddenly and, whirling round, snapped at Ralph's horse's forefeet. The stirrup-iron was still whirling in its gleaming circle. The dog, seeing it, became fascinated. Kate closed her eyes, but those of the dog remained fixed on the revolving steel.

When the girl looked again, the dog was dead, and Ralph was dismounting. His face was red with excitement and his horse's head was lowered, its sides heaving from the fatigue of the race. Kate slipped to the ground beside her companion.

"It's a big brute, isn't it?" she said.

"Yes," he agreed. "It's the 'Killer'."

"Are you sure?"

"Positive."

The dog's depredations had become serious. For several years it had killed sheep after sheep, and all the efforts of the doggers to trap it had been in vain. The Pastoral Protection Board paid two pounds for every dog's scalp, and as a further incentive John Thornton had offered a reward of thirty pounds for the capture of this particular dog. It was estimated that the "Killer" had murdered quite half a thousand sheep during the six years of its activities on the Barrakee run.

Several times it had been seen in the act by stockmen, and the tallied descriptions left no doubt as to the identity of the dead animal with the "Killer". Ralph produced his pocket-knife and skinned the beast from nose to tail, taking a thin strip of hide down its back. Rolling the scalp into a ball, he tied it to his saddle.

"We are not more than a mile from the tank, Katie," he said. "I vote we go straight there and boil our quarts. The horses want a spell."

"Very well. If they want a spell as badly as I want a panni-kin of tea, they must want it bad. And, by the look of the poor things, they do."

By the time the riders reached the tank the horses had cooled off, and, loosening the girths, they allowed the animals to drink before hitching the reins to the tank fence. A washing of hands followed, and then came the boiling of the two quart pots and making of tea. In the shade of the engine-house they ate their lunch.

The boy and girl were strangely silent during the meal. Kate was looking forward to the expression of joy on the weather-beaten, kindly face of her uncle when he saw the scalp and heard the story of the chase. But Ralph was think-ing of the Little Lady's talk with him about the girl at his side.

He had given much thought to Kate from that quite new angle. That he loved Kate he had not the slightest doubt. He had always loved her. He always would. But he had loved her, and did love her, as a sister only. He was not sure what the sexual love of man and woman, which should be the basic urge to marriage, really was. Never having been in love, it was not unnatural that he should confuse brotherly love with loverly love.

The result of deep cogitation was that he felt positive he would be happy married to Kate, if she could find happiness in being married to him. Any doubts as to the quality of his love for her were eventually banished from his mind in a laudable decision to please his foster-mother in all things.

A young man not yet twenty, his power to love was great. The almost worshipping love the Little Lady bore for him was every whit reciprocated. The tie between them, being without passion, was indeed a wonderful and beautiful thing, and in a similar way but lesser degree he loved Kate Flinders.

"I say, Katie," he said suddenly, "do you love me?"

"Of course," she replied, as if the fact were nothing out of the way. And then, looking at him, she saw that his dark face was deeply flushed.

"Yes, I know you love me that way, Katie," he said slowly. "But—"

He stopped suddenly on observing the blood mantling in her face. In that moment it came to him that never before had he realized how beautiful Kate Flinders really was, and for the first time he felt a leaping desire to possess her.

"But, dear, I want to know if you love me—if you could love me sufficiently well to marry me," he said. "You see, we have always got on splendidly, haven't we? And it occurred to me that it would be a really terrible thing if another fellow came along and collared you away out of my life, as it were. I

94

love you, Katie dear, and I am certain we should be happy. Besides, it would so please those at home."

He had taken one of her hands whilst speaking, and her eyes had fallen from his frank gaze. His last sentence took her mind back to that time she rode with her uncle, and the stumblingly-worded ambition of the big-hearted man who had been so good to her came back to her, as indeed it had done since repeatedly. John Thornton had planted the seed in her mind, as his wife had planted a similar seed in the mind of Ralph; and, both being heartwhole, the seeds of suggestion had taken root.

"What have you to say, Kate?" Ralph asked softly.

Suddenly she looked at him. He was very handsome, very gentle, brave, and clever; fine in every way. She admired him intensely.

"If you wish it, Ralph, I'll marry you," she said.

"Goodo, Katie darling!" he said, suddenly smiling. "This, I think, is where I kiss you."

"Yes, I think it is, Ralph dear," she agreed.

Chapter Sixteen

Three Letters—and a Fourth

RALPH THORNTON kept his two items of news until dinner was over and the family were sitting in the long main room of the house, part dining and part drawing room. Kate was playing softly on the piano an old Italian love song sent her by a girl friend in Sydney. Although she was quite happy about having consented to marry Ralph, she was perplexed. She felt that she was not so happy as she ought to be; that though her happiness was comforting it was not the tumultuous emotion so rapturously described by the novelists.

John Thornton was reading *The Pastoral Gazette*; his wife was sewing; Ralph, laying down a history of Alexander the Great, began to speak.

"Dad, Kate and I had two adventures this afternoon," he said. The girl, hearing him, played still more softly.

"Oh! And what were they?"

"We found a wild dog eating a sheep it had killed in the North Paddock." And the young man graphically described the chase, ending by: "I think, when you see the scalp, that you'll be pleased to divide between Kate and me your cheque for thirty pounds. It was the 'Killer'."

"The 'Killer'!" echoed the squatter.

"Yes. Fawn red coat, with almost black feet. Prick-eared and full curling red tail."

"That's the beast," John Thornton agreed. "Well! I'm mighty glad you got him, Ralph. Certainly, tomorrow I'll write you cheques for fifteen pounds apiece, and be very glad to do it. How will you spend yours?"

"With your permission, I should like to buy an engagement ring."

"An engagement ring!" the squatter echoed the second time.

Mrs Thornton ceased sewing and Kate stopped playing. Leaving the piano, the girl came into the circle and seated herself between the old and the young man. The latter was regarded by the Little Lady with startled eyes; by her husband with the suspicion of a frown.

"Have you become engaged, dear?" Mrs Thornton asked.

"Not yet, Mother. We agreed to wait until we received your permission," the young man replied quietly.

"Who, Ralph, is the girl?"

"Why, Mother, Katie, of course!"

The strained expression of the woman's face relaxed and gave place to a dawning smile, accompanied by a low chuckle from her husband. It was Kate who broke the silence by saying:

"I hope you are both pleased."

"Pleased! Oh, Kate! I have dreamed of your marriage to Ralph for years."

"Then, Mother, your dream shall come true." Ralph rose and stood behind Kate's chair, allowing his hands gently to caress her hair. He said: "Katie and I have decided that we love each other, that our marriage will cement the family more closely. We felt sure that you and Dad would be pleased."

"We are, my boy," said John Thornton. "Indeed, we are. You and Katie have made your mother and me proud and happy. But don't hurry things; you are both of you very young yet. Suppose we say five years, at least, for the betrothal?"

"Don't be so hard, John," entreated his wife. "Two years will be plenty."

"As you will, my dear. Do you want to be formally engaged?"

"We want to please Auntie and you, Uncle," Kate said softly. The squatter was on the verge of saying something when Mrs Thornton spoke decisively:

"Of course they do, John. They say they are in love with each other, and want some day soon to marry. What I should like would be to give a betrothal party. Let it be the evening of Saturday week, the day the Land Board sits at Wilcannia. Mr and Mrs Watts will be here that day, as well as Mr and Mrs Hemmings and the Stirlings. Let us call it a 'Surprise Party' on the invitations, and then towards the end you, John, can announce the engagement; and you, Ralph, can place the ring on Kate's finger. You must wire to Sydney tomorrow. Now, don't you think that's a good plan?"

"And who, my dear Ann, is going to pay for this party?" inquired the station-owner, with stern face but twinkling eyes.

"You, of course, dear. The bills will come in about the end of June, and you can pay them the same day you pay your income tax. Are you young people agreeable to the party?"

"Yes, Auntie," came Kate's eager response.

"Rather!" confirmed Ralph.

So the date of the party was fixed, and a few days later the elite of the Upper Darling received appropriately-worded invitations, invitations promptly accepted by all, whilst not a few implored information regarding the "surprise".

The day before the Saturday when the Great Land Lottery was to be held in Wilcannia was one of the two weekly mail days. Ralph received from a jeweller in Sydney, a diamond ring worth considerably more than his portion of the dog-scalp cheque. And, if he was pleased and not a little elated by the receipt of the ring, there was one other highly satisfied by the contents of his mail, and that was Bony.

The size of his mail was limited to three letters, and the first that he opened was from his wife, Laura, in which she gave him news of their three children, and evidence of her undying devotion, in a firm round hand, and quite passable grammar.

The second letter was contained in a plain foolscap envelope and was from Sydney. The message, however, was given in concise official prose:

Detective-Inspector Bonaparte. The plaster casts received recently, and numbered 1 to 4, have been examined. It has been established definitely that the print No. 3 is identical with that of the original stated by you to have been removed from the ground at Barrakee. If you decide upon an arrest, first communicate with the Senior Police Officer at Wilcannia, who has orders to carry out your instructions.

The letter was signed by the Chief Commissioner of Police at Sydney, and was read by Bony with a quiet smile.

"If I decide to make an arrest!" he said softly to a curious kookaburra perched on a branch over the second boat he was painting. "You seem to think, Mr Commissioner, that I am a policeman, whereas I am a crime investigator. And now for Mr Edward Sawyer's letter."

From its cheap envelope Bony took the following, written on cheap ruled paper:

Altunga Creek,
Vie Camooweal,
Queensland.

Dear Old Bony,

I quite thought you had been planted years ago. It was only the other day that me and Tommy Ching-Lung was talking about the little bit of tracking you done up here in nineteen-twenty. And now you resurrects and writes to a bloke.

Dear old Bony, when are you coming up here again? You'll find all the kids you used to talk to about the stars and things all growed up and thinking more of cattle, alligators and hard cash than of stars and all them elements you had in your head.

And now, Bony, about the gent you wants traced. You asked me if I remember ever seeing a tall, gaunt, cadaverous gent name of William Clair. Tall and gaunt were words I appeared to get the hang of, but cadaverous bluffed me at the post. I rode over to Blake's place and the next day went down to Moreno to try and dig up a dictionary, but we don't seem to be strong on dictionaries in these parts.

Anyway, two motor car explorers pulled up here last night, being afraid to sleep in the open on account of the alligators, and one of them told me the meaning of your foreign word.

That helped me to fix Mister Will Clair, but I reckon you've made a mistake in the gent's name. In nineteen-ten a tall, cadaverous, gaunt bloke with walrus whiskers hit the creek carrying a swag. I remember him because it's darned few what carry swags up here. This gent's name was Bill Sinclair, and for nine months he went black and lived with Wombra's push out at Smokey Lagoon.

I just got back from a trip to Wombra, who was looking younger than ever, though a bit worried on account of the police not liking the way he waddies his second best gin. Old Wombra remembers Sinclair. He says Sinclair was made second chief of the push because he happened to find Wombra up a tree, guarded by a particularly nasty bull buffalo.

Sinclair, it appears, was after a bloke called King Henry, a New South Wales abo who rated as Super Grand Master of the blacks' masonic craft. Wombra didn't tell me plain about the craft part of it, but putting two and two together that, I think, shows which way the steer bolted and explains, too, the reason of this King Henry gent being able to move about among Queensland blacks. By ordinary race rules a strange black gets a spear mighty quick.

But getting back to Sinclair, Bony old lad. This Sinclair palled in thick with Wombra and learned a heap of black's tricks. I asked old Wombra particular about boomerang chucking, and the old pirate told me that when Sinclair pulled out he could heave a war kirras as good as any of the bucks. In fact he won a kind of tournament the day before he left, and Wombra gave him his best boomerang as a sort of prize.

So that's that. W. Sinclair hasn't been up here since to my knowledge. What has he done? Run amuck or killed a money-wasting politician? If this last, let him go, Bony. He deserves a medal.

Well, so long old chip. Hop along this way when you go for your next walkabout. The wife and kids will be glad to see you. I got one wife and seven kids and gets two tax papers every year. Hooroo.

Yours till the alligators grow wings,
Edward Sawyer

Bony carefully re-read this boisterous letter from the far North-West of Queensland, and smiled with genuine pleasure; then, folding it, replaced it within the cheap envelope.

The writer was one of the many friends Bony's personality attracted to him. In those far-distant places the half-caste had devoted hours to the teaching of white folk's children—children who otherwise, on account of remoteness from a school, would have grown up unable to read or write.

The parents of these children owed Bony a debt of gratitude, the children themselves a much greater debt. There were dozens of white men scattered over the north of Australia who would have provided Bony and his family with accommodation and tucker for the rest of their lives.

And from several of these Bony's mind gradually reverted to William Clair. In Clair's bootprint No. 3, as well as the history of Clair's or Sinclair's sojourn with Wombra and his tribe, Bony had gathered sufficient evidence to justify the gaunt man's arrest.

He had not, of course, any direct proof that Clair killed the black at Barrakee. That Clair did kill King Henry he had no doubt, but what Clair's motive was still remained baffling. And until he, Bony, had laid bare the reason for that deadly pursuit of King Henry, which had been carried on patiently and relentlessly for nearly two decades before opportunity came for its terrible culmination, the half-caste felt that his work at Barrakee would not be complete.

That night he wrote a letter which he took to Thornton to address, and to dispatch by Frank Dugdale the following day.

The letter set the law in motion against the unsuspecing Clair, then living in solitude at the Basin.

Chapter Seventeen

The Great Land Lottery

BREAKFAST AT Barrakee the following morning was taken very early, because the Land Board, sitting at half past ten at Wilcannia, seventy-five miles down the river, wasted little time. An excited group gathered outside the double garden gates, where three cars were waiting.

Dugdale was driving the Barrakee car, and would have with him Kate and Ralph, who were going to Wilcannia for the trip and to shop, and Edwin Black, who with Dugdale was an applicant for land. Mr Watts was driving his own car and was accompanied by two boundary-riders and Blair, the bullock-driver, all applicants. The third car was owned by Mr Hemming, a station-manager, and with him were one of his jackeroos and two of his riders.

Mrs Watts and her family had come to the homestead and would remain there the day, helping with the preparations for the surprise party. Everyone was talking at once, all were keyed to a racecourse pitch of excitement. There is nothing that would more quickly damn any government of New South Wales than for it to take away the people's Land Lottery.

Frank Dugdale had just given a final glance to oil-gauge and radiator when John Thornton drew him aside.

"I wish you luck, Dug," he said earnestly. "Here is a letter addressed to the Board, in which I have stated that if your application is considered favourably, I am prepared to stock your block on very extended terms. Say nothing to the Board which is not absolutely to the point."

Dugdale accepted the proffered letter, and, looking straight into his employer's eyes, thanked him with his usual sincerity. From Dugdale the squatter turned to Blair.

Blair was dressed in a black suit that fitted him like a pair of tights, but with by no means the comfortable freedom of action that tights give. A black velour hat was set at a rakish angle on his greying head; new brown elastic-sided riding-boots adorned his feet. At a right-angle from his chin his beard, carefully trimmed, stuck out pugnaciously.

"Look here, Blair," Thornton said when he had drawn the little bullock-driver aside: "I want you to remember that it is most important that Tilly's Tank be cleaned out before the rain comes. If you get drunk, don't create a riot and get yourself locked up whatever else you do, for I'm relying on you to finish that tank-cleaning job."

"If Knowles and his demons wants their blasted jail white-washed, then they are going to shoot me in, drunk or sober, if I come out of a church or out of a pub," Blair said with conviction. "I might have just one snifter. But I am going to Wilcannia to gamble with the blooming Land Board, and not a publican."

"I am glad to hear that. The best of luck to you, Blair. You have now worked for me for more than fifteen years. Tell the Board that, and say also that if they grant you a block I'll buy you a house. Now, don't forget—only one snifter."

The little man, his short feet set at twenty minutes to four, looked up at the squatter with suddenly shining eyes.

"I didn't say I'd have only one snifter," he said slowly. "I said I might have just one, meaning more than one or none at all. Thank you for the offer of that house, though."

A chorus of "goodbyes" and "good lucks" floated through the still morning air, when the three cars moved off from the homestead. Dugdale, in the leading car, asked Ralph, who, with Black, was sitting in the rear, the exact time.

"Half past eight, Dug, old boy. Plenty of time, isn't there?"

"For us, yes. But Watts will have to push his light car. Hemming will have to step on it fairly constant. Keep a look out, will you? We must not get too far ahead."

"Why, Dug?" asked Kate. "They will be all right, won't they?"

"Other things being equal, they will," the sub-overseer told her, in an even tone of voice which required effort to maintain. "But we have no time to spare, and, the occasion being all-important to most of us, the occupants of any car that breaks down will have to be distributed between the remaining two cars. We couldn't leave one car-load behind to miss the Board."

"You're right, Dug. That would be too bad."

They had been travelling about an hour when one of the tyres blew out. The following cars drew up behind and many hands whipped off the tyre and replaced it with the spare. The change was made in a little less than two minutes. And then, later, Mr Hemming had tyre trouble which took longer to remedy, since he had punctured the spare the day before and had omitted to repair it.

Yet another delay occurred when thirty miles above Wilcannia, at a small station homestead, the owner and his wife would not permit them to go on till everyone had had a cup of tea and a slice of brownie. So that it was a quarter to eleven before they braked up before the Court House of what once was known as the *Queen City* of the West.

In the precincts of the commodious Court House were dozens of travel-stained cars, dozens of trucks, motor-cycles, and many buggies, buckboards and gigs.

In common with every applicant arriving at the Court House, the party from Barrakee made their way through a knot of men about the entrance, near which was a board bearing a typewritten list of names in alphabetical order.

The list comprised eighty names, those of the applicants to be interviewed by the Board during the third consecutive day of its sitting in Wilcannia. For weeks past the same gentlemen had travelled from township to township, and had examined hundreds of applicants: some further weeks would be occupied in travelling to many other townships to examine hundreds more. There were fourteen blocks of land thrown open for public selection, and probably there were eighteen to twenty hundred applicants hoping to obtain one of them.

The Barrakee overseer withdrew from the waiting knot of men, together with several others of the party whose names would not be called until the afternoon. Almost immediately on their arrival Edwin Black was called.

Dugdale gave him a reassuring nod and a bystander called "Good luck", when the jackeroo entered the room where sat the Board. He was within perhaps ten minutes, and emerged with a facial expression giving no indication of even hope. Then Blair was called.

Before starting for the door the little man re-set his black hat, and thrust out his chin as though to relieve the strain of the unfamiliar collar.

"Good old Fred," somebody sang out. There was a general laugh containing a hint of expectancy. "Don't forget to lay down the law, Fred," another voice said.

At the portals of the room stood Sergeant Knowles. Before him Blair paused, the light of battle suddenly dying in his eyes.

"Now, you ain't going to try to arrest me before I've had me say, are you, Sarge?" he said with genuine surprise.

"No, Blair. I have no intention of doing that," replied the policeman.

Reassured, Blair again re-set his headgear and worked his Adam's apple clear of the choking collar. Then, with a determined swagger, and his beard slightly raised in its angle, he entered the presence of the Land Board.

Before him he saw three men seated at three sides of a table covered with official papers. He was invited to be seated at the vacant side, and, having settled himself, sat with one leg negligently crossed over the knee of the other, the hat now pushed back low over his neck.

"Frederick Blair?" said the gentleman facing him.

"That's me," replied Blair.

The Chairman of the Board looked up from a paper and smiled. He and his confreres knew Frederick Blair. He pushed across the table a soiled Bible, and took from the secretary-member Blair's application form. The usual oath administered, he said:

"You have applied for either of Blocks three-ten and three-twenty, Mr Blair. What do you know of them?"

"I know more about 'em than I do the back of me 'and."

"Humph! What amount of cash have you, Mr Blair?'"

"I've got seven hundred and nineteen pounds, seventeen shillings, and ten pence in the Bank of United Australia," came Blair's somewhat surprising answer.

"Have you, indeed? Why, you could almost buy a small place, Mr Blair."

"You know darned well that I couldn't buy a small place for seven hundred, nor yet seven thousand," Blair burst out. "It ain't needful for me to tell you that nothing under twenty thousand acres in this district is any good to a bloke, and that the auction price per acre is round about twelve bob. How am I going to buy twenty thousand acres with seven hundred quid, eh?"

"It might—"

"You know darned well it couldn't," Blair shouted venomously. "'Ere are you throwing open a measly fourteen blocks when there's some twenty hundred men struggling to get homes, and that there Sir flamin' Walter Thorley owns half Australia, which belongs to no man but the Government, which is the people.

"Two thousand blokes, mark you. Most of 'em married and with a family, and the rest wanting to get married and have children; and you allow Thorley to own hundreds of miles of the people's land, employ a few abos and breed dingo, and see his bloomin' land once every two years."

"We must not discuss—" came from the chairman.

"Of course not," cut in Blair. "We must not take the name of the great Sir Walter Thorley in vain, but when there's a war we must fight for his land and his money-bags, eh? We mustn't say nothing, we must offer up thanks to the worst employer in the State and breeder of sheep-killers, and bless him for allowing us to live at all.

"I've been cheated out of my birthright, yes, me and hundreds of others. I got a right to have a wife, to have children by her, to make and have and hold a home. Can I ask any woman to marry me when I can't give her a home? Can I get a home when you won't give me the lease of any land? Can you open up the land as it should be opened when Thorley and all the rest of the absentee squatters have grabbed the lot? What flamin' use is it to the country to allow one man to own twenty millions of acres when that area would support one thousand families—that's what I want to know?

"Here am I," went on Blair with greater rapidity, "now fifty-two years old. All my life I bin on the Darling River. Twenty-one years ago I fell in love with a woman down in Pooncaira. For twenty-one years she's been waitin' for me to make a home. But my girl, aye, and me, too, will kick the bucket afore we ever have a home. Yes, cheated out of our birthright, two humans out of hundreds. That's all, gents."

Blair's eyes were suspiciously moist when he rose to his feet, at the end of this tirade, shouted in a loud voice. He had had his say, and felt like a man in the dock proven innocent.

"One moment, Mr Blair," came the chairman's tired voice. "As I tried to say, we cannot discuss the big leaseholders at these proceedings. We have to confine ourselves strictly to the present business, which is the allocation of land, and not the discussion of politics. The Board will give your application the usual consideration, and you will be notified of the Board's decision. You said just now that there are many married men with families in want of a block of land. Like them, you could have married had you wished."

"I could," replied Blair instantly. "But the men can't live with their families unless they work in or about a town. Being a bushman, I can't get a job in a town. Still, you're right, mister, I suppose. The woman and children first—after Thorley is satisfied. Good day-ee."

Head erect, the point of his beard horizontal with his nose, Blair marched out. If he saw the sergeant of police, or the waiting crowd, he made no sign. Passing through this latter, he stalked across the street and, entering an hotel, stood erect in front of a bar and ordered a double whisky.

Dugdale's interview with the Board was less dramatic. He answered the chairman's questions quietly and to the point. Thornton's letter, offering to stock any block he might receive, also spoke highly of the young man's character and abilities.

"I want this block, gentlemen, not only for the purpose of making money out of wool, but in order that I may marry and have a home of my own," Dugdale said in conclusion.

The chairman forced a smile. He had heard that plea so many times before. Privately he wondered how any man wanting to get married, and wanting a home, could be such an utter fool as to stay in the Australian bush.

When Dugdale found himself dismissed he was unable to decide what effect his present application had had on the members of the Land Board. He felt a little sick at heart. It seemed all such a gamble, a gamble with men's desires and hopes. Fourteen blocks among two thousand applicants. The odds against the home were about a hundred and fifty to one.

The three cars left Wilcannia about five o'clock, the occupants seldom speaking, the reaction of the gamble being felt. They would each experience the pleasure of anticipation for several weeks, until the post brought them the result of the Great Land Lottery.

In the second car, morose and silent, sat Frederick Blair. He was quite sober.

Chapter Eighteen

The Surprise Party

EVERY ROOM of the Barrakee homestead blazed with light. The wide verandas were festooned with Chinese lanterns, and hundreds of other coloured lights decorated the orange trees bordering the lawns.

Thornton himself was master of the ceremonies. Dressed in a well-fitting dinner suit, the white shirt of which accentuated his kindly weatherbeaten face, he announced the first dance at precisely nine o'clock, from the centre of the cleared dining drawing room. In one comer was the orchestra. One of the Misses Hemming and Miss Stirling agreed to take it in turns to play the piano, and they were supported by Frederick Blair with his accordion and Bony with a plentiful supply of gum-leaves. The tinkling of the piano, the organ notes of the accordion, and the thin wailing of the gum-leaf broke into the beautiful melody of *The Blue Danube*.

For at Barrakee the howling dervish charges known to moderns as dancing, accompanied by cacophonous bedlam, were not regarded with favour.

The big room was full of dancers, the verandas, too, provided excellent floors for many couples who disliked the crush. And over the lawns, lit by fairy lamps, the orange groves, and the dark, empty river beyond, brooded the soft gentle night of mid-May.

Kate had given Frank Dugdale her first dance, and while with leaping pulses and pounding heart he held her lightly, he whispered, with an unmistakable tremor in his voice:

"Will you give me the last dance, too?"

The question awoke her from a pleasant reverie. She was thinking how well he looked in clothes that sat on him with distinction. There was certainly no handsomer man present that evening, and he danced divinely. When she heard his whispered question she opened her half-closed eyes and found herself looking into his blazing orbs. For just a fraction of a second was he revealed to her, but only for a fraction, before the conventional veil of indifference again clouded his eyes.

"Well, what of that last dance, Kate?"

"I'm sorry, Dug, but I've promised it already," she told him, her voice low, her face flushed.

"I am sorry, too," he said, with evident disappointment. Then, in a lighter tone: "Who is the lucky man?"

She half-sensed the pang of regret in his voice, and experienced a peculiar sense of disappointment herself. With a shock of surprise she realized presently that for not a few minutes she had forgotten Ralph.

"I am not going to tell you," was her laughing response. "The surprise is going to be given before the last dance, and I'll promise you the dance before the surprise. And, Dug, you really should be grateful to me for that second dance. All the boys will be vexed with me for giving anyone two dances this evening."

"If there are any complaints, just refer them to me, please," he said. "Anyhow, this evening I shall dance with no other girl."

For the remainder of the dance he gave himself silently to the ecstasy of her close companionship and their spiritual union of music and motion. And, when the last notes, feelingly and lingeringly played, were struck, he awoke to realities as though he had been aroused from a sweet dream by the coming of an executioner.

At the end of the fourth dance Thornton besought the Reverend Mr Thatcher to carry on the duties of MC for a while. Mr Thatcher was the vicar of a parish about the size of Great Britain. Being equally proficient at motor-engine repairing, shooting and skinning kangaroos, and keeping the organ fund in a solvent condition, as he was at preaching a sermon at any time and in any place, Mr Thatcher was a born MC.

His freedom gained, John Thornton sought out Mr Hemming, and together they made their way to the small room where Nellie Wanting was acting as barmaid.

Mr Hemming managed a station belonging to Sir Walter Thorley some hundred miles north of Barrakee. In area the station he managed was larger than Barrakee, but his salary as manager was not as large as that of Mr Watts, the overseer of Barrakee. He was middle-sized, middle-aged, and middle-conditioned, and if his bank balance was invariably below par his spirits were invariably above. He had a good wife and a big family, and life would have been far more pleasant than it was if his titled employer would only have refrained from his biennial visit to the station.

"How did you get on with the Board today, Hem?" the station-owner said over his champagne glass.

"The same as usual, I think," Hemming replied. "The chairman said I ought to think myself a lucky man, being a station-manager, and having a good homestead for my family. Maybe he's right. I'm not grumbling about my luck. But I am sick and tired of Sir Walter, and constant orders to cut this and economize on that."

"That's his way of making money, Hem."

"Yes, but hang it all, John, you know as well as I do that twenty-seven shillings are kept every week from each man's wages for food, and, although the average station can keep a man comfortably on fourteen shillings a week, thereby robbing the man of the other thirteen, when it comes to keeping him on about four shillings and robbing him of twenty-three it's a bit thick."

"I quite agree, old man. It is a bit thick. Another glass of fizz?"

"Thanks, I will. I'll take one of these cigarettes, too. Have one?"

The squatter accepted one from the proffered box and silently watched Nellie fill their glasses. The music came softly to them, the echoes of happy voices from the lawns drifted in through open window and door. A moment later the two men went out and found a seat, where they smoked.

"About Three Corner Station, Hem."

"What of it?"

"How much money could you put up?"

"How much?" exclaimed Mr Hemming. "About two and tenpence."

For some few minutes neither spoke.

"The purchase price of the lease, Hem, will probably amount to fifty thousand pounds," resumed the squatter presently. "You're a young man yet, Hem, and you could make it pay well. If you like to buy it, I'll find the money, and we can come to an arrangement for repayment to suit us both. In ten or twelve years you should be clear of me."

Mr Hemming sat as though stunned. He was silent for so long that the squatter said:

"Don't you like the idea, Hem?"

The other found his voice and gasped:

"Say, John! Do you know what you are offering me?" he said, a break in his voice. "You are offering me a home and independence. You are offering me freedom from the slavery of Thorley, and you question my liking the idea. Are you sure you mean it?"

"Of course. Why not? We've been friends a long time."

"Then, John, you will have to excuse me at once. I must find my wife and tell her. The telling will be the greatest pleasure in my life; the next greatest pleasure will be when I tell Thorley to go and be damned."

Mr Hemming hastened along the veranda, leaving John Thornton chuckling. He liked Hem and knew him for a sound man.

"Oh! There you are. Why are you sitting all alone?"

Thornton looked up and saw his wife. Indicating Mr Hemming's vacated seat, he said:

"I have put it to Hem about Three Corner Station," he said, still chuckling.

"Ah! And how did Mr Hemming take it?"

"He has just rushed off to tell his wife."

"I'm as glad as she will be, John, but it is half-past ten, dear, and don't you think it is time for supper?"

"Yes. Is everything ready?"

"Everything. When this dance stops, will you tell them?"

"Very well, I'll go along in. Having a good time, sweetheart?" he asked gently.

"Just lovely," she said. "Ralph, I think, is in paradise. And Kate is there with him. Now go, the music is stopping."

Thornton rose, and, after playfully pinching his wife's ear, walked to the dining room, which he entered through one of the wide French windows.

"Fellow taxpayers and workers for the Governments of Australia, my wife and I think it time for supper," he said genially. "We must not abuse our strength by fasting too long, and strength is necessary to pay the tax-gatherers. Will you please partner all, and follow in line after the band?"

Shouts, encores and laughter greeted this impromptu speech. Blair and Bony stood up to head the procession of couples, and then striking up "For Australia will be There!" marched out of the room, across the veranda, and twice round the lawns before entering the big marquee at the bottom end of these.

A great display of viands to suit every taste was set out on a long table at one end of the tent, and every man waited on his supper partner. Seeing Mrs Thornton without a partner, Bony spoke to her.

"Madam, will you honour me by accepting my service?" he asked, making his courtly bow. She forgot his colour and his apparent station life: his bow and speech forbade remembrance. Taking the seat he offered her, she said:

"Thank you, Bony. I should like a glass of sherry and a sandwich. And," she added, when he was leaving her, "bring refreshment for yourself, and sit here beside me."

"I shall be charmed, madam," Bony said. And when he was seated beside her, he remarked:

"The party, I think, is a great success."

"I think so, too," she said. "Everyone seems to be happy."

They talked as equals, without condescension on her part or presumption on his. Nowhere but in the bush could that have been so. Even Blair, the only other person present outside the station homestead society, fitted naturally into the circumstances and was talking freely to his boss.

Mrs Thornton made a great impression on the half-caste detective. In her disposition he recognized gentleness and firmness, a wide charity of outlook and a great breadth of mind, apart from the capacity to dislike. He read, too, in her firm mouth and chin a powerful will, to which opposition was rather a spur than an obstruction.

After supper he and his musical colleague led the dancers back to the house, and again he played with unflagging verve on his succession of gum-leaves. It was one o'clock in the morning when Mr Thornton announced that but one more dance remained on the programme.

"Before this last dance I have an announcement to make," he said. He was standing on a foot-high platform, near the piano, and Ralph and Kate and his wife were with him. "It is the surprise," he went on, "to give you which is the reason for this party. Are you all quite ready?"

A chorus of "Yesses" answered him. He was smiling. He was very happy at this moment, and said simply:

"I have to announce the engagement of my son Ralph and my niece Kate Flinders."

No one spoke. Kate felt herself drawn by the squatter's powerful arm close beside him, then a little in front of him. Ralph, too, had been drawn opposite her. Looking into his dark face, she saw his eyes flash and burn into hers. He held his hands towards her and she gave him hers. She saw the sparkle of diamonds and the glint of gold, and felt the ring slipped on her third finger.

And then someone—she thought it was Edwin Black—sang in a clear tenor voice:

"For they are jolly good fellows!"

The whole company took up the refrain with enthusiasm, love and friendship fully expressed by a great people. With shining eyes a little moist, she looked at them; from one to another, from those in front to those behind them, and still further back.

And her wavering gaze finally and suddenly became fixed on the ashen face of Frank Dugdale.

He was right at the back, leaning against the wall as though for support. Without sense of time and with ever-increasing wonder, she examined each of his features in turn. And at last she was looking straight into his blazing grey eyes, and saw therein the horror, the agony, and the hurt.

Her heart stopped. The people, the room, life itself, became motionless. Her mind was capable of registering nothing but the white, stricken face over at the far wall. And then a brilliant rainbow colouring filled the air, the singing became softer, unreal, far away.

And the light fell upon the soul of Kate Flinders, revealing it to herself, showing her that at last she knew what love was, knew that she loved Frank Dugdale and had always loved him.

The orchestra began to play. The little crowd broke up into couples, and the couples began to dance. She looked at Ralph as though she were entranced. She heard him say:

"Come, dear! This is our dance."

Quite automatically she danced with her affianced husband.

But Dugdale went out and wrestled with a thousand devils until the dawn.

Chapter Nineteen

Blood and Feathers

AT TEN O'CLOCK in the morning on the following Monday, Sergeant Knowles and a trooper arrived at Barrakee in a motor-car. Mrs Thornton heard the car pull up outside the office, and asked Kate to see who were the callers. A minute later she welcomed them on the veranda.

"Why, it's Mr Knowles," she said in greeting. "Come in and have morning tea, do. Kate, run along and tell Martha. And why are you so far away from your post of duty?"

Talking gaily, she indicated chairs to her visitors, seating herself to permit them also to be seated.

"Trooper Smith and I have called about a little business matter," briskly explained the dapper yet athletic sergeant. "But the business can wait till after the morning tea, Mrs Thornton."

"Of course it can," the Little Lady responded. "If the tea-growers went on strike, I really don't know what we would do."

Martha, bearing a tray, arrived resplendent in white poplin skirt, emerald green blouse, and brown riding-boots.

"Good morning, Martha," Knowles said, without the faintest shadow of a smile on his brick-red face.

"Mornin', Sergeant," was the gin's simple answer, but her eyes rolled and she seemed ill at ease. Kate soon joined them. She said:

"I hope, Sergeant Knowles, that your jail doesn't want whitewashing. I'm sure Uncle would not like to lose Blair until his work is finished."

The trooper chuckled. The sergeant laughed right out.

"So you have heard of Blair's complaint?" he said. "No, we have not come to arrest Blair, this time."

"You appear to hint that you have come to arrest someone," ventured Mrs Thornton lightly.

"Where is Mr Thornton?" countered the sergeant.

"Good gracious! You are not going to arrest him, surely?"

"Oh, no! But I should like to see him presently."

"Then you will find him with Mr Mortimore and the carpenter down in the shearing-shed," the mistress of Barrakee told him, adding in a coaxing voice: "But really now, whom have you come to arrest? Tell us. We are always hungry for news and gossip."

The steely blue eyes of the sergeant twinkled genially. He saw that both women were burning with curiosity. Kate, he thought, looked pale and her eyes as though they required sleep.

"Won't you guess?" he teased.

"No," said Mrs Thornton firmly.

"Martha?" Kate guessed with a strained laugh.

"Quite wrong, Miss Flinders," interjected the trooper. "Well, you may as well know now as in a few hours' time. We have come to apprehend William Clair for the murder of King Henry."

For a moment the women were silent. Kate frowned. Mrs Thornton's breath was caught sharply and her eyes became veiled.

"Do you mean to tell me," she said, "that you are still worrying about the killing of that black fellow?"

"I don't worry about it, Mrs Thornton," replied the sergeant, well satisfied with the effect of his bomb. "The law does, however. The law never ceases to worry about an unpunished crime. The official memory is infinite. Now we must go along and see Mr Thornton. We want his cooperation."

"Then you will be going out to the Basin?"

"Yes."

"But you'll stay and have lunch before you go?"

"Thank you, we will."

"Certainly you will. I'll see about it at once. You know your way to the shearing-shed?"

"Oh yes! Thank you for the cup of tea."

The women of Barrakee watched the two uniformed men go out through the double garden gates, and climb into their car to drive the half-mile to the big shed.

"Well, what do you think of that, Kate?" questioned Mrs Thornton.

"It seems difficult to believe that Clair did it. But then, I suppose, it would be as difficult to believe it of anyone else one knows," replied Kate.

For thirty seconds the Little Lady gazed pensively across the lawn. Then, turning again to Kate, she said:

"If you'll tell Martha about the visitors staying for lunch, I'll go along to the store and get a few tins of ox-tongues. Martha is short of meat, I think."

Down in the shearing-shed, the squatter was planning some alteration in view of the coming shearing, and the policemen found him detailing to Mortimore the timber and iron necessary.

"Hallo, Sergeant!" he said. "More trouble?"

"For someone, yes. And a little for you, too."

"Oh!"

"From information received," this with a meaning look, "we hold a warrant for the arrest of Clair, now I believe at a place called the Basin."

"Yes, he is at the Basin. What's he done?"

"We have enough evidence to charge him with the murder of King Henry."

"Have you, now?"

The sergeant regarded Mortimore, then jotting notes in his order book, motioned the squatter to follow him outside. On the river-bank he said:

"What time do you reckon Clair will be home?"

"He is home all day," Thornton told him. "Clair is not boundary-riding. He's pumping."

"Oh! that makes it easier. He has no riding-horse out there?"

"No."

"How do you get to the Basin?"

"D'you know the road to Thurlow Lake?"

"Yes."

"Well, six miles from Old Hut Tank you will come to a gate," explained the station-owner. "Go through the gate and immediately take a secondary track to the right. From that gate to the Basin is thirteen miles."

"Good," replied the sergeant. "Mrs Thornton has kindly asked us to stay for lunch, and we have accepted. We'll get away directly afterward. Did Bony tell you anything?"

"Only that his suspicions rested equally on Clair and Martha and me."

The policeman chuckled. "Bony is a humorist," he said. "He discovered a footprint outside the lower garden gate miraculously saved from the rain. He knew a size 9 boot made it, shortly after the rain began that night. It's been established that Clair made that print. But the chief edifice of our prosecution is built from the material sent Bony in a letter from a pal of his in North-West Queensland. By the day of the trail we'll have affidavits and witnesses in plenty."

"But why did Clair kill the abo?"

"That we don't know," the sergeant admitted. "Bony appears sore on that point. Thinks that the arrest of Clair does not finish the case off artistically."

"Humph! If Clair is found guilty the case will be finished off all right," asserted John Thornton. "I must send a man out to take his place."

"Let him come out with us. There's room."

"No. I'll take him out myself. We can travel together."

"All right. Will you take Bony as well? Look all right if he accompanies you. No one then will guess his identity. Besides, he may pick up something valuable to us."

"Very well, I'll see him about it," agreed the squatter thoughtfully. "You go along to the homestead and make yourselves nuisances with the women. I want to finish this job."

After an early lunch the sergeant and his companion left ten minutes before the squatter, who drove his own car, and was accompanied by Clair's successor and Bony. Dugdale and Ralph were just riding in, and the latter waved to his foster-father.

The last thirteen miles of the journey over the secondary road was covered in slow time, since the little-used track was rough and covered with blown sand. The police car reached the Basin at about five minutes past two.

The Basin was situated on a wide circular flat, hemmed in by a mass of loose sand-hills. The hut was old, but weather-proof, and was built but a few yards from the sub-artesian bore, at which a small petrol-engine lifted the water into three large receiving tanks. Beyond the tanks ran two lines of troughing, each watering sheep in a paddock, a division fence separating the two troughs.

The police car pulled up at the door of the hut. The sergeant and his companion got out, the former knocking on the door. His knock being unanswered, he glanced at the trooper and, the two having drawn their heavy revolvers, he unlatched the door, and threw it inward.

"William Clair," he called.

There was no answer.

With that the two men entered. It might well have been that Clair was armed and desperate, but little thought of personal safety was in their minds. Clair's silence was ominous.

The hut was empty.

It contained no place for concealment. An iron cot at one end bore two hastily tossed blankets. On the table were parts of a carcass of mutton and grains of sugar mixed with tea-leaves. The open fireplace indicated that that day a fire had been lit, for smoke still curled upward from the almost consumed wood.

"Outside, Smith," snapped Knowles. "Look for tracks. Keep your eyes skinned. He may be hiding in the old shed over there. Search."

But Clair had vanished.

Thornton with Bony and the new man arrived by the time the sergeant had decided that Clair was not in hiding anywhere near the hut. He was annoyed but not balked. For here was Bony, Australia's King of Trackers. Mindful of the new pumper, Sergeant Knowles said, when he had explained the situation:

"What's your name?"

"I'm Bony," replied the half-caste innocently.

"Can you track?"

"A little bit," admitted Bony.

"All right. Get on this man Clair's tracks. He's wanted for killing an aboriginal called King Henry, so you ought to be interested."

"All right. Inside first. You all stay outside, please. And don't move about."

At the doorway Bony surveyed the interior. He noted the tumbled blankets, the accumulation of foodstuffs on the table, the wisp of smoke arising from the dying fire. He noted also the absence of the usual canvas water-bag, and the small tea-billy. Near the bed he saw a litter of feathers.

Entering the hut then, he removed the blankets from the bed. Beneath he found and examined what evidently had been a pillow. One end had been ripped open, and several downy feathers still adhered to the covering on the inside. From the bed he approached the table, observing the scattered tea and sugar. The meat had evidently been partly disjointed in a hurry, and the flesh was flabby, denoting that the ration sheep had been killed that day.

Bony sighed and smiled, and called the others in.

"Clair knows a thing or two which is going to make his capture difficult," he said. "I'm looking for a dish or bucket which has recently contained blood. We have no time to waste. Look around, some of you, outside."

It was the new pumper who found, at the back of the hut, the wash-dish in which were traces of blood and many white feathers sticking to it. When Bony saw it he nodded slowly and then, pointing to the telephone, said:

"Someone told him, Sergeant, that you were coming out to get him. Clair then took that dish down to the killing-pen, in which there happened to be a ration sheep, killed it, and caught its blood in the dish. The dish and the carcass he brought in here. He then cut off sufficient meat to take with him, filled his ration-bags with tea and sugar and flour, and put the full bags in a gunny-sack, with what cooked meat and damper he had by him.

"Next he rolled one blanket into a swag. Finally he removed his boots and socks and bathed his feet in the blood before dipping them into his pillow-case filled with pelican feathers. Allowing the blood to congeal and harden, thereby firmly adhering the feathers, he repeated the process till his feet were thickly encased with the feathers."

"Old abo trick!" Thornton exclaimed.

"Precisely! Clair knew that when a black fellow wants to avoid being tracked by an enemy he covers his feet with feathers," Bony answered calmly. "Feathered feet leave no mark, turn no stone, break no twig, and damage no grass where there is any."

"Damn!" growled the senior policeman. "Now, who the devil rang up Clair and told him we were coming?"

"Someone must have done so," insisted Bony. "Clair didn't just bolt when he saw your car coming through the sand-hills yonder. His preparations occupied quite two hours. He's on foot. Had you been mounted you might have run into him."

"And you mean to tell me you can't track him now?"

"Yes. Clair adopted the only method that baffles even the best trackers. If you circle that ring of sand-hills this quiet afternoon, you might see a very faint impression on the loose sand. But Clair would know that, and would not leave his direction so evident. When on fairly hard ground again he would circle in the direction he proposes to go."

Chapter Twenty

A Grain of Sugar

SERGEANT KNOWLES seated himself at the table with the air of a man weighed down by exasperation. Producing a watch, he set it before him.

"The time now is precisely twenty-one minutes to three," he said crisply, anger and chagrin in his tone. "We arrived here at a little after two o'clock. We find our man gone. From the preparations for his flight, Bony, what time do you think he left?"

"About midday," replied the half-caste promptly; then seeing the interrogative rise of the policeman's eyebrows, he added: "There are parts of blood in the dish not yet dry. The fly maggots on the meat left uncovered are about three hours old."

The uniformed man smiled acknowledgement of gifts greater than his. He said:

"Assuming that he lost no time after receiving the warning how long do you think it would take him to make all these preparations for a bolt?"

"From the way in which the sheep was skinned Clair didn't make his preparations in a leisurely fashion. He could not, however, hasten the drying action of the blood when fixing the feathers to his feet. I should think it would be all of two hours."

"Say ten o'clock." Sergeant Knowles was silent for a space. The others, standing about the table, watched him. Then: "At about ten o'clock this morning, you, Mr Thornton, and Mortimore, the trooper, and myself, were at the shearing-shed. Till then only two people knew that we were after Clair—your wife and your niece—and, according to Bony, Clair was warned about that precise time."

124

The squatter's tanned face flushed. A hard light came into his eyes.

"You are accusing either my wife or my niece?" he asked with surprising mildness.

"I am accusing no one, Mr Thornton. I am merely stating a summary of facts. However, there is this to consider. The conversation between them and myself occurred on the house veranda, and could easily have been overheard by anyone in the rooms on the one side, or concealed among the grape-vines at either end. It will be necessary to question the servants. What do you think, Bony?"

The detective-inspector smiled slightly.

"There is no definite proof that Clair was warned over the telephone," he said.

"Then how else could he have been warned? Are there tracks of any recent visitor, on foot or on horse?"

"No, Sergeant," Bony replied sweetly. "But there are minor ways of conveying a warning, such as smoke signals. I am inclined, however, to believe that the telephone was the method used, but we must remember that we have no proof. With your permission, might I suggest that the country is in a very dry condition; that the only watering-places are the wells and tanks and bores; and that your man must visit a well, tank, or bore for water? As there are so few wells, tanks and bores, why not have them watched?"

"What about the river?"

"There is too much traffic on either side of the river to suit Clair," replied Bony. "Clair will make for the safest place in the world—the Northern Territory. Whilst I take a walkabout around the place—for there's always the chance that Clair may drop something which would indicate his travelling direction—Mr Thornton, I am sure, would not mind making you a plan showing all the watering places." Turning in the doorway, he added: "If Clair has dropped so much as a hair of his head I shall find it. Don't wait here for me."

Pausing at the big car to remove one of the waterbags to take with him, Bony set off on his walkabout. Noting the encircling windswept sand-hills, he struck southward till he gained the long line of ridges and miniature peaks, thence to follow the ridges. And whilst he walked he read and thought, and the thoughts were not allied to the readings.

When he had completed the circle he seated himself upon the summit of a ridge, satisfied that so far he had followed Clair's mind correctly, for exactly west of the tank he crossed Clair's tracks, slight indentations here and there, as though a party of centipedes had held a dance on separated patches. Only upon that very soft sand would such faint indentations be left by feathered feet, and only then during a windless period.

Again Bony completed a circle about the Basin, but this time keeping about a mile out from the sand-hills. He walked rapidly, his head thrust forward and down, but his gaze kept continually on a point ten or a dozen feet in front of him.

A second circle two miles from the tank was completed, without result. The tracker kept moving with untiring effort, now and then stopping to make and light a cigarette and to take a single mouthful of water from the canvas bag. And whilst the walkabout was in course, whilst his eyes missed nothing of the passage of sheep, rabbits, kangaroos, cats, emus, birds and insects, his mind continually dwelt upon the mysterious warning given to Clair.

Who had been Clair's friend?

Bony sighed audibly, a happy contented sigh. Supposing the friend proved to be one of the servants, say Martha, then the affair would doubtless be explained by admiration or love. But supposing the informer had been Mrs Thornton, or Kate Flinders. If so, that would mean that the Thorntons were mixed up in this sordid murder, or at least knew more of what lay behind it than they professed.

What was Clair's motive? Why had he tracked King Henry for nearly twenty years, for Bony now firmly believed that the gaunt man was the white man Pontius Pilate said had died. The feud or vendetta had started at Barrakee, and had ended there. What caused the feud? What was the feud?

So far as the actual killing was concerned Bony had completely lost interest. He had indicated the killer to the police, and thus considered his work to be practically accomplished, for it must be remembered that the half-caste detective had strange ideas of the duties of a detective-inspector, and of an ordinary police-inspector, sergeant, or trooper. Where Bony's interest had been inflamed and was kept inflamed was the mysterious motive actuating the crime, and compelling that long tracking, murderous, relentless, covering nigh twenty years.

Until that day the whole affair appeared to be ranged outside Barrakee, the commission of the crime at Barrakee being merely a coincidence. But the warning to Clair was proof positive that someone at Barrakee had knowledge of the deed other than that elicited, and doubtless also knowledge of the motive. And if he or she possessed knowledge of the motive, even if no knowledge of the murder at the time of the act, that person was, likely enough, at Barrakee twenty years before.

Out came Bony's list of fish among which was a sting-ray. Producing a pencil, he placed a dot in front of all the names, bar three. For a while he closed his eyes and mused. Then suddenly he placed a dot before the name of Mrs Thornton. Five seconds later his pencil made a mark in front of the name of her husband, leaving then but one name unmarked.

"Martha!" he said aloud. "Martha was at Barrakee twenty years ago. Martha doubtless was in the dining room and heard the sergeant tell the Ladies of Barrakee what his visit was for. Martha is black: so was King Henry. There is undoubtedly more black than white in this affair. The moving finger is trembling, undecided, but inclined to point towards Martha."

Pocketing his list and pencil, Bony rose and started out on his third circle. The sun was going down. The air was rapidly cooling. He noted that the ants were more numerous and more industrious now that the surface of the earth was cooler.

Half an hour later, when the sun's rim touched the mulga scrub, he suddenly halted and stared fixedly at a point on the ground. Dropping the bag, he picked up a twig and with it began to tease a red meat-ant. The ant was carrying a particle of white matter and fought for several seconds to retain it. When finally it let fall its tiny load, Bony picked it up with the point of his penknife and laid it on the palm of an open hand.

He prodded it with his fingernail. It was hard, faceted, light-reflecting upon one side. It was a grain of white sugar. Clair had dropped from his ration-bags a fatal clue.

Chapter Twenty-One

A Bullocky's Camp on Sunday

HENRY McINTOSH was born and reared at Port Adelaide. His father commanded a tugboat and drank great quantities of beer, his mother's favourite poison was brandy; and, since poor Henry was fated thus always to occupy that unenviable position known as being between two stools, he "went bush" at the age of fourteen. Four years later he was still suffering from the chronic bewilderment caused by constant hammerings with kitchen utensils and iron-hard fists. However, going bush was Henry's salvation.

It was Sunday and he was engaged in boiling a pair of dungaree trousers, with the aid of a liberal supply of caustic soda to reduce the labour of rubbing them clean. Frederick Blair, attired in spotless undervest and white moleskin trousers, was reading, from a weekly paper, particularly obnoxious details of a then famous society divorce case.

And quite suddenly there rode into the camp Sergeant Knowles, accompanied by Bony.

"Good-morning, Blair," greeted the policeman civilly.

"Now if that D. hadn't found the bloke and the tart canoodling under the mulberry-tree, the husband—'Enery, you are not payin' attention. Wot's gone wrong with you, 'Enery?"

Blair gazed over the top of his spectacles with serenity. He was fully aware of the presence of the visitors. From Henry, Blair slowly shifted his gaze round over his shoulder and stared hard into the eyes of the mounted policeman. Deliberately he laid the paper down on the ground, and as deliberately placed his spectacles on the paper.

"Good day-ee," he said coldly.

"Good morning," Knowles repeated.

"'Enery, take the sergeant's annimile and tie it to that tree over there. Then git one of them feeds and shove it under the annimile's nose," Blair ordered grandly, adding, as though as an afterthought: "And, 'Enery, if the sergeant and me comes to an argument, you will not interfere."

Henry grinned vacantly and took charge of the sergeant's horse. As ordered, he tied it by its neck-rope to a tree. Bony tied his mount to another tree. Henry slouched over to where some twenty roughly-made big hessian bags were set together, filled with chaff and bran in readiness for the team's dinner, and from the outer edge took up two of the bags. Blair indicated the freshly-made billy of tea with his pipe-stem.

"Have a drink of tea, Sarge, and a bite of brownie," he said acidly. "You'll want all your strength. Good-day-ee Bony. Since when have you become a john's offsider?"

"Since yesterday, Fred," replied Bony easily. "Bill Clair escaped arrest yesterday, and I've been called upon to track him."

"Oh! And wot's Bill been and done now? The sugar is in the tucker-box, Sarge. Take plenty. It's fattening. You, too, Bony. Wot's Clair done?"

"I hold a warrant for his apprehension on a charge of murder, Fred," interjected Knowles. "Where is that brownie you spoke of?"

The sergeant was as much at home in a bullock-driver's camp as at a station homestead. With a pannikin of black tea and a slice of eggless cake he seated himself before Blair and allowed his eyes to go roaming about the camp.

"'Enery," remarked Mr Blair, "from a divorce we come to murder—sootable subjects for a Sunday morning. Who did you say Clair 'as bin and shot up, Sarge?"

"I don't think I mentioned the victim's name."

"Every day and all day, Mister Knowles, you are gitting cleverer and cleverer," remarked Blair with studied calmness. "However—" He picked up spectacles and paper, placed the former on his nose, the latter across his knees. Ignoring his guests, he said: "You will remember, 'Enery, that we were reading about the scene under the mulberry tree when we were rudely interrupted. It appears that the 'usband. ...."

Blair was too much for Bony. The half-caste choked, while Knowles joined in hearty laughter. Henry giggled and broke into a guffaw when the situation became clear to his slow brain. With slight jerks Blair's goatee beard rose. Seeing the sign, the sergeant interposed before the storm broke:

"Sorry Blair," he said with twinkling eyes. "But let's leave the husband and get back to Clair. I want him for the killing of King Henry, and Bony here says he believes Clair has come this way. Have—"

"Are you telling me, Sarge, that you are a-chasin' a white man for knocking an abo on the head?" Blair demanded.

"That is the strength of it."

"Then I don't wonder any longer that I've got to pay seven shillings in taxes on every pound of tobacco I buy," Blair gasped. "To think that I have to pay you, a full-blown sergeant, to go mooning about after a gentleman because said gentleman corpsed a useless, worthless abo. Now, wot do you think about that, 'Enery?"

Henry looked as though he knew nothing. Blair turned to Bony, saying:

"And wot makes you 'think' Clair came this way? If you're a tracker you should know whether he came this way or not, not 'think'."

"In Clair we have a man who is by no means a fool," Bony explained. "Clair adopted the blood-and-feather method of avoiding being tracked."

"Blood and feathers! Sounds like a Buffalo Bill penny dreadful," murmured Blair.

"Exactly," blandly agreed Bony. "It is the only method successfully adopted by the blacks to escape their enemies. I knew, however, that I should find evidence of Clair's passage, as I did; for I came across several grains of sugar which Clair had dropped, and that sugar was but six miles from here—in fact, directly between here and the Basin, where he was working."

"Well, now! Ain't that wasteful?" Blair said. "Fancy dropping sugar about the place, and sugar the price it is."

"I suppose Clair stayed here last night, Fred?"

"Oh, yes."

"Ah! And which way did he go when he left?" Knowles asked sharply.

"He hasn't left yet, to my knowledge."

The sergeant's eyes narrowed. Bony smiled. He was a better judge of human character than was his inferior in the force.

"Then where is he?" came the demand.

"I believe he is lying down in my tent," came the calm, ominously calm, reply. Immediately Knowles was on his feet. So, too, was the little bullock-driver. Henry's face widened in a grin of anticipation. Bony smiled again, but Bony's eyes were everywhere. And he was sure Blair lied when he admitted that Clair had been there the night before. Knowles moved towards the tent beneath a box-tree. Blair stood resolutely between it and the policeman. With studied deliberation he rolled up the sleeves of his vest to his armpits. In his eyes was a light of pure joy, whilst the tip of his beard was level with his nose.

"That 'ere tent is my property, my house," he proclaimed. "Unless you have a search-warrant you don't enter it."

"Don't be silly, Blair. Stand aside."

The little man backed to the door of the tent. The policeman followed.

"Come on, Sarge!" Blair pleaded. "You've been looking for a brawl for years. Just us two, now. A level go."

It might have been a "level go" had not Bony laughed.

A suspicion of disappointment clouded Blair's blazing eyes. And the sergeant, realizing that the little man was lying to gain a fight, to him the very breath of life, stepped back, and smiled.

"I suppose I shall have to show you a warrant, Blair," he said, pulling out of a pocket a bundle of documents. Selecting one, he showed it to the chagrined Blair, who, stepping aside, raised the tent flap and bowed mockingly.

Within was a stretcher-bed, and an assortment of blankets and clothes on the ground which evidently was Henry's sleeping place. Clair, of course, was not there.

Knowles glanced over the camp. A table-top wagon afforded no concealment, neither did a small heap of yokes and scooping gear. Seeing several bags of chaff and horse-feed, he said:

"Are you feeding the bullocks?"

"Looks like it," came the sulky reply. "No ground feed hereabouts, and them annimiles 'ave to work hard."

Bony walked about the camp, his gaze always on the ground. Whilst Knowles was fruitlessly questioning Blair, he made a wide detour and finally looked over and down into the partly cleaned-out earth tank or dam. It was when returning to camp that he saw and picked up a small white feather, a feather whereon was one smear of dried blood. It was, he knew, a pelican's feather.

The half-caste sauntered back to the baffled Knowles.

"If Clair has passed this way he has gone on," he announced. "I suppose Thurlow Lake is the next place west?"

"Yes," Knowles assented. Then, turning to Blair, he said with annoyance: "It won't help you to prevaricate. I want the truth now. Did Clair camp here last night?"

"I've told you a hundred times that he did," replied the little volcano, with a broad grin.

The sergeant snorted, or the venting of his exasperation sounded like it. He strode to his horse, followed by the still smiling tracker. Together they mounted. Together they nodded farewell to the now seated Blair. The spectacles were once more on the little man's nose, the paper on his knees.

"As I was saying, 'Enery, the 'usband and the D. came upon the sinful wife and—Oh, good day-ee, Sarge; good day-ee, Bony!—her lover beneath the mulberry-tree. Stay where you are, 'Enery, for a minute. Let them git well away. They're off to Thurlow Lake to take poor old Bill Clair, or try to. Now, shin up that tree, 'Enery, and watch 'em out of sight."

Henry climbed the tree pointed out to him. Blair read to himself for quite five minutes; then:

"Are they over the rise yet, 'Enery?" he asked.

"Just on the top, Fred," announced the watcher. "Now they 'ave gone."

"Goodo! Just stay there and keep a look-out for a bit. They might circle and come back."

Blair sauntered over to the feed-bags. He pulled several away till he came to those in the centre. These, too, he moved.

"Righto, Bill, old lad!" he said. "The coast is clear."

Up from a narrow deep hole William Clair arose as Venus from the sea. His limbs were cramped. He said:

"I'll never bash no more abos, Fred."

Chapter Twenty-Two

The Pool

WHEN THE squatter remarked to Kate Flinders that he thought Ralph was thinking out some problem he was nearer to the truth than he suspected. Exactly what the problem was the young man did not know, nor did he realize even that he was working out a problem. When he told his foster-parents that he would prefer to become an ordinary station hand to reaching the summit of Church or State service, he was voicing what was really the mysterious lure of the bush for those born in it, as well as for many born out of it.

What seafarer, compelled by old age to live always ashore, does not long for the sea, the smell of the sea, the moods of the sea? The scents, the moods, the changing yet eternal aspect of the bush of Central and outer Central Australia had become necessary, impelling, to Ralph Thornton during his last college term. Unconsciously throughout the long years of his childhood the bush had got into his blood, calling with increasing insistence in these latter years that were shaping his manhood.

Having drunk afternoon tea in company with the Little Lady and discussed Clair's impending arrest, the young man procured bathers and towels and walked up the river to a deep hole where the water was crystal clear. On that late afternoon the air, too, was crystal clear, and warm despite the lateness of the autumn. He felt an unaccountable gladness that he was there walking beneath the grand old gums bordering the dear old Darling, which now had ceased to run. The bed of the river was quite dry along the stretches between the holes at the bends, and in the hole at the station Ralph saw Frank Dugdale fishing. He was glad Dugdale did not wish to accompany him.

Ralph's bathing-pool lay half a mile up from the blacks' camp, a twelve-foot hole in the bed of the river, with a diameter of twenty feet or so; and at last the young man stood in his bathers on the brink, looking down in a fascinated manner at the white sand bottom showing in large patches between the gnarled snake-like limbs of sunken tree-snags.

One particularly large patch of clear ground lay right below him, and whilst watching he saw the graceful form of a superb codfish glide slowly across it. It was a large fish, and the magnifying thickness of the water made it appear larger than it was. Ralph seated himself at the edge of the pool to watch it.

The young man had seen the fish at every visit. He knew precisely where that fish retreated when the water was disturbed either by his body or with stick or stone. It took refuge among some heavy snags lying to one rocky side of the pool. The entrance of the refuge was plainly visible, and it was an entrance which Ralph believed could be closed by removing a short length of snag lying across another and heaping up several other snags.

If the entrance to the fish's lair could be closed against the fish, it was his intention to take with him a black fellow's shortened throwing-spear and give battle to the cod. For the fish was as quick as lightning in action, as wild as the wildest dingo, and the most exciting moments so far in the young man's life had been the taming of wild things.

When again he moved, the fish was immediately below him. Ralph rose with that stealthy slowness of movement which had characterized his actions when he had caught and saddled the outlaw horse—the stealthy slowness which appears to hypnotize the creatures of the wild—the kind of movement which very few civilized white men had retained, and which is to be seen in perfection among uncivilized North American Indians.

Drawing back from the edge of the pool, Ralph climbed the steep river-bank and reached the gum-tree that was leaning over the water. And there, taking his stand on one of the limbs thirty feet above the pool, the venturesome youth manoeuvred his position till he was right above the mass of snags which formed the fish's lair or retreat.

There he waited, judging the depth, ascertaining the correct springing kick the branch would give when he dived. Lithe, supple, and beautiful, his body showed darkly against the green foliage of the tree, like a statue of Adonis set high against a background of climbing vines.

The fish investigated a mussel-shell that closed abruptly and clung with amazing strength to a large slab of rock. A yabby or gilgie, a miniature crayfish, partly emerged from its hole, in which position it remained as if daring the fish to make a dash. A small school of fish swam languidly over the largest of the sand patches and braved the cod lying in the shadow by swimming closer at their peril. For the great fish was suddenly among them.

Ralph saw them but as silver sparks eddying and swirling about the green, flashing killer. It was then that his body swooped down to the pool and disappeared below its surface with hardly a splash. He and the cod arrived at the fish's lair almost together, the cod about a second too late.

The boy beheld the fish back-water, as it were, with great swiftness. Looking up, he saw the agitated surface of the pool reflecting the trees and sky above in a shimmer of green and silver. He stood gripping one snag to keep himself down for a second or two, deciding which of the others to try to move to block the fish's retreat. It was the short cross-length which must be taken out, and, giving it a tug, he found that its long submergence had covered it with fine slimy growths.

A swift stoop, and he filled his hands with sand to make them grip. Then, bracing himself with one foot against the lower snag, he pulled with all his strength.

The cross snag gave way. The upper snags came to rest upon the lower. The entrance was sealed, the fish balked. Ralph bent his knees to give him the spring to the surface. He straightened them suddenly in the spring. But he did not rise. His right foot was caught between the lower and the next snag.

A tug, and his foot was still imprisoned. A greater effort brought no release. A surge of terror swept over his mind, such terror as not even nightmare had brought within his experience. Realization that he was caught, doomed to death, seemed to stun him as effectually as a blow to the head. Then quite suddenly his stunned sensation gave place to a great calmness, during which his mind raced as never had it raced before. Strangely, however, his mind was already becoming detached from his body, as a separate and independent entity.

"It is the finish," cried the struggling entity. "God! it's the end. Dug is miles away and will give no help. Oh, Mother, how grieved you will be! They'll come searching presently, Father and Dug, and some of the men. They'll look down and see my white body, still and limp, see my wide mouth and staring eyes. Oh! I can't—I can't hold out much longer. I must open my mouth—I must. If only I had a chance!"

Then came to him a greater terror than the last—the final terror of dissolution, instinctive in us all. It caused Ralph's thoughts to become chaotic, his limbs to thrash in one supreme struggle. He heard the air bubbles rising from his mouth, heard the gurgling cry for help those bubbles contained. His sight failed and revived almost the next moment. The pain of his clenched jaws became an intolerable agony whilst the conflict between the mental and the physical worlds drew to a close.

And when the inevitable moment came—when at the very climax of horror, Ralph's mouth opened wide—it was to draw into his red-hot lungs clean, beautiful air.

So this was death! The pain had gone, as had gone the roaring in his ears. Death was not so terrible after all. In fact, it was delightfully restful. A soft, yielding something supported his neck and shoulders. And how strange it was that in this dark, restful world a crow would mournfully caw-

caw! And then the young man's eyes were open, and he was looking up into other eyes—big black eyes filled with wistfulness, a mistiness of unshed tears. And when his gaze became properly focused he saw that he was looking into the lovely face of Nellie Wanting, the aboriginal girl.

"Stay still, Misther Ralph," she implored softly. "Bime-by your strength come, and we get out."

She was standing on a narrow ledge of rock, the water reaching her breasts. She held Ralph closely against her, his head supported by her shoulder, his neck encircled by her arm. Her free hand was clutched against the rim of the pool for support.

When the young man realized that he was alive—realized that the air was flooding his lungs—he began to laugh for very joy. Returning strength surged through his body, the confident strength of youth. His voice trembled, however.

"Let me go, Nellie. I'm all right now," he said.

But, though she loosened her clasp of him, she did not entirely let him go; wherein she was wise, for it required effort on Ralph's part to clamber out upon the dry rim of the pool, where reaction robbed him of strength once more, and he was violently sick.

The sickness passed quickly, however, and, raising his head, he forced a smile at the anxious girl sitting in her drenched clothes beside him. Then giddiness overcame him, and when he lay down and closed his eyes the girl reached over, and, taking up the towels, covered him with them.

"Lie still!" she whispered. Her voice was rich and sibilant, soft and caressing. Moving her body, she came to sit closer to him, supporting herself by one arm whilst leaning over him.

"How did you get me out?" he murmured.

"I saw you go down," she explained. "Me been down there, too. Those tree-snags, they like dingo-traps. And when you didn't come back I run much. I look down and see. See you caught in trap." She shivered as with chill, but it was with the vivid memory of that moment. "You struggle," she went on simply. "No good. So I went down to free you. Oh, Mister Ralph! I were such frightened. I—I thought you died—dead."

The young man again looked up at her. He made no effort to rise, though he was feeling much better. He experienced a growing sense of wonder, akin to amazement, for he saw quite suddenly how beautiful she was, how beautiful the outlines of her body where the damp cheap blouse clung to it. With increasing wonder he noted the bigness of her eyes, widely opened by memory of his peril. Yes, he realized that her terror was on his account and not on her own. He saw, at first with bewilderment, and then with rapidly-growing clearness, that her eyes were misty, brimming with tears, happy tears, and it seemed that this post-drowning life was beautifully different from what it had been. Slowly he raised his hand and touched her cheek, on which glinted a single tear.

And she, seeing the growing glory on his face, bent forward swiftly and kissed him on the mouth.

That kiss! Electric fire rushed through his body and surged about his brain. The recent experience was forgotten, the whole memory was dead, it was the very first moment of real life. When she quickly drew away from him, momentary fear and shyness pictured in her face, he raised himself and sat in such a way that their heads were close together, and almost face to face.

"Nellie, what—what has happened?" he whispered.

For a long moment she stared at him without answering. Then softly, so softly that her voice sounded like a zephyr among tree-leaves, she said:

"Oh, Misther Ralph, don't you know?"

He knew! Instinct told him. It was quite unnecessary for anyone to tell him that she loved him, and that he loved her— had loved her always.

He took her face between his hands, and slowly, very slowly, drew her near, nearer, till his lips were pressed fiercely against hers, returning, with man's awakened passion, her kiss.

Everything was forgotten but the amazing glory of that moment, a glory that whilst he lived would never cease to shine. He forgot himself, who and what he was—forgot the Little Lady, so proud and happy in him—forgot the beautiful Darling of the Darling whom he was to wed.

And on the bank of the river above them, his face white with anger, one hand savagely bitten on by his teeth, the other clenched about a fishing-line, there stood Frank Dugdale.

Chapter Twenty-Three

Bony is Surprised

ASSURED THAT her hero was thoroughly recovered, of which the ardour of his kiss seemed sufficient proof, Nellie became a thing of heredity and instinct. With surprising swiftness she sprang up and ran away, along the dry river-bed towards the camp, ran with wide eyes and parted lips; full of fear of what she had done, what had been done to her; full of hope yet dread that the young man would pursue her as the bucks of her tribe had pursued their women for ages past.

Ralph, however, did not follow. Still seated, he watched her flying feet and graceful figure till she disappeared round the first slight bend; and then, his blood still aflame and his pulses throbbing wildly, he snatched up his towels, rushed up the bank, and hurriedly dressed. And it was whilst lacing his shoes that Dugdale joined him.

Immediately the young man looked up into the sub-overseer's face he knew that Dugdale knew, had seen, what had happened down there beside the pool. The first thing to banish Nellie momentarily from his mind was his recent closeness to death, and that gave place to the memory of his position in the world. The blood crimsoned his face. As a heavy load suddenly laid upon him, he felt self-accusation, self-contempt, and shame.

"Hallo, Dug!" he said, without looking up.

Dugdale sighed, but said nothing. At last the shoes were laced. Ralph picked up his towels and rose to his feet. Tears of mortification clouded his eyes:

"I suppose you saw?" he questioned, faintly defiant.

"Fortunately, Ralph, I did."

"Why fortunately?"

"Because, sooner or later, you would have been observed. It is better that it should have been me than—Kate."

"But, hang it, Dug! There's no harm in a fellow kissing a girl is there?"

"Little harm, perhaps, in an ordinary chap doing such a thing—me, for instance—but a lot of harm for Mr Ralph Thornton, promised in marriage to the Darling of the Darling, to kiss a gin." Dugdale paused, then repeated, with emphasis: "A gin, Ralph."

The sting conveyed by that "A gin, Ralph" angered the young man, into whose eyes leapt a cold glare. Yet, even while his gaze was held by that of the older man, the fact that Nellie Wanting was a gin caused that feeling of shame to reassert itself, and suddenly Dugdale found himself faced by the straight young back and the bowed head.

To the sub-overseer the agony of loss occasioned by the engagement of his idol to his employer's son had been softened by the knowledge that Ralph was a fine, sterling boy, who should, and would, prove worthy of such a gift. The very last thing Dugdale had expected of young Thornton was that he should have forgotten his colour. To him, those kisses meant far more than a mere flirtation. The thought, so dreadful to him, was that the boy's lips, which had touched Nellie Wanting's mouth, would likely enough be pressed to those of Kate Flinders, the loveliest and purest girl in Australia, before that day was wholly gone.

Poor Dugdale! He had never seen in any woman's eyes be she white or black, that which Ralph had seen in the eyes of a black "gin" that afternoon.

And poor Ralph, too! Alive with the joy of youth, aflame yet with the glory of a lover's first kiss, ignorant of the irresistible forces drawing him, for ever drawing him, along one inevitable road! Knowing that he had done wrong, done his wife-to-be a greater wrong still, it came with a shock of surprise to him that he did not feel sorry. There was a tremor in Dugdale's voice when he spoke:

"Ralph, old boy, let's forget it," he said. "You have a great future and a great happiness before you. Live only for those two things. Great God! Are they not worth living for?"

The young man swung round, his face still reddened.

"What has all this to do with you?" he demanded.

"I am thinking of your father, and the Little Lady, and Kate," came Dugdale's answer, whilst they stared into each other's eyes. "Three people, Ralph, whose kindness and generosity I can never repay. Surely you can understand the hurt they would receive if they knew about this flirtation. Cannot you see for yourself that the terrible part of the affair is that Nellie Wanting is black?"

It required Dugdale's almost brutal plainness of speech to bring home to the young man the enormity of the thing. The younger man's eyes fell. He bowed his head, and Dugdale, racked by disappointed, hopeless love, worked heroically, like the man he was, to bring his successful rival back to the path of rectitude.

"If Nellie had been a white girl," he said, "I would have urged you to confess to Kate and ask forgiveness. The insurance of happiness must be paid by confession, and forgiveness. But confession of this would not insure happiness. How could it? It is best, as I said just now, to forget the whole wretched affair. Don't you think so?"

Ralph did. He was utterly miserable, utterly puzzled.

"You are right, Dug," he said a little wistfully. "I—I've been a beast, and I can't marry Kate now."

Dugdale laughed softly. He slid an arm through that of Ralph and gently urged him into the homeward walk.

"Don't be an ass, old boy," he pleaded. "You are not the first poor devil to be tempted by a woman, remember. And remember too, that you can't insult Kate by jilting her. The country would lynch you, for sure. Besides, there's Mr and Mrs Thornton. You'll see that in an hour or so. You will become more cheerful and look upon yourself not as a beast but as a temporary fool. Hark! There's the dressing-bell. I'll race you home. Ready?"

Under the now lightening load Ralph laughed chokingly and assented. The half-mile to the homestead was covered in record time; and, after his toilet, when the dinner-gong sounded, Nellie Wanting's lovely face had dimmed, and Nellie Wanting's kisses had ceased to thrill.

But later the young man retired early to his room with the excuse that he was tired, and Dugdale returned to the hole below the garden and fished for hours in the kindly darkness.

So it happened that no one heard of Ralph's diving adventure until Bony gleaned it from old Sarah Wanting a week later.

The attempt to arrest Clair had been less than a nine days' wonder. The attempt had failed utterly. The gaunt man had disappeared. Regarding this, the police, reinforced by several troopers, were confident of ultimate success, in spite of the fact that the majority of the bushmen were wholly sympathetic towards Clair. Had Clair killed a white man it would have been quite different.

Bony sensed the sympathy. He was, however, quite indifferent to Clair's fate. He was now giving all his mind to discovering who was the person who warned Clair of the coming of the police. The mystery of King Henry's death was a mystery no longer, but the mystery behind the murder was still to be solved.

The half-caste had infinite patience. That was the keystone of his success. He made open love to the sceptical Martha, he took rations along to Pontius Pilate and spent hours in the blacks' camp. And it was after leaving the camp late one night and whilst returning to the homestead in his noiseless fashion that he was suddenly halted by the sound of whisperings.

Bony kept quite still. Presently he observed a deeper shadow in the general darkness under the gums. From that shadow came the whisperings and occasionally the sound of passionate kisses.

It seemed then that Bony was as much interested in lovers' meetings as he was in the atom and in Napoleon Bonaparte.

He sat down on the ground just where he was. He sat there for half an hour till the lovers parted. He was still sitting there when Nellie Wanting passed him on her way back to the blacks' camp, and when she had gone he rose silently to his feet and followed the man.

He followed him across the billabong to the lower end of the tennis-court, along by the court, and across the cleared ground between it and the offices. There was a light in the jackeroos' sitting room, and when the door was opened to admit the newcomer it revealed Ralph Thornton.

Bony was astonished. He would have been less surprised had the lover proved to be Mr Thornton himself. For hours that night the detective-inspector lay pondering over the import of that lovers' meeting.

Chapter Twenty-Four

The Cemetery Clue

DURING THE last week in May a great rain fell over the whole of the eastern States. Many places in Southern Queensland received over eight inches, whilst the reading for the week at Barrakee was four inches and a half.

Everyone was delighted, for plentiful grass and herbage were assured for the stock and continuous employment made certain for all hands. Probably the most joyful man in New South Wales was Mr Hemming, now free from the great Thorley and master of Three Corner Station. Mr Thornton had paid forty-five thousand pounds for the property and, given average luck, the little sheepman would pay off the debt in ten years.

The action of giving Mr Hemming so wonderful a life was typical of the squatter of Barrakee. He was generous to a fault; but the safeguard to the fault was the Little Lady, and to her in this matter Mr Thornton made final appeal. She was the last tribunal, and her decision was always final, based as it was on her womanly intuition of the character of the person to be helped or benefited. And the joy of the two personages of Barrakee over the rain was no less keen than that of Mr Hemming and his wife.

The rain had come just in time to be of great profit to the ewes and lambs. The season promised to be an excellent one. Blair had finished cleaning out Tilly's Tank with three days to spare, and was brought into the station to cart wood for the winter and the coming shearing. He continued to find life a matter of great importance, and the secret of Clair's whereabouts was well kept by himself and his offsider.

Bony also was preoccupied by the seriousness of life, for he had discovered a most important clue, yet one which deepened the mystery he was so determined to solve.

It was late one afternoon in early June that he had strolled up on the sandy plain at the back of the homestead and visited the cemetery. The visit had not been premeditated. In fact, Bony had taken little heed of his meandering footsteps, his mind being occupied by the secret love meetings between Ralph Thornton and Nellie Wanting.

Now, among other things, Bony was a gentleman; which is to say that he practised the virtues of gentlemen as exemplified by the great Napoleon. Above all, Bony was intensely moral. The loose-living customs of the civilized aborigines, and the majority of white people as well, found no favour in the man who tried to pattern his life on that of his hero.

Ralph interested him because Ralph was a mystery, and the mystery to Bony was what the young man found in Nellie Wanting that he did not find in Kate Flinders. Regarding the Darling of the Darling as the most beautiful woman it had been his privilege to look upon, he was convinced that Ralph was indeed favoured by the gods. Yet here was this young man, hedged about by parental love, engaged to be married to an angel on earth, secretly meeting a black girl and, to do that, risking all worth having in life.

Where the half-caste was undecided was whether he could presume so far as to inform Ralph that his amour was discovered, and to advise him to put an end to it. Ralph was proud. He was a squatter's son. Bony was a half-caste and ostensibly a mere station-hand. An alternative was to put Mr Thornton in possession of the facts. Yet another line of action was the moving of Pontius Pilate and his people far up the river. That could be easily done through Sergeant Knowles, but at the same time it would remove a source of information which Bony still hoped would yield the solution of the greater mystery.

So much did these thoughts engage his mind that he failed to observe that he had entered the wire-fenced cemetery, and indeed was sitting on one of the graves. And it was whilst still in deep cogitation over the lesser mystery that there grew, as it were, before his eyes the lettering on a plain granite headstone. Bony's thoughts were suddenly wrenched away from Ralph's amour to the name, cut deeply into the slab. With widening eyes he read:

"Mary Sinclair. Died, February 28th, 1908."

Sinclair! Where had he heard that name? No, he had not heard but read it. It had been written by his old friend in North Queensland, among other details of the strange white fellow who had been made a sub-chief of a tribe ruled by one Wombra. His friend had named Clair Sinclair.

And now, here was Mary Sinclair, a Mary Sinclair who had died more than nineteen years ago. And it was from nineteen to twenty years ago that Clair or Sinclair had started out after King Henry. The triangle again, the eternal triangle. Was Mary the sister of William? Was it because of Mary that William had killed King Henry? The dates coincided strangely.

Bony got to his feet and began to pace to and fro between the graves, his mind racing in and out among little illuminated patches amidst encircling darkness, his hands gripped before him, his eyes almost closed. He had hoped that the solution of the mystery would have come from the blacks' camp, as indeed it yet might, but always something turned up or happened to point to the homestead of Barrakee.

Hoofbeats of a horse caused Bony to pause in his walk and, looking up, he saw Mr Thornton, mounted on a black mare, riding towards him from the road. After the disappearance of Clair the squatter had wondered why the detective elected to remain, since the case appeared to be complete. Bluntly asking Bony for his reason, he had been told with equal bluntness that the case, so far as he, Bony, was concerned, was not complete, the motive for the murder being still unknown. This being a matter of indifference to the squatter and considering also the fact that Bony was doing good work about the homestead for which he was not being paid, Mr Thornton had not pressed the subject. On reaching the cemetery he smiled with his usual friendliness, saying:

"Good evening, Bony! Looking for inspiration among the tombs?"

Bony returned the smile, and proceeded to roll a cigarette.

"Inspiration comes to me; I never seek it," he said. "The favoured of Dame Fortune is he who ignores the jade. Is it not wonderful how in so little time the grass is already growing? In a week or two the ground will be covered."

"It is wonderful—no doubt of that," Thornton agreed, seating himself on the foot of Mary Sinclair's grave and pulling out his cigarette-case. "It would be better, though, had the rain come a month sooner, for then the grass would have been better able to weather the frosts we are sure to have at the end of the month."

"Well, well! Let us be glad that the rain has come," Bony murmured. "It is as well, perhaps, that we cannot order Nature to act as and when we like. Just imagine now, if the great ones of history had possessed that power! Philip of Spain would himself have accompanied his armada and ordered the sea to remain calm; whilst the Emperor would not have been beaten by the cold after the burning of Moscow. Speaking of the dead, would you mind telling me who are the dead around us? Edward Crowley—who was he?"

They both glanced at the expensive monument to Bony's left.

"He was the only son of Jim Crowley, the man who formed this run a hundred years ago. Edward was sixty when he died." The squatter pointed out a grave over which stood a cross of red gum. "Harold Young sleeps there. He was my first overseer, and was drowned when foolishly attempting to swim his horse across the Washaways."

"Ah! Sad indeed. Your own son nearly lost his life not very long ago in the Darling."

"Do you mean Ralph?" Thornton demanded in surprise.

"Yes, I do," replied Bony. "He dived into a deep hole about a mile and a half up the river, with the foolish idea of blocking a fish lair with some sunken snags. It appears that, when he moved one of the snags, others fell and caught him by the foot, keeping him prisoner."

"Oh, this the first I've heard about it. Go on."

Bony's inherent love of the dramatic was fully aroused. He went on:

"As I have stated, your son's foot was caught by the snags he had loosed twenty feet under water. He was unable to free himself, and he would assuredly have been drowned had not someone dived down after him and engineered his release just when the boy was at his final struggle. In fact, your son was that far gone out of this life that, even had his final struggle released him without other help, it is doubtful if he would have survived had she not brought him to the surface."

"Great heavens, man! She! Who was this she?"

"A woman of my people—Nellie Wanting."

"You don't say so!" Mr Thornton regarded Bony with a look of slow-dawning admiration. "Well, she had grit, that girl. I thought the youngster had something on his mind. Doubtless he said nothing of it, fearing to worry us, especially his mother. But I must at least thank Nellie Wanting personally. The devil, now! Had the lad been drowned it would have killed my wife. How did you find out about this, Bony?"

"I learned the details from the girl's mother," the detective answered. "I would, however, deem it best if you did not make any mention of it. You see, the young man himself not having told anyone, it might be for the best to respect his motive for silence. Perhaps I have been indiscreet?"

"Not a bit of it," Thornton assured him warmly. "But I must talk to him in a guarded way to be more careful and take less risks. In any case, I would like to reward the girl's pluck. Tomorrow I'll give you a fiver to give to her."

"That, I think, would be appreciated," Bony returned. "However, we are getting away from the dead who are still close to us. Who and what was this Mary Sinclair here?"

Mr Thornton looked sharply at the indicated headstone. For a second he hesitated. Bony noted it, but when the squatter quickly turned his eyes on the detective Bony was regarding yet a further headstone.

"Mary Sinclair was our cook and died of peritonitis," Mr Thornton said, and at once regretted mentioning the cause of her death.

Bony appeared little interested, however. He asked about the fourth grave, and was told that the occupant had been a boundary-rider who was thrown from his horse and killed.

"Is it correct that we are to expect a flood?" asked the half-caste, deftly turning the subject.

"Reports have it so," Thornton replied. "Most of Southern Queensland is under water, and all the tributaries of the Darling are running bankers. It would not surprise me if we should have a record flood, and I am hoping we don't get it till after shearing. I have been intending for years to bridge the Washaways, but have always put it off. But let us go. I am getting cold."

"Ah, yes! The sun has gone. Do you ride on. I shall not forget to call for Nellie's present in the morning."

They parted with friendly nods, but when Thornton had left him Bony's face grew serious.

"So she was the cook, eh?" he murmured.

Chapter Twenty-Five

When Black is White

I F MR THORNTON had been aware of the gradual change in his son, Kate Flinders had been acutely aware of it. There were several points that constituted the change which had seemed to begin on the night of the surprise party.

At first, Kate thought that the change might be in herself, because after the revelation that she loved Frank Dugdale she knew she regarded her betrothed in an entirely different light. The unenviable position in which she found herself she faced with courage. No doubt existed in her mind that she loved Dugdale and that he loved her, and had she been offered her freedom she would have felt both relief and joy. But she had not been offered her freedom, and, knowing that she could not expect it to be offered, she determined that at least she would try to banish Dugdale from her thoughts and be loyal in them to Ralph. And the basic reason for this decision was that her marriage to Ralph was actually desired by the two people whom she loved so well.

For Kate was nothing if not loyal. Her promise given she would keep it, and resolutely crush down any feeling for Dugdale beyond the old light-hearted friendship. But it was a task terribly bitter, so bitter that the joy of life was dulled, while to make matters worse Ralph had grown preoccupied, his usual affectionate attentions slowly becoming more indifferent.

The day after Bony discovered the clue in the cemetery was brilliantly fine, and for several hours during the morning Kate was busy among her hens and broods of early chicks. It was whilst feeding the latter, in the bottom end of the garden, that Bony paused in passing, and spoke.

"It should be a matter of pride, Miss Flinders, having all those chickens out so early in the year," he said, removing his old hat and standing before her bare-headed.

Kate smiled. Of all the hands on her uncle's run the half-caste aboriginal was the most interesting. He was, in fact, not a little "intriguing". Several exceptionally educated and refined men had worked on the run at various periods, men whose presence there as station-hands was mystifying; but until the appearance of Bony she had not met a man so deferential to her sex, so frankly admiring of her looks for beauty's sake. There was, too, something so easy in his speech, as though, whilst recognizing the difference of their social status, his worldly wisdom entitled him to address her at all times.

"I am proud of my chicks, Bony," she said smilingly.

"They are, if I may guess, Buff Orpingtons, Miss Flinders."

"Your guess is right; they are."

"Ah! Excellent table birds, indeed, but not so excellent in producing eggs as, say, the Black Wyandottes," murmured Bony.

Kate stared at him, and then burst out laughing.

"Is there any subject you are not well up in?" she asked.

"Too many, I am afraid," Bony admitted. "Just now I am reading Hepplewaite's treatise on the general paralysis of the insane, a subject of which I am lamentably ignorant."

"Do you know, Bony, that every time you speak to me you make me feel that my education has been dreadfully neg-lected?" she said, with another laugh. "But why in the world are you interested in insanity, of all things?"

"Because I am interested in all things, the human mind particularly. When a human being commits an act there is always a cause before it and effect after it. For instance, when a man who all his life has dressed in quiet colours suddenly takes to wearing violently-coloured socks and ties, it may be assumed that the thought has entered his mind that no longer is he young. The subsequent act proves his desire to retain his youth, at least, to make other people think he is still young and—er—daring. But the subsequent effect is to make other men regard him as—what shall I say? Vulgar, no; loud, yes. That is the effect—loudness."

Kate could not refrain from a slight start. The threatened abnormal charge of blood to her face made her turn her head to the task of adding a little more food to the chicks' pan. What a strange coincidence that Bony should have said that when Ralph's sudden liking for vivid colours was one of the points of the change in him she was noticing! Or had Bony noticed it, too?

"There is no cause without effect," Bony went on. "At one time a friend of mine died of the disease I am now studying. It was unaccountable, for he was healthy and of healthy parents; but, when he was admitted to a home for such sufferers, it was found that for many years he had been addicted to opium. The doctors said that opium was the cause. Undoubtedly it was the cause of his death, but there must have been a cause leading to the first indulgence. And that, the real cause of my friend's death, was disappointment in a love-affair."

"Then I hope, if I am ever disappointed in a love-affair, I shall not be so very foolish," Kate said, still busying herself with her chicks.

"I thought of something much more drastic when I was thus disappointed," Bony remarked, sighing.

"You!" Kate flashed round, but Bony was already leaving her. He smiled slightly.

"Even I, Bony," he said softly. "Good morning, Miss Flinders!"

The detective was much pleased with this conversation, which had its cause and would have its effect. He had learned that Kate had noticed Ralph's growing predilection for colours, and also he had learned that Kate was suffering from a disappointment in love; because, though her face was turned from him, he noticed the blood, which had come into her face on his introducing the subject of disappointed love, spread to her neck. But Bony thought that it was over Ralph. He was not to know that it was on account of Dugdale.

Leaving the garden by the wicker-gate, the half-caste crossed the billabong and sauntered up the river-bank with the intention of visiting the blacks' camp, and when almost there he saw Nellie Wanting crossing the dry bed on her way to the homestead. Bony slowed in his walk and awaited her under one of the gums.

"Good morning, Nellie!" was his greeting when they met.

"Good day-ee, Bony!" she replied in her soft drawl.

"We are well met, Nellie, because I was coming to talk to you on very private business." Bony seated himself on a fallen tree and motioned to her to sit beside him. Then, abruptly: "Are you in fun, Nellie, or do you love Mr Ralph Thornton?"

The girl, who had seated herself, sprang up. She looked at Bony as though he had struck her.

"What—what for you say that?" she demanded, the whites of her eyes very plain, her scarlet lips held apart whilst she waited for his answer. Then, since he did not reply immediately, she whispered: "What do you see, what do you find out, eh?"

"I have seen enough to make me feel very sorry for you, Nellie," Bony said at last. "It would have been better if you had fallen in love with poor old Bony, who has a gin and three little children. You don't expect Ralph Thornton to marry you, do you?"

"But he loves me," she said simply.

"Does he? Are you sure he does, just because you want to believe he does? Ralph Thornton can never marry you, Nellie."

Quite suddenly she sat down on the ground at his feet and burst into sobs. Bony's great heart throbbed in pity. He saw the shaking shoulders and the bowed head. He saw with infinite pity the cheap cotton blouse, the cheap but spotless navy-blue serge skirt, the flesh-coloured stockings, and the brilliantly polished high-heeled shoes. Wearing a grass-plaited sarong, he thought, she would have been a queen. Wearing the clothes of a white girl, decking herself to please her lover's eyes, she appeared a travesty of womanhood, a travesty and a tragedy. Leaning forward, he placed a sympathetic hand on her short black curls.

"You think he play with me because I am black," she sobbed. "But he love me. He tell me so again and again. I love him, yea—oh dear! I love him. He drown, and I pull him out. I save him, and he belonga me all right now. I love him long time before I pull him out of hole, but he love me then and always ever after. He marry me and I go away long way off with Ralphie. He make me call him Ralphie. Even if he won't marry me, no matter. I go way with him, I go bush with him, and help him—bush all alonga me. I wanta go, he wanta go. He want me and I want him."

The man found himself regarded by tear-drenched eyes.

"Oh, Bony—dear old Bony!—done you see my Ralphie all belonga me, and me all belonga him?" she pleaded.

"What does your mother say about it?" Bony inquired.

"Ole Sarah—she dunno. You no tell her, Bony."

"What do you think she would say if she did know?" the half-caste persisted.

For a while Nellie was silent. Then:

"She no say nothing."

"That may be. But what do you think Mrs Thornton say when she know her son has gone bush with you, Nellie, you, a gin?"

"What matter what she say, then?" Nellie countered naively.

"A great deal, my girl, a great deal. They would very soon have your lover back. And you would be ordered off the run, kept away like—like a dingo. Can't you understand that?"

"They'll never find us when we go bush. We'll be, oh! so clever. We'll have plenty tucker and walk, walk, walk all day, far, far away."

Bony sighed. It was evident that the affair was already becoming serious, and that young Thornton was planning to make an irrevocable outcast of himself. For an outcast he would assuredly become if he took the girl away into the bush. Had the two met in the far north of Queensland, or the Northern Territory, the public eye would have been closed in a portentous wink; but here, in New South Wales, the home of the bluest-blooded squattocracy, such a course would result in utter social damnation.

So Bony played the age-old trump card, the chief trump card of all:

"But the time would come, Nellie, when out there in the bush he would begin to think of his father and mother and the home he had left. He would look at you. And you would see in his eyes the longing for all those things he had lost."

"I won't let him think of that," she said fiercely. "I shall love him so, so much that he would not have any time to think like that."

"You won't stop him thinking when you lie asleep," Bony pointed out gently. "And you will know, girl, that he is there living like we black people because of you. You will know that you have dragged him down to our level, he who now is so proud, so white, so high."

Nellie made no reply to that. Bony had let her see the matter from an entirely new angle, had started a train of thought which kept her silent. Still he urged further:

"You don't know it, Nellie, but you are an exceptional girl. I have studied you. In spite of the loose morals of your people, made loose because the iron tribal customs of old have been swamped by the white man's damnable civilization, you are a thoroughly good girl, a throwback, as it were, to your ancestors of five hundred years ago.

"Just think now. Suppose you let Ralph take you away into the bush. It will be lovely to be wrapped in love for a little while—and a little while it will be, in spite of what you think. Love will sleep one day, and he will awake to see how deep

158

has been his fall because of you. Now, suppose you say to yourself: 'I love my Ralphie so much that I won't let him fall because of me. I'll make him stay as he is. I'll watch him grow older, see him boss of Barrakee, see him become so fine, and I shall be able to say to myself: 'Ralphie, you have become great because I love you so much that I would not let you sink to be an outcast, a wild man, a dingo.' Would not that be so much nobler, Nellie, wouldn't it?"

Whilst he spoke the girl watched his face with growingly shining eyes, but when he ceased speaking her voice was caught by a sob, and suddenly the tears fell from her eyes and rolled unchecked down her cheeks of black velvet. And then, as suddenly as the tears came, she caught him by the knees and lowered her face upon them. For a long time they remained like that, the girl passionately weeping, the man softly caressing her hair.

"Bony, oh, Bony! you is right," she cried. "I go away now, this minute. I go down to Three Corner Station, to Mrs Hemming, who want me. Ralphie! Oh, my Ralphie! What shall I do?"

Chapter Twenty-Six

In a Cleft Stick

THE MAIL from Bourke arrived at Barrakee at noon on Tuesdays and Fridays, and it was the same day on which Nellie resolved to steal away from Ralph that the official notification reached Dugdale that he had drawn one of the prizes in the Land Lottery, to wit, Daly's Yard block.

The lucky prize-winner and young Thornton had been out riding most of the day, and immediately on their return they had gone to Mortimore for their mail. Dugdale's eyes glittered when he read the contents of the long official envelope.

"I've been allotted Daly's Yard, Mr Thornton!" he told the squatter, who was writing in his own portion of the office.

You have, Dug? Well, my congratulations!" Thornton said, genuinely pleased. "Now, I suppose you'll be wanting to leave us."

Dugdale became serious. Here at last was decent excuse to tear himself away from Barrakee and all the bitter-sweetness of his life there. But what at one time had seemed desirable now threatened to be a wrench.

"Well, yes; I suppose so, Mr Thornton," he admitted. "There is, of course, no immediate hurry. Say, after lamb-marking."

"Fine, Dugdale! We start lamb-marking next Monday. We'll be at it for about a fortnight, or a little over, as usual. Go, then, and look at your land, and then come to me, and for what financial assistance you may need you know you have only to ask. If you serve yourself as well as you have served me, you will succeed. Honestly, I am sorry to lose you."

"It is kind of you to say that and to offer assistance," Dugdale told his employer-friend warmly.

Within a few hours everyone in the back country knew the names of the winners and the names of the prizes won. Just before the men's dinner gong was due to sound Dugdale had a caller in Fred Blair.

"I've come ter offer you me congratulations," Blair explained. "I'm mighty glad you got a block, and as usual mighty disappointed the Board won't give me one. My gal, who has been waiting all these years, will cry her eyes out. She always does."

"I am sorry you weren't lucky, Fred," Dugdale said sympathetically.

"Not half so sorry as I am meself, Mr Dugdale," Blair rejoined grimly. "Still, it's no use singing about it. What you must do now is to head a syndicate of a few blokes to take a try in Tattersall's. The Golden Plate is to be run on August 2nd, and you'll be just in time. Tickets, one pound three and sixpence; first prize, twenty thousand quid, second, ten thousand, third, five thousand. What about it?"

"Yes, I am agreeable, Fred."

"Good!" Blair went on: "You've got the luck now, and, while you're getting the run of it, put your name down first. Be sure your name is first, now. Put me down, too, and 'Enery McIntosh, will you?"

"I will."

"And you'll do it tonight before midnight," urged Blair seriously. "Tomorrow your luck might be out."

Dugdale laughed. "And what shall we call the syndicate?" he asked.

"Why—Daly's Yard Syndicate, of course."

"All right, we'll do it, Fred," Dugdale agreed.

"Good! If we don't pull in the winning horse, my name's not Blair."

And so it happened that the Daly's Yard Syndicate—consisting of Dugdale, Mr Thornton, Ralph, Blair and McIntosh—was formed, and five tickets bought in the Golden Plate Sweep.

Dugdale's luck was a subject of the dinner conversation that night.

"I am so glad he drew Daly's Yard," Mrs Thornton remarked to everyone, the others at table being her husband, niece, and "son". "But I shall be sorry to see him go. I like Dugdale, and I liked his poor father."

"His father would have been proud of him had he not—had he lived," the squatter said, leaning back in his chair in a suddenly reflective mood. "It must have been a terrible thing for the son, faced by the manner of his father's death. However, he has proved his worth. He will get on all right, no doubt of that."

"He will find life very lonely there by himself," Ralph put in. "He will find he'll have to look out for a wife."

Whilst speaking he sat his chair in a manner that could not now be described as graceful. He lounged rather than sat. Wearing a black dinner-coat, this and his shirt and tie were faultless; but round his waist he wore a cummerbund of brilliant blue, and from his shirt-cuff there hung a silk handkerchief of the same colour.

Apparently neither Mrs Thornton nor her husband noticed the incongruity of dress, or the slipshod manner of sitting at table he had fallen into. The effect, however, was not lost on Kate Flinders. To her the young man had visibly changed during the few short months since he had finished with college. It seemed that he was quickly losing the polish that a first class college had put on him; and Kate observed this progressive deterioration with an acute sense of regret, as well as anxiety, concerning the hidden reason for it.

The imminence of Dugdale's departure for his block also weighed heavily upon her soul. He had become, as it were, a part of Barrakee; and, since she had known she loved him, it was a little balm to know she was near him. But now he was going away—probably right out of her life—the loss that was coming to her was overwhelming. And here was Ralph cynically saying that Dugdale would be obliged to seek a wife.

"You are right, dear," Mrs Thornton agreed, bestowing on the young man an affectionate smile. "But I think he will find it hard to secure a good wife. Nowadays the girls won't stay in the bush. They must be in the cities, gadding about in clothes which I consider indecent. What the world is coming to I don't know."

"Do you hear that, Kate?" the young man said laughing. "You'll have to lengthen your dress."

Kate was daydreaming, but awoke with an answering laugh when directly addressed.

"Lengthen it," she cried, with assumed gaiety. "Why, when I go to Sydney again I shall be obliged to shorten it, if I would avoid being laughed at."

Ralph turned to the Little Lady: "There, Mother," he said. "Even in our own family do we find the sinners."

"Some were born many years ago," interjected the squatter, with twinkling eyes.

"I know," Mrs Thornton countered. "Why, last year, when we were in Melbourne, I saw a woman of forty dressed like a girl of fourteen."

"I was not referring to the age of the sinners, my dear Ann. I was thinking of the time when quite a young man—before I met you—I went to a music hall in Sydney. And there I was duly shocked at seeing a dancer in a dress much longer that is worn by the average woman today. Each new fashion shocks us at first, till the next shock makes the previous shock seem old fashioned."

Mrs Thornton sighed. "Yes, John. Perhaps that is it. We are growing old fashioned, you and I."

Dinner over, they played cribbage, and when Mrs Thornton announced her intention of retiring Kate rose, too, to leave with her. Ralph kissed the Little Lady affectionately. Kate he kissed with equal warmth, whispering:

"Goodnight, Kate. I am sorry I am so poor a sweetheart."

The girl's eyes widened with surprise, and she would have replied, had not Ralph gone over to a chair, where lay a novel he was reading. Was Ralph tiring of the engagement? Was he thinking of asking for his release? And then Dugdale's white face and burning eyes, when he looked at her that night of the party, made her catch her breath.

And an hour later, when she fell asleep, Ralph Thornton was in his room, looking through his clothes. First he selected an old suit and a pair of riding boots, which he placed on a chair. Then he chose a complete change of underwear.

On the floor he spread out a bed sheet, and on that he laid two blankets. On top of these he put the underwear, his shaving kit, a hairbrush and comb, an old hat and a few soft collars. The long sides of the sheet he turned in, and then rolled up the whole into a cylinder, which he strapped. He had created a bushman's swag. From deep in one of the drawers of the chest he produced a hessian sugar bag, containing smaller calico bags of flour, tea, and sugar. Yet another bag of cooked meat and bread he added to those in the hessian bag, and the neck of this gunny sack he loosely connected to one of the swag straps with a towel.

His preparations complete, he changed into the old suit and donned the riding boots. He was ready for his Great Adventure. With the swag slung over his back, balanced by the gunny sack hanging in front of him, he picked up an old billy and silently opened the door. Two minutes later he was walking through the garden to the bottom gate.

Beyond the gate he halted. It seemed that he was waging a battle that had often been fought before without decision. There he stood on the fine edge of the divide. Behind the gate lay his home, his inheritance, the woman he loved as his mother, the big generous man he looked up to and admired as his father, the pure lovely girl who was to be his wife. Before him, across the billabong, a little way up the river, awaited the goddess of love, that beautiful black girl whose arms were so soft and clinging, whose kisses were so passionate, so full of the very essence of love's perfect joy.

For, though he had decided, the decision had been arrived at only after much mental struggle. He fully recognized the consequences of the step he was about to take, yet there was that lure of the bush, that call to his blood, that pull at every fibre of his being which at last had become irresistible. His mind was chaos. One side of him appeared to cling passionately to home and love, whilst the other demanded that wonderful freedom from all restraint, compared with which the freedom of Barrakee was as artificial as that which is conceded to the more favoured animals at the Zoo.

The hesitation disappeared of a sudden. He almost ran across to the riverbank, and hurried up the empty river till he arrived at the fallen red gum at which he had always met Nellie.

There was no one, however, awaiting him. But stuck in a cleft stick, so placed that he could not miss seeing it, he saw a dainty silk handkerchief which he recognized as one of his gifts to Nellie Wanting. The handkerchief was wrapped about a folded piece of paper. With a sense of calamity he struck a match to read the almost illegible scrawl:

I can't come (he read). It would be no good for you. I'm black, you white. Goodbye my Ralphie—my Ralphie.

The young man's mind ceased to function for a while; Bony's note, written with Nellie Wanting's sanction, had the effect of a stunning blow.

Chapter Twenty-Seven

A Cold Camp-Fire

By MID JUNE the lamb-marking was in full swing. Every man on the station was working at full pressure, and extra men had been put on for the occasion. Watts, the overseer, was in charge of the camp, with Ralph as second in command, and during the marking the camp was moved to four points on the run to which the flocks were taken by the riders under the direction of Frank Dugdale. Mr Thornton himself undertook a roving commission, accompanied often by his niece.

The Western Division of New South Wales had become a comparative paradise. The frost of mid-winter not having yet come to cut down the growing grass, the whole world was covered in brilliant emerald, whilst the full water-holes and clay-pans sparkled like huge diamonds beneath the mildly warm sun. It was the kind of weather that makes man and beast very glad to be alive.

Perhaps the worst or hardest of the work was the marking, done by George Watts himself. He had a surgeon's hands, plus the knack of mental concentration, which enabled him to keep at his labours at extraordinarily high speed. For an hour at a time Watts kept moving up and down the line of lamb-catchers, followed by Ralph with ear-markers and tarbrush. At the end of each hour the young man was permitted to use the knife under the calm directions of the master, who whilst supervising Ralph rolled and smoked a thin cigarette.

Yet, in spite of the interest of the work, and the gaining of essential experience, young Thornton's mind was not in it. Watts was too busy to notice his preoccupation at the time, but subsequently events recalled those evenings by the camp-fire, when Ralph sat and stared silently into the glowing embers.

166

Warring for the soul of Ralph Thornton were two separate influences, influences that had well nigh assumed personalities like those of Dr Jekyll and Mr Hyde. Each influence, backed by distinctive desires, was pulling in opposition to the other, and it seemed to him sometimes that the struggle going on within him would drive him mad. It was as though he stood on the very summit of a high ridge, with the ineffable lure of the bush, typified in Nellie Wanting, trying to pull him down on the one side, and on the other the civilizing restraint of Barrakee and the conventions embodied by Mrs Thornton.

Of this strife the two women concerned were utterly unconscious. Neither was aware of the other's opposing influence—the one sure of her affectionate domination, the other resigned to the surrender of hers. Mr Thornton realized in a dim, careless way that the lad was thinking out some personal problem, whilst Kate Flinders believed it also, and believed, moreover, that the problem was a basic reason of the gradual change in his habits.

It was Bony, the half-caste detective, not a student but a professor of human nature, who saw so plainly the perpetual struggle occupying Ralph's every waking moment. But, though Bony was witness of the battle, was conversant with the personalities, he could not fathom the underlying reason. To him Ralph had become an absorbing study, so much so that it almost excluded from his mind his real business at Barrakee.

A battle of lesser intensity was being fought in the heart of Kate Flinders, but of this battle Bony knew nothing. To the girl it was unutterably distressing to be betrothed to one man and wholeheartedly in love with another. Her sense of loyalty was outraged, for, no matter how she tried to banish thoughts of Dugdale, the sub-overseer's personality would obtrude, making her feel a traitress every time Ralph kissed her, which fortunately had now become a rare occurrence. As to the kissing, Bony wondered if Ralph occasionally, when kissing his betrothed, consoled himself by imagining it was Nellie's lips he was kissing. Actually Kate had wondered twice whilst being kissed if Dugdale's kisses would be fiercer.

She could not help it. The thought came involuntarily and horrified her. It made her both grieved and ashamed. Yet how could she ask Ralph to release her? How could she disappoint the Thorntons who had been ever as a father and a mother, surrounding her with their protection and love?

And it was these thoughts that filled her mind when in company with the squatter, who himself drove, but more slowly than Dugdale, the big station car about the run. The thoughts and the growing forebodings made her silent till her uncle rallied her with teasing questions or some joking remark.

Many times did they come upon a great flock of sheep being taken to or brought from the lambing camp. The squatter, of course, knew precisely where those flocks were, but coming upon them invariably took Kate by surprise. At the first sight of the moving mass, with its attendant horseman and lolling-tongued dogs, Kate's eyes searched hungrily for the graceful figure of Dugdale, sometimes on a grey gelding, at others on a spirited bay mare with white feet.

And when they did come upon him her heart fluttered and her eyes sparkled till she remembered Ralph, and then the sun appeared to lose its light, and the sudden glory of the world die down to a dull drab.

It was thus they came upon him when engaged, with the help of three riders, in moving a flock of ten thousand sheep towards the marking camp. When the car slowed, Dugdale cantered over to it and, dismounting, removed his wide-brimmed felt to Kate.

"Good afternoon, Kate. Good day, Mr Thornton," he said levelly. A quick glance at the girl, another at her uncle who was watching the milling flock, and a second look, longer and searching, at the girl.

"Gad! how lovely she is today and for always," was his thought.

And hers, when her eyes that were in danger of telling too much, fell aside: "Always cool and good-looking, and so efficient. How can I—Oh, how can I help loving him?"

"How are they travelling, Dug?" asked the squatter, referring to the sheep.

"Good," answered the sub-overseer. "Mr Watts still has ten hundred at the yards, so I am not hurrying these."

"That's right, Dug. How are the lambs going, do you think?"

"I should say about eighty per cent, if not a little higher."

"Humph! That rain came just in time." For a while Mr Thornton again regarded the flock, and absently looked at the slow-moving riders, none of whom carried a stock-whip, for he would not allow a man working sheep even to crack a whip. Cracking of whips, or any methods designed to hurry sheep unduly, the squatter frowned at, and it was these little points, among others, which had made him so successful a sheepman.

"Who owns that brindle dog working close in?" was his next question.

"Sam Smith."

"Is it a pup?"

"No, second year. One of Elsie's pups."

"Oh!" Elsie was a famous kelpie bitch belonging to the overseer. "Well, it looks as though it'll never make a good dog. Keep your eye on it, Dug. I noticed it biting just then. Tell Sam to make it work wider or—shoot it."

"All right. Sam, I think, reckons it to be no good, but his other dog is sore-footed and he is giving it a spell."

"Well, we'll get on. So long, Dug."

"Goodbye! Goodbye, Kate!"

"Au revoir, Dug."

And when the car moved ahead Kate dared not raise her eyes and look at him, yet she could not refrain from looking back to see him vault into the saddle and canter off easily on his return to the sheep.

Half an hour later they came to a winding creek in which was a chain of water-pools.

"What about a drink of tea, Kate?"

"I would like it, Uncle, if we have time to boil the billy," she said with an affectionate smile at his consideration, well knowing that, had not she been with him, he would never have thought of it.

So, while he gathered a few sticks and made a fire, afterwards putting the billy against it, she undid the strap securing the small "tucker-box" to one of the running-boards, and produced tin pannikins, a bottle of milk, tea, sugar, and sandwiches. He came across, got the tea-tin and with it returned to the billy; and there, whilst waiting for the water to boil, stood idly looking about the scene, sylvan and lovely. She saw him frown, saw him hesitate, and then watched her uncle walk away for some fifty yards and examine the ground about a large box-tree, growing at an angle of forty-five degrees from the ground.

Circling the tree, he looked as though searching for tracks, and, his actions puzzling her, she called out:

"What are you trying to find, Uncle?"

"I am reading a story," he called back. "Come and read it, too."

She rose and joined him. At the foot of the box-tree she saw the ashes of a recent fire. A little away from it were three chop-bones, picked clean by the birds.

"The story reads that someone has camped here," she said lightly.

Nodding, he said reprovingly:

"You've only half read it. When did that someone camp here?"

"Really, I couldn't say."

"Three nights ago a slight shower fell," he reminded her. "See! Here are the marks of the raindrops on the bare places. Here is a footprint on bare sandy ground on which are no marks of raindrops. The fire is too old to have died out this morning, so that it was made the night before last. The person who made it was a big man—anyway, he wears a larger boot than I do. Look!"

Placing his foot over one of the few tracks plainly visible, he showed her how his boot fitted inside it. Then, looking up at the interested girl, he went on:

"Excepting the possibility that one of the temporary hands has large feet, there is no one on the run who wears bigger boots than I do but Martha. None of the temporary hands have been to this part of the run to my certain knowledge, and Martha hasn't left the homestead. Of course the fire may possibly have been lit by a wandering swagman, but I much doubt it, as we are so far off any track. It is my conviction, Kate, that the person who made that fire and evidently camped here for one night is none other than the missing William Clair,"

"Uncle!" Kate was surprised more by the mention of the name than by the reasoning.

"It is a fact," Thornton said when, reaching the boiling billy, he dropped a small handful of tea in it, and allowed it to boil for six seconds before taking it away from the fire. "Poor devil, it must be a terrible thing to be hunted like a wild beast."

"Awful," agreed the girl.

"I suppose—" Her uncle regarded her with suddenly twinkling eyes. "I suppose, if Clair made his appearance now, you would wish to give him up."

"No! No, I would not wish it, nor do it if I could," she said slowly. "The black may have provoked Clair, even attacked him. In any case, Clair is white, and King Henry was black. He should certainly be punished, but not hanged."

"I think I agree with you," he said. "But then, as your aunt said recently, I am old fashioned. We old people and our people before us regard and regarded the lives of blacks very cheaply. They regarded our lives and our stock equally as cheap."

Kate shivered. "I hate black people," she said. "Every time I look at them I go cold, especially when I see the whites of their eyes. If one came for me, or ran after me, I'd die."

"Well, perhaps I am wrong, and, as a JP, I should not say it, but I shall be sorry when they get Clair."

"They may not get him," she said softly.

"Oh, they will eventually," he opined. "They've drafted over a dozen troopers into this district to track him down. Likely only the rain has saved him up to this, by filling more water holes than the troopers could watch. Yes, they'll get him in the end, but when they do I do not think we shall ever know why Clair killed King Henry."

Chapter Twenty-Eight

Pincher Joe

DURING THE last week of the lamb marking there came to Barrakee, walking up river, a person whose baptismal names were George Joseph Sparks. Doubtless, forty years before, he had made a man and a woman very proud of his freshly started career; but the pride of his parents had not been transferred in later life to the policemen who handled him, or to the citizens who lost through his mental complaint—called "petty theft" when the sufferer belongs to the masses and "kleptomania" when he or she adorns the higher social strata. In that underworld to which Sparks belonged he was known, if not respected, as "Pincher Joe".

He was a little man with a small head, and hands apparently created for wandering gently into other people's pockets. Dirty hands they were, however; grimy, not with labour, but from an intense dislike to labour, even that of washing them. Never in all his life had he looked directly into the face of a human being, nor had he ever worked or done anyone a good turn disinterestedly. Yet, in his way, Pincher was a great man, a man who can be likened to the great Napoleon himself, in that he never missed an opportunity. That is, in Pincher's case, an opportunity to steal.

It was precisely five o'clock when he reached the shearing-shed at Barrakee: his mind uneasy, his nerves shaken, his temper ruffled by two meetings with suddenly appearing police troopers since his departure from the township of Wilcannia. The cursed troopers had wanted to know all about him, where he came from, where he was going—as though he would trouble to remember whence he had come, or to plan whither he would go. All that he did trouble about was the low condition of his tucker-bags.

At the shearing-shed he boiled his quart pot and made his tea strong by the simple process of allowing it to boil for five long minutes. This he cooled rapidly by another simple process: that of raising the quart pot high above his head and emptying the contents into an old ant-cleaned jam tin held on the level with his knees; then pouring the decoction back into the pot, and repeating as required. Had not the man's ferret eyes been so serious in expression, the action would have been comical. Sweetening his tea with sugar taken from a calico bag which, like his hands, required much soap and water, the gentleman from nowhere, bound for nowhither, with years yet to go, sat on his swag and drank daintily. He would have eaten also had the cook on the station lower down given him anything to eat.

At five-thirty the hands' dinner gong sounded, and, allowing a just measure of time to elapse, Pincher Joe rose languidly and sauntered up to the men's kitchen, on the back door of which he timidly tapped. Where he stood he could not see the cook at his stove, but he was able to see the whole dining table, at which sat a Chinaman—evidently the gardener—and two station men. Pincher surmised that the remainder of the hands were out in the lamb-marking camp. And then, with surprising suddenness, he was confronted by Rainbow Harry, the cook, so nicknamed because of his love of colouring the sweets and brownie. He used also, at times, colourful language.

"Wot-cher-want?" demanded Rainbow, with that fierceness of expression reserved in particular for tramps.

"Can you spare us a bit of tucker, Cook?" whined Pincher.

"You—you blank Wooloomooloo rat!" Rainbow snarled. "Why, it was you wot pinched me watch up at White Gate last August."

"No, I didn't, Cook. I was never there—straight."

"No, of course you wasn't. Am I blind?"

"No, you looks orl right."

"Am I a liar?"

Pincher hesitated for a split second. Rainbow roared:

"Am I a liar—am I? I arsts you."

"No, Cook," the little man said with sudden fervour.

"Then you go and git your tucker off'n the bloke you sold me watch to," ordered Rainbow, with a hint of triumph in his hoarse voice.

"But I ain't got a bite, dinkum, Cook, I ain't," Pincher whined in desperation.

"Give him a bite to eat, Harry," urged Bony, who sat at table intensely amused. Pincher flashed him a look which only hinted gratitude. Rainbow raised his hands on high and swore shockingly.

"No!" He thundered the word and, stooping, glared at the little man on the doorstep, adding, as though to emphasize his decision: "Go away, you rat! I'll teach you to pinch me watch wot I paid six shillings for in nineteen-twelve. Go up to the big 'ouse. The cook there don't know you."

Pincher Joe faded away. For a minute no one spoke. The men thought Rainbow overhard; for, no matter the personal disagreement, it is the unwritten bush law to hand out food to the calling sundowner. And then upon Rainbow's face there slowly dawned a grim smile, culminating in a chuckle. He said:

"'E don't know that Martha is still cooking up at the Government 'ouse kitchen. Martha 'as bin waiting for years for Pincher Joe, 'cos 'e stole her haluminium fry-pan once."

Hungry and disconsolate, a martyr to the world's dis-approval of his solitary talent, Pincher Joe made his way along the fence of the Chinaman's garden, deciding before he reached the end of it not to proceed to the homestead kitchen by the main route, which led past the offices and jackeroos' quarters, but the other way, round the bottom end of the garden. So intent was he on filling the void paining his stomach and inventing an opening speech for the coming interview with the homestead cook that he failed to observe Bony following him, still interested and amused.

In all great crimes that are found out the criminal makes one mistake that lays him low. Pincher's mistake that evening was omitting to look behind for possible enemies. As Bony would have put it, Pincher's cause was hunger, but the effect was so amazing that Pincher's art was minimized to the ninety-ninth degree.

Whilst sidling along the wire and bamboo fence of the homestead gardens and lawns, the little man heard the homestead dinner gong. There were no sounds of human activity beyond the fence, and this Pincher attributed to the fact that nearly everyone would be out engaged in the lamb-marking. Pausing for some two minutes, during which he heard a fly-proof door spring shut, he went on again till he arrived before a small wicket-gate giving on to a concrete path that ran along the side of the house, round a corner, and straight to the kitchen. He opened the gate and passed within. He walked the path and finally reached the house.

All the doors of the rooms on that side were wide open. He passed one room that evidently was occupied by a man, for male apparel was in evidence, and male hair brushes lay on the dressing table. It was in the third room into which he looked that, on a well equipped dressing table, he saw, fastened to the edge of the mirror by a pin, a ten shilling Treasury note.

And straight away the little man had another attack of his chronic complaint, kleptomania. Electric tremors shot up and down his arms, pricking sharply the balls of each finger and thumb. The other objects within the room magically dwindled into a blurred nothingness, but the note itself seemed magically to fill the whole world. One sharp glance about him, and the little man was in Mrs Thornton's boudoir.

Pincher Joe found it impossible to move quickly enough towards that magnetic Treasury note. For one second his long tapering fingers appeared to hover over it; the next the note lay snugly in an inside pocket. And then, as though eased from pain, as though the attack of kleptomania had subsided,

Pincher Joe sighed, a luxurious sigh, a sigh of blissful content. But, following closely upon the sigh, almost cutting it short, came another dreadful attack.

The glitter and glint of gold and silver flared into his brain like powerful searchlights. There, on the dressing table, lay silver backed hairbrushes, a silver backed hand mirror, a gold plated pin and brooch box, the colour and the sight of which caused Pincher's eyes to protrude and his fingers to tingle again. Pincher Joe became a live wire.

The silver and gold dressing table appointments were thrust into his gunny-sack. Article followed article with lightning rapidity. Into the bureau drawers delved his flickering hands, to reappear and disappear into his sack. A beautiful inlaid mahogany sofa-chest was ransacked in like manner until the sack was bulging full, when the attack passed off once more.

It was then that Pincher looked carefully out of the door-way. Observing no one, he slipped out, following the concrete path to the wicket-gate, unhurriedly, casually, for he was nothing if not an artist in the make believe of innocence and absence of guile. Forgotten was his hunger in the fiercer hunger of gloating over his newly acquired treasures. Forgotten the insults of cooks, the rude inquisitiveness of policemen, the hate and envy of him by the world he preyed upon. For within his sack he possessed gold and silver as good as legal tender—objects of beauty which the magic of a "fence" would transmute into a long succession of amber-froth-tipped drinks and delectable "eats", such as cheese and bacon and tinned fish.

Once outside the garden gate Pincher Joe quickened his pace. Since it was too far to the shearing-shed, since it would take too long to reach there, he walked parallel with the river gums till he espied a bower of seclusion within a clump of tea-tree bushes. Once there, within his bower, with the sun-tipped gum-trees beyond the shaded bushes, Pincher Joe took out of his bag the treasures he had secured, with an expression on his face like that of a child with its arm plunged into a lucky dip at a church bazaar.

There came into the light of the fast ending day the silver backed hand mirror. At it he looked lovingly—that is, at the back of it and its chased handle. His reflection in the glass interested him not at all. The little box of gold made his eyes shine as stars seen through a fine high level haze. The hair brushes parted his lips in a grin of avarice.

These things he placed in turn beside him. He brought out a pair of cheap scissors, twined about with a length of silk thread. A narrow leather waist belt followed, then came a china pot of sweet smelling cream. A long gold plated box containing two valuable rings and an assortment of the odds and ends apparently so necessary to a lady's existence made him suck in his breath, but his breathing became normal once more when he took from his bag a small framed photograph of Ralph Thornton riding a horse. That he contemptuously tossed aside.

For a little while his hand delved into the bag in search of small objects that might be there, ignoring a larger object which stretched the bag in a peculiar manner in one place. A common steel thimble was added to the pile at his side, as were an expensive fountain pen and a memorandum book. And, finally, the delving hand brought out a piece of wood, round and angled and polished. At this Pincher Joe frowned in perplexed annoyance.

He wondered why on earth he should have gone to the trouble of stealing a common black fellow's boomerang.

And then the voice of doom fell on his ears. It was a still small voice, yet a voice that filled the sky and trembled and throbbed among the trees and the bushes, and penetrated to every fibre of his being with its awful hint of punishment. That voice was worse, far worse, than the laying of hands upon his shoulders.

"Quite a nice little collection, Pincher," remarked the soft drawling voice; and, looking round sharply yet furtively, the little man beheld Bony regarding the contents of the bag with extreme surprise.

"It ain't none of your business," Pincher whined.

"There you are quite mistaken," Bony murmured, recovering from his surprise and regarding Pincher with the interest bestowed by a botanist on an unfamiliar insect. "I am afraid, Pincher, that, to use an Australian aphorism, 'your eggs are cooked'. Precisely, in what room did you—did you discover these things?"

"Wot's the odds?" the little man demanded, adding hopefully: "As you've foxed me, let's go fifty-fifty."

"Try and remember what room it was," insisted Bony.

"What room! What are you driving at?"

"I want to know what room you stole those things from."

Looking for one fraction of a second into the detective's eyes, Pincher saw in them that which caused the return of his habitual whine when confronted by—to him—an enemy.

"It was the third round the corner," he said thinly.

"Ah!" After that understanding exclamation Bony sat and stared at nothing so long that Pincher became uneasy.

"Well, wot about going fifty-fifty?"

Bony looked at him. Putting a hand in a trouser pocket he brought out a small metal object, the only proof of his connexion with the police force. Pincher Joe's face became ashen.

"Shall we say three years' hard labour for this?" inquired Bony blandly. "Or would you prefer to run your hardest down to the shearing-shed, stop there long enough to pick up your swag, and then run again till you are right off the station of Barrakee?"

"I—I—" stuttered the little rat. "Jer mean it?" And at Bony's nod he leapt to his feet and made possibly the record sprint of his career. The exhausting and humiliating adventure had left him, however, one drop of balm—the Treasury note.

For perhaps five minutes longer Bony sat and pondered over the strange way in which Fate had given him this incriminating clue. At equal distance from the centre to the extremities of the boomerang were the marks of Wombra's tribe, the marks that had distinguished the wound on the gum-tree near which King Henry had been killed. Of all the puzzles of the many that kept this particular murder shrouded in mystery, what was Mrs Thornton doing with that boomerang in her boudoir?

Bony rose to his feet and stuffed the heap of articles within the gunny-sack. Walking back to the wicket-gate, he decided to empty the bag out inside the room from which the objects had been taken and quietly retire. No one observed him enter the homestead garden, and he was convinced that he would achieve his object right up to the moment he met Mrs Thornton coming out of her room, her face a picture of anxiety and astonishment. Seeing Bony, she exclaimed:

"Someone has been here and stolen all my dressing table things."

"Ah, but fortunately, Madam, I was able to intercept the burglar," he said grandly. "Whilst I was recovering the plunder, however, he managed to escape. You see, he was examining the contents of his bag when I came upon him. Putting them back, I brought them here at once."

Just outside the door stood a small occasional table, and on this Bony set out the stolen articles. At sight of the boomerang Mrs Thornton paled; and, when Bony bowed himself out, it was with difficulty that she managed to say:

"Thank you, Bony! Thank you!"

Chapter Twenty-Nine

Dugdale Departs

DURING THE time that the bullock team was being used for carting wood at the homestead it was Blair's custom to draw his wagon against a fence running behind the trades shops. It makes yoking and unyoking bullocks much more easy if they can be jammed against a fence. Henry's duty after breakfast was to ride out to one of the home paddocks and muster the team, whilst during his absence Blair obtained their midday lunch and attended to any fault among the gear.

With the lunch in a gunny-sack the pugnacious bullock-driver was passing the jackeroos' quarters when there came to him Frank Dugdale, a strange light in his eyes, and in his hand a telegram.

"Read that, Fred," he said, with unusual excitement. A few seconds were necessary for Blair to find and adjust his spectacles. Aloud he read deliberately:

"Daly Yard Syndicate drawn my horse Eucla in Golden Plate. What will you lay off to win?"

It was signed by the owner of Eucla, a famed Australian horse-owner. Blair read it out once more. Then, as deliberately as he spoke, he removed his spectacles and placed them in an inner pocket. For a moment he stared at the younger man.

"Now, isn't it right that a man lucky enough to draw a block in our Land Lottery is lucky enough to draw a good horse?" he said. "The proof that I think Eucla the best horse entered for that race is that I sent away five pounds yesterday to put on him. We've got to square the owner, or he will scratch his horse and we'll only get a few pounds out of it. The prizes are big, Mr Dugdale. What does the boss say about it?"

"He suggests betting the owner two thousand Eucla will not win, fifteen hundred it won't secure second place, and a thousand he won't get in third."

"Yes, that ought to do," Blair agreed.

"Very well; I'll wire him to that effect. By the way, I am leaving Barrakee today, you know. Would have been gone weeks ago, only Mr Thornton wanted me to stay till the end of July."

Blair looked up at Dugdale, the habitually severe expression of his grim face relaxing into one much softer.

"Today, eh?" he said. "Well, I wish you continued luck. You're the overseer, I'm only the bullocky, but we never clashed with you. Good luck to you!" And with that they parted with a handshake, never dreaming of the manner of their next meeting.

Dugdale was leaving that afternoon, driving a motor-truck he had bought and intending to reach his block via Thurlow Lake. The morning was occupied in packing his belongings, quite voluminous in bulk, being the gathering of years, and it was about eleven o'clock when he had finished and Mr Thornton led him into the office.

"Sit down, Dug; I want to talk to you," opened the big bluff squatter in his kindly way. "Have a cigarette?"

Dugdale nodded and selected one from the box pushed across the writing table. Thornton leaned back in his chair and regarded the young man pensively.

"You and I have always got on well," he said slowly. "I like a man who sticks to his work, not only sticks to it but studies it. When I came to Barrakee first I paid cash for the lease, and that expenditure left me tight of money. For the first twelve months I spent only fifteen nights here; the other days and nights I was out on the run. I spared neither myself nor my wife then, but now we don't regret it. How much money have you got?"

"About four hundred pounds," was Dugdale's unhesitating reply.

"Go careful; you'll want every penny of it. Make the hut on your land serve you for at least a year. Never spend a penny 'less you are forced to, yet pay cash for everything. The deferred-payment system is our greatest curse. Today is August 1st. I have told Watts to have two thousand six-tooth ewes yarded at Thurlow Lake on the 7th. He'll lend you a man to get 'em to your place, and as you have plenty of feed and water you should do well. I'll let you have rams next month, or October, and here is an order to Mortimore to start you off with three months' supply of rations. However, before you go to him, run in and see Mrs Thornton. She wishes to speak to you.

"I think that's about all, Dug, excepting that I am always here if you get into any difficulty or want assistance. And, Dug, if you get tired of squattering, your job is always open to you."

The station owner rose to his feet, smiling.

"But the sheep, Mr Thornton!" Dugdale expostulated. "When will you require payment? I can't possibly pay cash for them."

"When you take delivery of them Watts will ask you to sign a document. I am selling them to you at fifteen shillings a head. My opinion of you is good, and I am going to back my opinion by leaving you to pay when you like within the next ten years."

They stood facing each other across the table. The young man's face was flushed, and his eyes were suspiciously moist:

"Thank you, sir," he said softly, holding out his hand.

He found Mrs Thornton in the garden.

"You asked for me?" he said, smiling.

"Yes, Dug. I wanted to invite you to lunch with us before you leave." She stood, frail and pale, yet indomitable in spirit. Only a little woman, yet holding a personality of surprising power.

"That is very kind of you," he said.

"It is not often, fortunately, that my husband and I lose people we like," she went on gently. "I am sorry you are going, yet glad you have the opportunity of doing well for yourself. We shall miss you, and I think Ralph will miss your steadying influence. Is it right that you will be living alone in an ordinary hut?"

"Why, yes, Mrs Thornton, till I can afford to build a larger house."

She sighed. Then:

"You will find it lonely, Dug, and you will miss your home comforts. I suppose you have no curtains to hang before the window?"

"No. I never thought of curtains," he admitted.

"I expected that," she said. "So I sent Kate in to make you up a parcel of things—curtains, a table cover, a small carpet, a fire fender, and what not. And then there is a small box of preserves and jams and pickles Kate and I made. They will, I think, be so much better for you than the tinned stuff. And, Dug, never forget us, will you? We would like to have you think that this is your home, and we your people."

He found himself unable to speak.

"We all have our worries and our battles," she went on softly. "And the older we get the more we enjoy battering down our worries and winning our battles. Your father and we were great friends, and we hope his son will always be our friend, too."

"Perhaps my father would have won his battle had my mother lived, and she had been like you," he told her, with choking voice. "Certainly she could hardly have been more kind than you."

And quite suddenly the calm, efficient Dugdale took her hand in courtly fashion and kissed it. "Please accept my thanks—no—my gratitude—for granted. I cannot say what I would like." And, bowing stiffly, he left her to regard his retreating figure with suddenly shining eyes and flushed face.

The lunch in Dugdale's honour was a great success. The squatter talked sheep, and his wife housekeeping. Ralph rallied from his lately growing silence, and even Kate—Kate, whose heart was slowly breaking—forced a laugh now and then, and a bantering suggestion that Dugdale should buy a cookery book.

"I shall be satisfied with baking-powder bread, and meat grilled on hot coals," he told her, keeping well hidden the agony which was becoming almost unbearable. "And when I tire of that, I shall doubtless find an excuse to come to Barrakee for a meal."

"Then you will be finding excuses fairly often, because you will soon tire of baking-powder bread and grilled meat," she told him with a laugh.

"You will have to do as I suggested some time ago, Dug," Ralph put in. "Which is to hunt up a wife to keep house."

Dugdale looked at everybody but Kate when he replied:

"Then, I think I shall find myself blocked at the outset. I am sure no woman would want to live in a boundary-rider's hut."

"Women have done it," Kate murmured.

"Would you live in a boundary-rider's hut with me?" asked Ralph.

"I would live anywhere with the man I loved." And so well did she play her part that even Ralph thought that the man she loved was himself. His gaze fell to his plate. He felt like Judas.

The conversation ran on gaily till the end of the meal, when they all rose and accompanied Dugdale to his loaded truck. Cranking the engine, he slowed it till it ticked over gently; when, beginning with the Little Lady, he shook them by the hand, coming last to Kate, at whom he smiled in his old quizzical fashion. She returned his clasp with a soft pressure, and his smile with plucky lightness; but when he drove away she left the others, walking slowly to the garden gates, and then when out of sight almost running to her room, where she flung herself with abandon on the bed.

Ralph had his arm through that of Mrs Thornton when they, with the squatter, sauntered back to the house. The latter was saying: "I had a letter from Hemming this morning. He tells me that his place is in fine fettle."

"Oh, I am glad of that," Mrs Thornton exclaimed.

"But they find the homestead much larger than Thorley's place," Thornton continued. "The house contains sixteen rooms, and Mrs Hemming has had great difficulty in securing maids. She was indeed thankful when our missing Nellie Wanting turned up asking for a job."

"So that is where she went to, John? You know, I cannot understand to this day why she so suddenly disappeared."

Ralph Thornton, with eyes on the ground and quickly throbbing heart, said nothing.

Chapter Thirty

Bony Sees the Light

AUGUST 2ND was a memorable day in the history of Barrakee.

When Blair was driving his team from the homestead for the daily load of wood, the squatter told him that if he liked he need bring only a small load, so as to be back in time to hear the result of the momentous race. Blair smiled in his grim way:

"Eucla will win, so there is no need for me to worry, or wait for the result I know already," he said.

So at about three o'clock the Thorntons assembled on the veranda and the squatter proceeded to tune in on the expensive wireless set. Very shortly he got Melbourne just in time to allow them to hear the result of the three o'clock race. After that followed market reports and a short lecture on the art of fattening pigs, a subject that interested the station-owner but not the ladies.

Mrs Thornton was sewing, Kate pretending to listen but her thoughts far away, Ralph also was pretending to be interested in pigs, but it was only pretence. Back at the office door stood old Mortimore, watch in hand. Behind him was the telephone, and fifty miles west at Thurlow Lake Dugdale sat with the receiver against his ear. Then, clear as a bell, came the announcer's voice one minute after the great race. It said:

"Result of Golden Plate Handicap at Mooney Ponds— Eucla, one; Teddy Bear, two; Gentleman Jack, three. Time, one minute thirty-seven seconds."

The four listeners smiled at one another. The squatter rose and walked to the end of the veranda, and, hearing Mortimore respond to his call, announced the horses' names as

187

given. And at Thurlow Lake Dugdale put back the receiver and shook hands enthusiastically with the overseer.

"Twenty thousand pounds free of income tax, less two thousand pounds to be paid the owner, is eighteen thousand pounds," Thornton murmured. "Five into eighteen thousand is three thousand six hundred pounds."

"What are you going to do with all that money, John?" inquired the Little Lady, a hint of mockery in her voice.

"I am going to divide with you and Kate," he replied instantly.

"Oh, Uncle! You are a dear," Kate burst out. "I want some clothes badly."

"You will be able to buy one or two things with twelve hundred pounds," the squatter told her gravely.

"And you, Ralph? What are you going to do with your share?" again asked the Little Lady.

"I am going to divide with you and Kate," he said, mimicking the squatter's voice.

"But that wouldn't be fair," Mrs Thornton urged. "Kate and I would then have double what you and your father had. And it was your money and his that bought the two shares."

"Well, let us pool our two shares, then, and divide among the four of us, Dad," Ralph suggested.

Thornton laughed softly and agreed. It was then that Mortimore called him to the office and there he found Dugdale wishing to speak to him on the phone.

"Our luck is right in, isn't it, Mr Thornton?" the squatter heard over the wire. "About those sheep," Dugdale went on. "I shall be taking delivery on the 7th, two thousand at fifteen shillings, and I shall pay cash for them, Mr Thornton."

"But that is not necessary, Dug," expostulated the squatter.

"Ah, but it is. I remember your saying that it was wise to pay cash for everything."

Secretly delighted with Dugdale's principle, Mr Thornton still urged his extended-terms offer, but Dugdale persisted and finally won.

188

"I think, Dug, that it would be as well if you came for those ewes on Friday the sixth," Thornton said reflectively. "The Paroo is flooded as far down as Wanaaring and the river is rising rapidly at Bourke. We are in for a big flood, and the Washaways are sure to run. Ask Watts to have the sheep in the yards there for certain Thursday night."

"Very well, thanks. But how will you get those out-back sheep in for the shearing?" asked Dugdale.

"We shall have to muster and get them this side of the Washaways before the flood comes, Dug. I should have had the bridges made."

Coming up the river road about this time, Henry McIntosh walked beside the bullock-driver.

"Your share of that twenty thousand, 'Enery, works out at about three thousand five hundred pounds," Blair was saying, certain sure that Eucla would win. "Now, wot I want ter know is, wot are you going to do with all that 'ere cash?"

"I dunno, Fred," replied Henry, with his usual vacant grin.

"Well, you ought to," Blair's beard twitched, and his eyes glared. "People who don't know wot to do with their money shouldn't be allowed to 'ave any."

"Well, wot are you going to do with yours, Fred?" countered Henry, after a full minute's pause.

"I'm going to git married," announced Blair, with studied casualness.

"Wot!" Slowly a grin started to spread over Henry's face. Blair saw it, and up rose his beard; and as quickly as it rose, so quickly did the grin subside.

"As I just said, 'Enery, I am going to git married now that I am a blooming capitalist. And you, 'Enery, are going to be my best man and valet. You are never going to leave me while Bill is dependent on us for a bit of tucker. So there! Don't you think I am going to allow you to go and git drunk, and tell the whole blooming world where Bill Clair is hid up."

"But I am not going to git drunk," protested Henry.

189

"No, you are not going to git drunk, 'Enery. I am going to take great care that you don't."

They fell into a lengthy argument about this, which lasted till the team drew the load against the wood-heap at the shearing-shed; and later neither of them would tell their fellow workers precisely how they intended spending their fortunes.

Naturally the winning of the sweep was the sole topic of conversation at dinner that night. Rainbow Harry suggested that, as a particular friend of his invited him and several others to Wilcannia on the occasion of winning a hundred pounds, it would be considered the thing for Blair and McIntosh to invite all the hands on Barrakee to spend a month with them at Broken Hill. O'Grady, the station engineer, seconded the proposal; but Johnston, the carpenter, thought that, if the two lucky winners were each to make their friends and comrades a present of a hundred pounds, their illustrious names would be handed down to posterity.

The discussion threatening to become heated at the end of the meal, Bony, an interested but silent listener, rose from his place, and, getting his hat from the bunkroom, walked away past the pumping plant and finally seated himself on a log at the upper end of Dugdale's favourite fishing pool.

It was growing dark and the air was cold and frosty. Below was the dimming sheen of water; above the shimmering lights of brilliant stars. Other than the far, dull murmur of men's voices there was not a single sound to disturb the silence.

But of his surroundings Bony was oblivious. His mind was still centred on the fact that Mrs Thornton had the boomerang with which Clair had killed King Henry. The recurring question, which the half-caste worried as a dog will worry a bone, was: How did the Little Lady become possessed of the weapon?

Had it been any other boomerang, at once it would be obvious that it was merely a curio; but it was outside all probability that here on Barrakee there were two boomerangs originally belonging to members of Wombra's tribe in far-off Northern Queensland. Yet, if it was the actual weapon, which Bony was compelled to believe it was, why did Mrs Thornton have it in her boudoir? If she knew its late ugly history, why had she not destroyed it? And, knowing, what was the connexion between her and Clair?

Assuming that there was such a connexion it was obvious, too, that it was the Little Lady who had warned Clair over the telephone—a timely warning which had enabled him to escape the police.

Bony's mind travelled backwards to the point when Clair had just set off tracking King Henry. At about that time, Mary, the cook, had died. Mary was Clair's sister. Was there a connexion between her death and Clair's vengeance? If so, how did Mrs Thornton come to be mixed up in that, or was the Little Lady's warning, plus her possession of the boomerang, just feminine sympathy for a wanted man?

It was more than an hour later that Bony thought he saw the light. Subconsciously aware that he was chilled to the bone, the discomforts of his body were nothing in the sudden elation of his mind. He rose to his feet with the suddenness of one who has arrived at a long-debated conclusion. His reddish-black face was lit by the lamp of triumph.

"Ah!" he whispered. "That must be it. It must be. It accounts for all things. I must find that doctor."

Chapter Thirty-One

The Coming of the Flood

THE MORNING after the day on which the great sweepstake prize came to Barrakee it was seen that the chain of pools along the river bed had been joined by the first freshet presaging what eventually became the greatest flood recorded during the white man's occupation of the country.

Countless millions of tons of water spread over millions of acres of country in the south-west of Queensland and north-west of New South Wales were rolling slowly but irresistibly southward down the Darling and the Paroo, as well as the dozens of creeks forming the network of tributaries of those rivers. From the vast watersheds the waters converged upon the Darling at Wilcannia.

There is nothing spectacular in these floods. There is no sudden rush of water sweeping everything before it; rather does the water creep, filling first the deep channels, then rising slowly to push its way out into the shallower channels, in a further and final rise sweeping over the flats and low-lying country, submerging ground thought to be above the reach of floods.

One week after the first water appeared at Barrakee it ran fourteen feet deep along those stretches that had been dry. It was the first stirring of a sleeping giant, whose awakening brought disaster, sorrow, and retribution to the people of Barrakee. For, to carry the simile further, when the giant yawned and stretched his sinuous self he took as his own young Ralph Thornton.

Not a soul saw him depart, but in the morning Bony read the story on the ground. Picking up the young man's tracks at the garden gate opposite the billabong, the half-caste traced him for nearly two miles down the river, past the shearing-shed, past the old hotel site, to a point in a river bend where a boat had been drawn into the bank.

As plainly as though Ralph had told him, Bony knew then whither he was bound and the object of his voyage. The young man had heard a pretty lubra's voice calling, calling, for ever calling him from down at Three Corner Station, between Wilcannia and Menindee. Throughout long nights and longer days Ralph had heard the call; his heart was being strangled by those influences which no longer puzzled and frightened him, because they had become so felt that it was useless to resist them.

The river had taken him, had claimed him. The bush with its indescribable lure, a lure a million times stronger than that of the sea, had drawn him. Nothing—devoted love of the Little Lady, generous love and pride in him of the squatter, the promise of the prettiest girl in Australia, careful rearing, wide education—not all these together had availed to balance that insistent, insidious, luring call.

His head bowed in thought, Bony walked back to the homestead. He knew the way the lad had taken, he knew why he had taken it, and he knew the victorious force compelling the lad to go without a word to his foster-parents, not even leaving a note in part explanation. Nellie Wanting was the immediate influence, but behind her was a much greater one.

At the shearing-shed he was met by Mr Thornton, whose face was a picture of anxiety.

"Have you tracked him, Bony?" he demanded when yet several yards separated them.

The detective nodded.

"Great God man! If you have found his body, it will send his mother to her grave," Thornton burst out.

"Let us go yonder to that heap of building material and talk about it," suggested Bony, in his wonderful kindly way.

"But have you found him? Is he dead?"

Bony seated himself and gently urged his companion to sit next him.

"It would be better if he were dead," he said softly. "Much better."

Thornton stared at him uncomprehendingly:

"Then let me have it, Bony. Don't keep me waiting." His face was very white, his eyes very brilliant, his lips were trembling. Bony decided that he could not give the full terrible truth of what he knew and what he suspected with such reason. He softened the blow by giving only what he knew, and that, in all conscience, was hard enough. He said:

"Your son walked past here very early this morning, carrying a heavy load. I suspect the load was a swag and a supply of rations. Going on past the old hotel site, he turned into the bend and there he boarded a boat he had hidden in a patch of fallen tangled gum-suckers."

"But why? Why? Why?" demanded Thornton.

"It is evident that he has gone down-river," Bony went on. "Curb your impatience, Mr Thornton, and try to keep calm, I beseech you. Young Ralph had—I should say has—a sweetheart—a secret sweetheart who is not Miss Flinders. He used to meet her every evening at a place between your house and the blacks' camp."

Thornton sighed; it sounded like relief. It was a bitter disappointment; it would give deep pain to his wife and his niece; but—it was better, far better than death. Yet Bony . . .

"But you said that the lad would be better dead. Why?" he asked. Bony looked him straight in the face.

"Because the sweetheart is Nellie Wanting," he said.

For several seconds Thornton and the half-caste continued to stare at each other. Then suddenly the squatter threw back his head and laughed. The idea of Ralph sweet-hearting with a gin! It was ludicrous. Such a fine lad, well reared, well educated, a fine intelligent youth, engaged to be married to a lovely, a pure, a wonderful white girl. And while he laughed, with a hint of hysterical relief in the timbre of it, Bony slowly averted his face and stared unseeingly at a meat-ant being slowly eaten by a dozen smaller sugar-ants.

"What a joke!" the squatter gasped.

"I never joke," Bony said quietly. "Life is too full of tragedy for me to joke. I wish it were a joke for your sake, and more so, much more so, for the Little Lady's sake."

And then it was that Thornton realized that he had been told the simple truth. The laughter died away and his face became grey and drawn.

"But why—for God's sake, Bony—why Nellie Wanting?" he managed at last to whisper.

Bony was tempted to tell him of his suspicions, but somehow they and the stunned man at his side did not seem to fit.

"Because, I suppose, he loves her. Listen!" And he related his witnessing the meetings, told in full his interview with the black girl, of the message he had concocted with her consent which was left in the cleft stick, of Nellie Wanting's departure for Three Corner Station.

"Even now I can't believe it, Bony. Indeed, I can't. It seems so utterly at variance with logical human behaviour," groaned Thornton. "The lad must know the consequence of this. It will break the heart of his mother, who adores every hair on his head; it will make him an outcast; it will bring me to the dust. Dear God! What have my wife and I done to deserve this? Is this to be our reward for lives of endeavour, for our strict obedience to His law: 'Do unto others as ye would they should do unto you'? My wife—God help her! God help her!"

Bony was moved as rarely his career allowed him to be. To his critical gaze this generous man's soul was laid bare. Plainly was it to be seen, guiltless of wrongdoing, guiltless even of wrong thinking. Big in all things as in stature, Thornton's grief and abasement were terrible to behold. Bony held out a straw:

"There may yet be time to stop him," he pointed out.

"Ah!" Thornton grasped the straw. "I'll send riders down the river to watch at the points of the big bends. I'll drive myself down to the Three Mile bend above Wilcannia. Surely he will not have got that far?"

"No, he will not have got that far," Bony agreed; but added a suggestion:

"Don't send the riders. The fewer people who know of this the better. Ring up Sergeant Knowles and get him to arrest Nellie Wanting. He'll do it on any old charge; and, once we have the girl safe out of the way, then we can await your son at Three Corner Station. But first let us phone Mr Hemming to make sure the gin is still in service there."

"By gad, Bony! We may be able to avert this disaster after all," Thornton exclaimed, hope revived, despair banished. "If only we can prevent their meeting, I'll see that the boy doesn't make a fool of himself, and us, even if I have to chain him to a post at night."

Bony's sigh was inaudible. Into his mind flashed the picture of a wise king seated amidst his courtiers at the edge of the ocean. Yet, if King Canute could not stay the tide, they at least might stay, but not avert for ever, the destiny of Ralph Thornton and Nellie Wanting.

When they arrived at the office the bush detective was out of breath. The impatience of Thornton waiting for the connexion with Three Corner Station was nerve-racking. Then:

"That you, Hemming? Yes. Thornton speaking. We got your letter all right. Yes. Is Nellie Wanting still with you? What! Disappeared three days ago! Do I know where she is? I wish to God I did!" And the receiver crashed on the desk.

Chapter Thirty-Two

The Passing of Clair

FRANK DUGDALE removed the bridle from his horse with deft fingers, patted its sleek neck and allowed it to walk away to a sandy place for a roll before drinking. Midway between the little harness-horse and his hut he scanned the sky with hopeful expectancy. From north to south, across the meridian of the sky lay a knife-like edge of dark clouds moving slowly eastward. They massed from the meridian to the western horizon and promised rain.

It was about four o'clock when the new owner of Daly's Yard paddock, now called Eucla Station, entered his house. It was a spacious single-roomed hut with logged sides and iron roof. The inside was spotlessly clean. A camp stretcher-bed was placed in one corner. A table with a sheet-iron top stood in the centre. At one side was a stack of rations set upon petrol cases.

A bushman's home indeed, yet possessing much more comfort than the average. Over the table lay spread a blue cover. On the centre of this stood a brass oil-lamp. A single curtain cut in two guarded the window by day, whilst a roller blind excluded the night. Above the bed Dugdale had made several shelves, which carried many books, not all of which were novels, whilst on the floor lay an exquisite dark-green carpet.

In the wide, cavernous fireplace the occupier made a fire and set thereon the tea-billy. The several minutes whilst it came to the boil were spent in bringing in the evening's supply of wood, and that job completed and the tea made Dugdale lit his pipe and lounged in his home-made easy-chair for a quiet half-hour's thinking, whilst the fire burned down sufficiently to produce cooking coals.

At last Dugdale found himself a settled pastoralist. He owned the leasehold of twenty-five thousand acres of first-class country, each two hundred and fifty acres equal to one English acre. He owned two thousand splendid breeding ewes and two fine presentation hacks. He had plenty of money in the bank, plenty of feed and water, and unlimited scope to exercise his organizing abilities. Of the solitude he took no account. He was the odd man in a thousand who could live in solitude contentedly; nevertheless Dugdale was sad at heart.

Of what benefit to him was luck, the luck of drawing the land, the luck of winning the sweep, the luck of being befriended by a man of Thornton's stamp? What was the use to him of a good living here alone, when his heart ached for the unattainable?

His pipe went out, and moodily he stared into the subsiding embers. The ambition of his life had been attained, and after all it was but ashes. For ahead lay all the years, empty years, when work would be mechanical, without object.

He was aroused suddenly by the first few drops of rain pinging on the corrugated-iron roof, and, since it was coming dusk, he arose and lit the lamp. While he prepared the oven and mixed the dough for a baking-powder loaf, the raindrops increased slowly, until when he sat down to dinner of grilled mutton chops and potatoes a steady downpour had begun.

The meal eaten, he washed the utensils, looked in the camp-oven, shovelled a few additional live coals on the lid. It was now quite dark. The rain had become a continuous roar on the roof; he could hear the water running down the rain-gutter outside.

He lowered the blind, and, donning a gum-coat went out and chained up his two sheep-dogs. And when he returned he found that his cat had come back from hunting and was drying herself before the fire. The cat had to have her saucer of condensed milk, the loaf had to be taken out of the tin and stood on one side to allow the steam to escape, and fresh water put in the billy to boil for eight o'clock coffee.

Such was Dugdale's home life, similar in every detail to the home life of hundreds of bushmen.

For an hour he read a novel. For another hour he played musical selections on his portable gramophone and drank his coffee and smoked. And then he went to bed.

Still the rain fell. Lying in the firelit darkness he estimated the fall to have totalled already fifty points. He was on the point of falling asleep when there came a squelchy footstep from outside. The uneasy dogs barked. The door was flung inward, and into the hut lurched a tall, gaunt man.

Dugdale was out of bed in a flash. From his side of the table he stared into the deathly white face of William Clair, the wanted man, the hunted man. Clair rocked to and fro on his feet. The firelight revealed his blue eyes burning with strange brilliance. He was hatless. He carried no swag. His coat was open. The dirty-white shirt was smeared with blood.

For several seconds the two men remained thus, and, when Clair coughed significantly, Dugdale remembered the lamp and lit it.

"Good evening!" was what Clair first said, a smile, a pitiful smile, breaking over his bloodless features.

"You are hurt, Bill," Dugdale said in reply. "Sit down in that chair. I'll get you a drink of coffee."

The home-made chair threatened to collapse when the gaunt man fell into it. With shaking hands he greedily snatched the proffered cup of coffee, still steaming hot. The giver crossed to the door and closed it. Then he placed a bucket of water over the fire and added fresh logs.

"How did you get hurt, Clair?" he asked kindly.

The gaunt man, looking up, smiled wanly, the smile that of a philosopher who scorns pessimism:

"I met Sergeant Knowles," he said, with difficulty. "We had a word or two. The gentle sergeant shot me because I could not agree to accompany him to the hangman." Suddenly his bantering tone changed to one of entreaty. "He plugged me through the left lung, just above my heart, I think. I woodened him with a waddy but he'll come-to presently and is bound to make for this hut. And before he gets here I must write a letter for you to take to Mrs Thornton."

"Very well, Clair. But first we must have that shirt off and the wound at least washed."

"That can wait. We have no time now," Clair insisted. "Get me paper and things quickly; I must write while I am able."

Lurching to his feet, he stumbled to a cane-bottomed chair and dragged it and himself to the table. Dugdale hesitated for a moment, then got a writing-block, pen and ink, and envelopes. Clair began instantly to write, careless of the drops of rain falling from his hair to the paper. The younger man stirred the embers, and, going to a chest, brought out a pair of blankets which he laid out near the blaze.

The suddenness and the circumstances of Clair's appearance had partially stunned him. His first thoughts were of Clair's wound, his second of Sergeant Knowles lying somewhere out in the rain, knocked senseless. And, whilst his first duty to Clair was clear, he was undecided what his duty was to himself and to the State. For even Dugdale, orthodox and precise, regarded the killing of a black fellow as of little account.

The scratching of the pen continued rapidly for five minutes, then stopped. Dugdale heard the sheets being ripped from the pad, and again the scratching of the pen, addressing an envelope.

"Dugdale!"

"Well, Clair?"

Dugdale went to the table beside the gaunt man. Clair, who was supporting himself with one hand and one wrist from falling forward, stared into the younger man's face with bloodshot eyes. Nodding to the letter, he said with difficult slowness:

"You would render a service to the Little Lady, wouldn't you?"

"Certainly I would," Dugdale agreed.

"She has been very kind to you, as she has been very kind to dozens of men and one or two women," Clair went on. "She was very, very kind to my poor sister, and, because of her kindness, I am going to pay the price. You pay your debt, too, Dugdale, by taking that letter to her directly it is daylight. The flood is coming down, but let neither water nor policeman stop you getting that letter into her hands as quickly as possible. You understand?"

"I understand about the urgency of the delivery, but don't understand what is behind it, Clair. Anyway, that is none of my business. If it is necessary for the Little Lady to have your letter, as you say, she shall have it."

Clair pushed himself upright and wiped his mouth with the back of his hand. There was blood on his hand when again it was used to support him. Dugdale took the letter and placed it under his pillow. Clair began again to write, but this time what he wrote was short and needed no envelope.

"Read that, and give it to Knowles when he comes," urged Clair, and began to cough alarmingly. Dugdale gave him a towel before bending over the writing-pad, on which was written, in a shaking, spidery hand:

August 12th, 19—.
I killed an aboriginal named King Henry at Barrakee on the night of Saturday, March 5th, with a boomerang. I threw the boomerang and missed the throw in the dark. The boomerang returned to my feet. Him and me both dived for it. I got it, and while he was stooping hit him once on the head.
William Sinclair

"Sinclair?" Dugdale echoed.

"Yes. My name is Sinclair, not Clair. Get me a drink of coffee, please. Let—me—lie—down. I'm—crook—"

"Just a second, Bill," the younger man entreated. "You are soaking wet. Let us get your clothes off first. Come now, old man. Hold on."

Sinclair, as he had named himself, had gone limp. Dugdale found it necessary to hold him with one hand whilst he removed the sodden coat. Somehow he managed to get the gaunt man down on the blankets, when he cut away the blood-soaked shirt with a table-knife.

As Sinclair had said, he had been shot through the left lung, dangerously near his heart. The wound had ceased to bleed outwardly, and the young man washed it gently and wrapped about it a sheet snatched from his bed. His bed blankets he laid over the dying man.

Above the roar of the rain on the roof the alarm clock ticked as loudly as a grandfather clock, and the falling embers rattled in the fire. There was nothing more that he could do till day came: little, then, since it would be impossible to run the truck over the now soft track. And out there in the rain, in the pitchy darkness, another man, probably hurt, was either lying senseless or wandering about aimlessly searching for the hut and succour. Entirely on this latter account Dugdale drew aside the curtains and raised the blind. The lamplight might serve as a guide.

For nearly an hour Clair was unconscious. His coat and trousers, which Dugdale had set close to the fire, were then dry, and for something to do he folded them neatly and placed them on the table. It was then that Sinclair opened his eyes, in which at first was a vacant stare; but quickly understanding and memory came into them.

"Promise to deliver the letter, Dugdale," he struggled to whisper.

"I promise."

"And, Dugdale, in my coat-pocket is a wallet. Take that to the Little Lady as well. Promise!"

"I promise, Bill. Can I get you anything?"

"Coffee."

Dugdale filled the cup, and, kneeling, slid an arm beneath the gaunt man's head, which he slightly raised. But Sinclair had forgotten his need. He was murmuring:

"Grandfather Sinclair was a commander of a King's ship. Father Sinclair was a magistrate. Present Sinclair and sister Mary were orphaned, young and penniless. But we Sinclairs had our honour. For twenty years—the stain—was there. Present Sinclair goes out—without stain."

Since the dying man refused to drink, Dugdale put aside the cup, laid him down again, and wiped his blood-stained lips. He seemed to sleep. The chest rose and fell, but slowly. Dugdale, seated beside him, watched and waited. He had never before seen the coming of death; but he knew he would face it soon.

Seemingly far away a horse neighed. It was his own horse; he recognized the note. The dogs barked furiously. Two minutes later slow thudding hoofs sounded from without. Clair opened his eyes.

"The—sergeant—comes," he whispered. "Apologize— to—him—for me—Dugdale. Must have—head—no—bad head."

The door was opened suddenly. A tattered uniformed figure stood within the frame. Clair sat up, and in a loud voice cried:

"Thank you, Little Lady! You are safe."

And, when Dugdale caught him, William Sinclair was dead.

Chapter Thirty-Three

Two Resolute Men

SERGEANT KNOWLES appeared as though he had rolled in the mud; which was precisely what he had done, albeit unconsciously. The dark blue tunic was covered with a mass of red-brown clay, his khaki breeches were in a similar plight. He had lost his hat.

Apparently the significance of the scene which met his gaze when he opened the door was borne in upon him; for, when he closed the door, he removed his tunic and seated himself in the easy-chair at the dead man's feet before he spoke. Then:

"Well, that's that," he said grimly. "I gave Clair every chance, but he would bolt. Got anything to drink, Dugdale?"

Dugdale covered the face of the dead, kneeling by Clair's head to do so. Over the body the two men regarded each other. It came dully to the younger man that, if Clair was to have been hanged for killing a black, what a paradox it was that another man should be licensed to shoot him because Clair disliked being hanged.

Rising without reply, he "bulled" the coffee—or, in plain English, added hot water to the coffee remaining in the billy. Bringing a fresh pannikin, he filled it and set it at the sergeant's elbow on the table.

"You appear to have had a wild time of it," he said.

"One of the wildest. If you've got any aspirin, for the love of Mike give me four tablets in a little water. My head is split right open and the halves are clapping together."

Dugdale gave him the aspirin, and the policeman, having taken the dose, followed by a few sips of coffee, leaned back in his chair and closed his eyes. Dugdale found his pipe and tobacco.

Five minutes passed thus. At the sergeant's feet was a small pool of water that had oozed from his leggings and boots. Although he had removed his tunic he was no drier, for his shirt and vest were soaked. Watching him, Dugdale saw the frown between the eyes fade out and the grey eyes open.

"That's better," Knowles sighed. "Clair hit me mighty hard. When did he get here?"

"About three hours ago."

"Did he! Well, he walked three miles to get here. Where was he hit?"

"Just above the heart."

"So! It's a wonder he got here. Well, I'm sorry he's dead, and yet I'm not sorry. He died a man's death, which is better than the law's death. Is there any coffee left?"

"Half a cup," Dugdale answered. "Drink it, and I'll make more and cook you a couple of chops. I've no cold meat. I'll lend you a shirt and a pair of pants, too, if you like."

"You're a saint. But first of all I must see to my horse. It's a great beast that. Waited beside me till I came to. Can't understand why Clair didn't take it, unless Pronty wouldn't be took."

"What happened?" asked Dugdale.

"By a strange coincidence, both Clair and I were making for this hut of yours. I came on his tracks just this side of the Paroo, and just before it started to rain, and when they debouched on to a wide sandy plain I saw Clair in the middle of it. He was on foot and had no chance to get away. When he saw me he made no attempt to get away. He stopped when I called upon him to do so, laying down his swag but still holding a heavy waddy, which he was using as a staff. That I told him to drop, getting off my mount as I said it. I told him to hold out his hands for the bracelets. He did so, and just as I was about to snap them on he lowered his head and rammed me in the middle.

"The force of his head in my solar plexus paralysed me. He began to run. My horse was feeding, drat him! some fifty-odd yards away. I pulled my gun and called to him to stop. He was making for the Parro, on the cracked dry bed of which he would have defied me till dark, as my horse could never have faced the ground. You know the kind of place I mean. This was about an area of some ten acres. As he would have beaten me to it and wouldn't stop, I aimed low, and fired. But, damn it! a policeman isn't always using his gun. I didn't allow for the kick-up.

"Clair dropped—I thought dead. Even then I couldn't stand. I was doubled up for quite three minutes longer. When I was able to straighten up I went over to Clair and, when within a dozen feet of him, he jumped up and threw his waddy at me. There had been plenty of practice behind that throw. I saw the waddy coming at me, and no more.

"When I came to it was dark. My moke was still feeding about. I could hear the champing on the bit. Since then I have been circling for hours, so it seemed. Not a blessed star for a guide, and as dark as the tomb. Bit of luck seeing your light."

Certainly Knowles had been unfortunate. Dugdale knew that he was right when he said Clair could have defied him once he got to that terrible patch of cracked ground on the Paroo bed. No horse could have crossed it, and, had the sergeant followed on foot, leaving his horse, the odds between the two men would have been in Clair's favour. It was the clumsy way of trying to arrest Clair, or Sinclair, that was impressed on Dugdale.

"Well, I'll go and unsaddle my moke. Will he get a feed if I turn him loose just outside?"

"Yes; plenty of grass," Dugdale informed him.

"Good! But first we'll move the corpse over there to the back wall. That his clothes?"

The younger man nodded.

With the dead man covered from sight and removed farthest from the fire, the policeman went out into the rain once again. Dugdale heard him call to his mount, heard the animal whinny a reply. He put on a fresh billy of water and went to the meat-safe for the chop. And, while he was cutting off sufficient for a meal for them both, he remembered Clair's injunction to take his wallet also to Mrs Thornton.

While he held the wallet in one hand and the coat in the other, Sergeant Knowles re-entered the hut.

"You've no business to touch those clothes," he said sharply.

"I am taking from them what Clair told me to take," came doggedly from Dugdale.

"Then you can't. What is there belongs to the law. Give the wallet to me."

Knowles advanced a step. Dugdale slipped behind the table.

"What the devil is the matter with you?" demanded the policeman. "You can't have that. Clair's possessions become the property of the State until they can be handed to his lawful heirs."

"I am sorry, Knowles," replied Dugdale, with paling face. "But with almost his last breath Clair gave me certain instructions about the wallet, and I promised to carry them out; as I shall do."

Knowles measured his host grimly. He saw the determination in Dugdale's jaw. Yet his duty was plain. As the representative of the law, he must take possession of the dead man's effects.

"I'm in no condition for a brawl, Dugdale," he said. "Don't be a fool. Give up that wallet and let's eat. I'm famished."

"We'll eat, certainly—but I keep the wallet."

"All right: have it, then."

Knowles slipped to the door, locked it, and pocketed the key. Without haste he approached the table, seized the lamp, extinguished it and placed it on the mantelpiece.

"Now, Dugdale, for the last time, give me that wallet," he said savagely. Across the table, their faces lit by the ruddy glare of the fire, they faced each other, both equally resolute. Then, nearly as quick as light, the sergeant sprang on the table to vault it, and at the same instant Dugdale dived beneath it and suddenly straightened, heaving upward table and policeman on his back.

The capsizing table upset Knowles' balance a split second before his hands left it to follow his flying body. Instead of landing on his feet, he fell flat on his back, his head thudding on the carpet.

Dugdale, free of the table, jumped round to meet the next charge. The table stood on its edge. Two seconds passed and Sergeant Knowles did not appear. Slowly, cautiously, the young man edged round the wall to a point where he could see beyond the table. His nerves were taut with excitement; he was prepared fully to fight to the last gasp to retain the wallet and carry out Sinclair's instructions.

And then the strain snapped and he could not forbear a laugh. It had been so absurdly easy. The argument had ended before it had properly begun. Yet he must be careful. A picture of Clair shamming death till his pursuer was near him came to Dugdale. Perhaps the sergeant was shamming, too.

First he must have more light. Reaching up behind him he took down the lamp, and, setting it on the ration heap, lit it without taking his eyes off his adversary.

The policeman lay quite still, his eyes closed. He hardly breathed, and Dugdale sighed with relief at finding he was breathing, for he had conceived a horrible fear. His subsequent actions were almost mechanical. The idea dominating his mind was the fulfilment of Sinclair's mission. What the dead man had written and what documents his wallet held Dugdale felt were no concern of his, but he had come to understand that Clair's death and Mrs Thornton were inexplicably mixed up, and that it was of vital importance to the Little Lady that she should be placed in possession of the wallet and letter as quickly as possible. That being the case, his course was as clear as daylight.

From the sergeant's tunic he secured the shining hand-cuffs. Then he took a chance. He dragged the insensible man to the open space before the fire and handcuffed him by one wrist to the heavy easy chair he had made with heavy cut timber and wire. It was a piece of furniture not to be moved with ease. Still, as a further safeguard, he lashed the sergeant's feet securely against the long fire-poker, which served as a splint and would prevent him from drawing up his legs to release himself with his one free hand. And that done, Dugdale proceeded to revive him.

Knowles was a sick man when he came to, and Dugdale made him as comfortable as the circumstances permitted with rolled blankets and his pillows.

"You'll be wanting more aspirin," he said, overdosing the groaning, swearing man.

"By Heaven, Dugdale! You'll suffer for this. You must be mad about the wallet. It can do you no good. In fact, you'll get jail for it for sure. I'll see that you do; you can leave that to me."

"It doesn't matter much what you do—after I have carried out Sinclair's commission."

"Sinclair? You mean Clair."

Dugdale moved the lamp and held Sinclair's confession for the sergeant to read.

"Sinclair told me to give you that," he said. "You'll find it on the table when I've gone."

Leaving Knowles then to recover fully from the effect of his second head blow, the younger man grilled chops and made coffee. The sergeant's portion he cut up and fed to him with a fork, not daring to loosen the manacled wrist.

Knowles made an effort to eat. Dugdale ate more than he required, for he wanted a reserve of strength. It was then about four in the morning.

At five he went out for his horse, which he brought back and saddled. The policeman's horse followed, the two animals remaining quietly outside whilst Dugdale made his simple preparations. First he made sure of the wallet, and in it he placed the letter, the wallet finding a safe depository in an inside coat-pocket.

"You seem determined to go the whole hog," observed Knowles, watching him with hard eyes. "Don't be a fool, Dugdale, and serve a period in jail. Release me and hand the wallet over, and I'll cry quits."

"Sorry," came briefly from Dugdale. He placed a suit of spare linen on the table, together with a clean towel. "There is water to wash in the bucket here," he said. "Here you'll find some dry things. Over in the safe is meat and damper—help yourself." For a moment they regarded each other grimly. "You may jail me, Knowles, as I expect you will," the young man went on. "In fact, you may do your damnedest—it cannot be helped; but I would have you understand that what I have done regarding the wallet, and what I am going to do, benefits me personally in no way whatever. You've hunted Sinclair and you've got him. You should be satisfied, and not try to frustrate his last wishes regarding his property."

"I do what is my duty, and I shall continue to do it."

"Of course you will, Knowles," Dugdale told him, taking from the policeman's tunic the key of the handcuffs. "Here is the key to your release. I expect you will try to overtake me, but you'll be wasting your time, as I ride one of the fastest horses in the west."

Dropping the key beside the sergeant's free hand, Dugdale went outside and vaulted into the saddle to start off on the wildest ride of his life.

Chapter Thirty-Four

Crossing the Paroo

DUGDALE RODE Tiger, the deep-chested, powerful-loined grey gelding, at an easy canter. At the least he had nine or ten minutes' start of Sergeant Knowles, and was confident that, should the policeman overhaul him, he could keep well ahead. His plan was to cross the Paroo directly east of his hut, and, when through the boundary of his block and on Barrakee Station territory, to strike north-east to Thurlow Lake homestead, a distance of about forty-five miles. He calculated that Mr Watts would willingly loan him a good mount for the remaining fifty miles to Barrakee homestead.

This route, doubtless, he would have altered had he known that Sergeant Knowles, instead of pounding after him, rode south of Eucla for twelve miles, to a hut where he knew there was a telephone. For the sergeant of police was no fool. He knew his district thoroughly. Therefore it was easy for him to deduce the fact that Dugdale was making for Thurlow Lake by following his tracks for a mere mile. Also he realized that he was in no way fit for a gruelling pursuit Indeed, he was a very sick man.

The rain had stopped, though the sky was still overcast and threatening. The clay-pans were full, the hard places treacherous and like greasy boards, so Dugdale rode circumspectly, choosing the softer, drier ground of the sand ridges. Constantly glancing behind, he came at last to the wide circular plain in which Sinclair's encounter with Knowles had taken place, and, passing across this, mounted to the summit of the mulga ridge bordering the Paroo.

The Paroo is like no other river in the world. It has no defined channel other than a strip of flat grey-black country varying in width from half a mile to three miles. Only once during the memory of the white man has the Paroo run the whole of its course. This was the second time. Subjected to mere local rains, the creeks draining the surrounding country empty their water into the Paroo, where, after running a little way, it disappears down the wide erratic cracks. Some places, notably that to which Sinclair tried to escape, are so criss-crossed by cracks a foot wide and many yards deep on rubbly subsiding ground that no horse could possibly cross them. The cracks scar all the remainder of the flat ribbon of river country in lesser degree, and anywhere where stock cross they have made a beaten track.

At the point opposite that where Dugdale rode over the sand ridge there was one such pad, a few hundred yards above the place where Sinclair had thought to defy Sergeant Knowles. It was the pad both he and the sergeant had used the day before. Now it was covered with water.

The young man reined in and gasped. Whilst he knew that the flood down the Paroo was approaching, he was astounded to see that already it was between him and Thurlow Lake. Slowly, irresistibly, it was moving down to join the floodwaters of the Darling.

How far down was the head of it? Would he have to ride forty miles to cross by the bridge three miles above Wilcannia? Aghast, he turned his horse south, and followed the stream. Two miles down he was halted by a creek discharging a bank-high stream of reddish water from the clay-pans a few miles westward, water accumulated by the rain of the last night and not by the general flood rains of a few weeks earlier. The chances were that the creek waters would fall in five or six hours—but the Paroo water would be rising.

"Tiger, old man, you've got to swim," Dugdale remarked to his restive mount. The creek banks were steep, but where the flow entered the flat country they shelved away into gentle slopes. The current was strong, and the horse objected to entering it; yet there was no time to be lost in gentle persuasive methods. Dugdale dismounted and cut himself a switch.

Only after punishment from switch and spurs did the grey abandon his resistance and sidle into the rushing torrent. He whinnied with fright when swept off his feet, but swam gamely while being swept out into the broader stream of the Paroo. With voice and rein his rider urged him towards the same side of the Paroo as the creek, well knowing that once in the Paroo proper the water would be only a foot or two in depth, but the grey black bottom would be almost as bad as a quicksand.

Even as it was, when the horse, having swum the creek stream, found bottom on semi-black soil and sand, it was only with difficulty that it reached dry land. After that Dugdale rode at a hand-gallop for four miles, and then, crossing a sand-pit at a wide bend, he gave an exultant shout; for there, but half a mile ahead, was the edge of the creeping flood.

The edge of the flood consisted of a floating mass of logs, boughs, and sticks, branches of trees and rubbish. Even from the shore he could see that the mass was crawling with snakes, bulldog-ants, goannas, lizards, and even rabbits. It was being carried along at about four miles an hour.

He rode on a further mile. The main course there was a little more than a mile across—dry ground, but rubbly and soft from the recent rain. Was it possible to cross before the flood travelled that one mile? He thought not, and rode on.

For another half-mile he cantered, deciding to cross where a dead box-tree stood at the point of a wide bend; but when he reached the tree he pulled up sharply, for, beyond it, the Paroo bed was covered with water, which, whilst mainly flowing down, was also creeping up to meet the main flood.

Dugdale knew then what was happening, and what he would have to face if he attempted to cross between the two masses of water. The main flood was flowing through the cracks, deep below the general surface. Somewhere below him the subterranean stream had met an obstacle in the shape of a sand-bar, and, being unable to pass, was rising up the cracks to the surface. In very short time the dry ground opposite would be covered by the rising water and the meeting of the main with the subsidiary flow. If he was to cross, he must cross instantly.

He was fully aware of the risks he ran. He knew that when the water in the ground cracks rose to a certain distance from the surface, the surface would dissolve in mud exactly as sugar dissolves in tea. If that occurred whilst he was crossing, his horse would be inevitably bogged and he himself likely enough to be bogged as well, and finally overwhelmed by the water while stuck fast. Yet these risks were dismissed from his thoughts almost as soon as they occurred. Sinclair's urgency for the letter and wallet to be delivered to the Little Lady as quickly as possible was sufficient spur to one who almost worshipped her.

Whipping his horse to a gallop, he retraced his tracks for a quarter of a mile, to where the red sand-hills along the east side of the river were a mile and a half distant. Here he reined his mount to the right and dashed out on the rubbly, sticking mullock intersected by a mad mosaic pattern of cracks yards deep.

Having been bred on Barrakee, where no such country existed, Tiger was at once at a great disadvantage. The irregularly spaced islands of firm rubble hindered his swinging stride so much that he was forced to proceed in a series of hops and jumps. More than once a hind-hoof slithered into a crack, and only by a miracle did he keep his feet.

His attention divided between the treacherous ground and the coming water, Dugdale helped his horse as much as possible with rein and knees. So imminent was the danger around and below him that he then did not notice the sun shining through the first rift in the clouds, forgot entirely Knowles' probable pursuit, even his own mission.

The recent rain had made the rubble—in size varying from marbles to small oranges—pudgy outside but still as hard as flint inside. This rubble clogged the horse's hoofs, forming great balls beneath each which eventually flew off, whereupon the clogging process was repeated. Tiger broke out into a white lather of sweat; his breathing rasped through scarlet nostrils and grinning teeth. The first half of the crossing was far worse than a ten-mile gallop.

And it was about halfway that the animal misjudged a short leap and dropped both hind feet into a crack. Prepared though he was, Dugdale was sent hurtling over the gelding's withers and landed with stunning force. In his turn he felt in a lesser degree the sensations of Sergeant Knowles when hit by Sinclair's waddy and later tricked by Dugdale in the hut.

Dazed, semi-conscious, the young man lurched to his feet, the reins fortunately still in his grip. The horse scrambled forward and out of the crack, mercifully uninjured, but the rider swayed on his feet with giddiness. For an entire minute the earth spun round and over and under with the sky, and only his iron will prevented him from lying down until the effect of the fall had passed.

Knowledge, however, of the creeping waters kept him up, whilst clinging to a stirrup-leather for support.

"Gad, Tiger, that was a buster, to be sure!" he gasped at last, and then when his vision cleared he added: "You're in a nice state, old boy, but we're not across yet."

Once more in the saddle he urged Tiger, trembling and afraid, again into the leaps and hops, so unnatural to an animal of Tiger's youth and freedom of action.

Three minutes later, when yet more than a quarter of a mile from high ground, he heard the sinister rush of water down in the cracks, water that "clucked" and "guggled" and "swished", water that was rising slowly to the surface.

The rubbish-littered lip of the main flood was less than a quarter of a mile from him. He could see the sinuous movement, the rise and fall of dead limbs and branches rolling over and over. And at less, much less than that short distance, he saw the silver glint of the water lower down moving upward to meet the main flow.

At that instant Dugdale knew that he had about one chance in a hundred of ever gaining firm ground. The beckoning sand-hills looked so close that it seemed possible to lean forward and touch them.

Now the upper surface of the ground was beginning to sink. He could discern the sheen of water less than a foot down in the cracks, water of a million eyes winking up at him malevolently. Tiger floundered worse and worse every second. Pools were forming between the two waters, ahead, behind, and on each side—pools that assumed sinister personalities. Dugdale felt as perhaps the escaped convict feels with a circle of armed warders creeping upon him.

Fifty, forty, thirty yards off now was the barrage of rubbish, with its six-yard vanguard of frothy water. Three hundred yards now separated horse and rider from the shelving red sand. Tiger's speed, in spite of prodigious efforts, had dropped to the pace of a walking man.

The next hundred yards took an eternity of terrific effort. A million times worse was the second hundred yards, and before ten of the remaining hundred were covered Tiger suddenly sank.

The mud and water reached Dugdale's knees. The horse screamed once, just before the whirling, floating, reptile-covered barrage rolled upon horse and man.

Chapter Thirty-Five

A Nice Day

THERE WAS in all that long, many-curved line of sticks and branches not a log of sufficient buoyancy to support a man of Dugdale's weight. When the horse sank to its shoulders, its rider threw himself sideways out of the saddle, whereupon he slushed cheek-down into a two-foot ridge of froth covering a further foot of water. Bunching his knees, he raised himself sufficiently to see a rotten fence-post within reach.

A red-hot iron was thrust through his right hand when a bulldog-ant bit; a cold contracting thing wrapped itself about his other wrist, but pain and sensation were hardly felt in that supreme moment wherein the earth vanished beneath the mass of cracking, lurching, upthrusting snags and branches. And then, as suddenly as it had come, so the barrage passed horse and man, leaving them in comparatively clear water.

Again Tiger screamed, this time with pain, not fright. Dugdale guessed that some venomous insect had taken refuge on his sweat—and mud-covered body and then proceeded to assert its irritability. The pain of the bite or sting proved to be the horse's salvation, proved to be just the necessary stimulus applied at the right moment; for Dugdale saw his animal make one tremendous effort to reach the high ground. He could never decide whether it was chance or equine sagacity; but Tiger lurched a little sideways, almost gained his feet, slithered forward two or three yards, sank deep with only his head out of the shallow water, paused for one more tremendous effort, moved forward again—and, amazingly, found his feet, and stood still.

The sluggishly moving water did not rise to Tiger's fore-knees. He trembled violently, and finally looked back with wide eyes at his rider. Mud and water dropped from him. He had become a brown horse. Dugdale saw that Tiger by miraculous chance stood on firm ground, and that if he could join him he might find a way, a causeway, from the island of firm ground to the shore of the river.

He was still clutching the rotten fence-post, and when he removed his left hand a small brown snake reared its graceful head and hissed. Had the snake been less frightened it would have struck, and without thought Dugdale flung up his arm sharply, whereupon the reptile was sent far into the water. Beneath him the ground felt slushy and glutinous, and only by lying full-length, allowing the water partially to support him, was he able to pull himself forward towards his horse. And then he found that Tiger stood on hard red sand.

For a full minute he patted and coaxed and generally worked to reduce Tiger's almost humanly hysterical fright. The slowly-moving water was imperceptibly rising and bore on its dark-brown surface countless half-drowned insects. Dugdale, without conscious thought, removed a dozen harmless ants and one of the ferocious bulldog-ants from the fidgeting Tiger, as well as several that clung to himself; and then, sliding one foot forward at a time, gingerly prospected for a firm crossing to dry land eighty or ninety yards distant.

In such manner did he fortunately find a way, his animal reluctant to leave the safe spot he had found, yet obviously frightened by the conditions surrounding them; and when at last they did clear the Paroo river, the bed behind them was no longer dry.

Dugdale first of all removed his coat. Then off came Tiger's saddle. The saddle-cloth he used to wash the animal down, and when again clean and saddled Tiger appeared little the worse for the crossing. The next matter of importance was the condition of Sinclair's letter. It was soppy from immersion, and the bearer of it was obliged to lay it against a sand-ripple facing the sun to dry. Sinclair's wallet was less affected, a cursory examination showing that the water had not penetrated to the folding pockets. After that there was nothing to do but wait till the letter dried.

The adventure of the crossing had in a way calmed Dugdale's mind sufficiently to allow of consecutive thought on what had occurred and what the future might hold in store. While riding towards Thurlow Lake at a quiet amble, knowing that he was safe from personal pursuit by Sergeant Knowles, Dugdale made up his mind to experience a trying time at least from the further activities of the police sergeant.

From his official standpoint Knowles had been right in his demand for the handing over of Sinclair's property, because the wallet had been Sinclair's property and now was the temporary property of the State. That Dugdale refused to divulge the name of the person to whom he was to take the wallet made it quite evident to the policeman that the act was perpetrated to benefit Dugdale or one of Dugdale's friends in an unlawful way, because, Sinclair being dead, there remained no one to prove Dugdale's words.

A southerly wind blew chillingly through the rider's wet clothes, and he urged Tiger into an easy canter. Arrived at the boundary-fence, he lashed the top wire to the bottom wire with his waist-belt, and had no difficulty in getting the horse over, this being a method Tiger was quite used to. Pressing onward, yet without undue haste, horse and rider finally came in sight of Thurlow Lake homestead about three o'clock in the afternoon.

Half an hour later he was close enough to see the several boundary-riders standing in a group near the horse-yards, and of these he made out Fred Blair and his bullock-wagon offsider, Henry McIntosh. That these two were now occupied on horsework was obvious to him, because it had been essential to get all the sheep east of the Washaways before the flood waters divided the run into two, and to beat the flood every available man was necessary.

What Dugdale didn't know was that the three men talking to Blair and McIntosh had been waiting at Thurlow Lake since nine o'clock that morning for the express purpose of apprehending him, the three men in question being members of the police stationed at Thurlow Lake in the general search for Sinclair. They were not wearing uniform: each of them appearing to the observer as either a jackaroo or a well-dressed ordinary hand.

Two of them had already had the pleasure of meeting Blair in their professional capacity. Consequently Blair knew them. Knowing, too, that they would be loath to devote their time, urgently needed in the search for Sinclair, to escorting him to the jail at Wilcannia, Blair was airing his view about policemen in general and these three specimens in particular. It was as well, perhaps, that Blair did not know that the search for Sinclair was over.

Dugdale rode up to the stockyard and dismounted. Nodding to the others, he said to Blair:

"Is Mr Watts home, Fred?"

"Just come in," Blair replied, the heat of argument still in evidence on his brick-red face and in the angle of his beard. "I think he is in the office."

"Thanks! I want to see him."

But as he moved towards the house the three plainclothes men edged around him. Blair saw the movement, the significance of which brought a gleam into his eyes.

"Mr Dugdale?" inquired a big, raw-boned man, evidently the senior officer.

Dugdale paused in his walk. Upon him also the significance of the three men about him was not lost. He saw now what their avocation in life was. They were too hard, too suspicious, too efficient-looking to be anything but bush-troopers. Allowing Tiger's reins to drop to the ground, where upon the animal stood and would continue to stand for hours, he braced his shoulders and gave answer in the affirmative.

"Then I am going to arrest you for being in possession of stolen property," the leader said grimly. "You will be charged with having removed from the clothes of William Clair, now deceased, a leather wallet and contents, and a further charge will be laid against you of having assaulted Sergeant Knowles, causing grievous bodily harm. Just to save trouble, give me the wallet."

Dugdale stood with his hands on his hips, the ever-ready poise of the fighter. The information that Sinclair was dead shocked Blair into immobility, because less than twenty four hours previously he had seen, spoken to, and supplied the gaunt man with rations. The matter of the pocket book was a puzzle. The outstanding facts were that Clair was dead, that Dugdale had his wallet, and that Dugdale had fought the sergeant either to obtain or to retain the wallet. Natural instinct prompted Blair to side with Dugdale. Still Blair waited.

To ask why Frederick Blair so loved fighting is to ask why a dog loves to chase and kill a cat. The love of fighting may have been inherited, for Blair's grandfather had been a notorious blackbirder, almost officially designated a pirate. The little man lived some three hundred years too late. Even in Bully Hayes' time he would have secured worldwide fame; because, not only was he a natural fighter, but he also was a natural leader. Suddenly he seized McIntosh's arm and drew him aside.

"When I w'istles, 'Enery," he said, "you bolt to the stock-yards and turn out all them 'orses. Then you come back and have Tiger waiting and ready for Mister Dugdale to git away. Savvy?"

Henry intimated with his usual grin of vacancy that he did savvy, and the grin was still a grin when Dugdale's fist crashed into the police leader's face and Blair whistled precisely one second before ramming his head between another policeman's legs and heaving him over his back like a bag of potatoes.

Now, when a ten stone man hits a twelve stone man a glancing blow on the lower jaw, it seldom occurs that the bigger man goes to sleep. The leader of the police party was but slightly jarred. Like Blair, he, too, loved a fight, and with a broad grin of joy stepped in with amazing swiftness to return the punch. But somehow his fist shot skyward. A volcano opened the earth beneath him and sent him up in a parabolic curve which ended when he returned to earth on his head.

A lesser man's neck might well have been broken. In any case, the twist it received whilst his body was still in the air was infinitely worse than Dugdale's smash to the jaw. When finally his body did come to rest with a dull thump, it was to feel the not inconsiderable weight of Blair, who jumping high, landed with both feet on the small of his back.

The third policeman had got a ju-jitsu hold on Dugdale and the second was gathering himself to fling his weight into the melee. Blair saw Dugdale's helplessness, saw his captor's broad back, saw the third member of the enemy forces charging upon him, heard the leader coughing up sand and gasping for wind.

The little man gave vent to a roaring laugh of ineffable happiness. The tip of his beard was level with his eyes, blazing and alight with glory. Ignoring the charging policeman, he estimated the distance between the back of Dugdale's captor and himself to a bare inch, took a short run, launched himself in the air with terrific velocity, and crashed the ju-jitsu expert's legs from under him. Never losing an instant, he was on his feet before Dugdale and his captor found the ground. Laughing again, he ran to meet the second policeman who was closing in upon him, ran forward as though eagerly welcoming a long lost brother, and smote that man between the eyes so mightily that he dropped as though dead.

Knocked down and winded though he was, the ju-jitsu expert merely exchanged one paralysing grip for another. He was master of the art, yet was unfortunate in having devoted his art to the subjugation of Dugdale and not of Fred Blair. Whilst Dugdale was a straightout boxer who could be overcome by the other two policemen, Blair was a rough-and-tumble, eat-'em-alive-oh! whirlwind fighter, bringing to his

222

aid extraordinary nimbleness of feet, terrific punching ability, strong teeth, and dexterously used boots.

Having put one man to sleep and observing that the leader would require just two more seconds to get the "crick" out of his neck, Blair proceeded to finish the liberation of Dugdale already begun.

The expert had his victim down under him. He was on his knees holding Dugdale's arms in a bone breaking grip. Blair mounted the broad back like a little child riding on its father's back at home. But there Blair's childlikeness ended. He slid one hand over the crown of the expert's head and, twining his fingers in the hair above the man's forehead, began to pull backward. The pull being anything but slow or gentle, it was a wonder Blair did not pull either the policeman's head or his scalp off. As it was, the expert became the victim and bellowed.

Just then, however, Blair was picked up like a noxious insect by the big leader and hugged in a breathless grip. He saw that Dugdale managed to worm his way out from beneath the expert's body just before that performer recovered from his surprise; and then, finding that his head was lower than the big man's face, so that he could not knock it out of shape with the back of his head, Blair devoted a few seconds to tattooing tender shins with the heels of his boots.

That eased the situation but did not relieve him of restraint. Hearing the smack of fist against flesh somewhere outside his line of vision, Blair laughed again, and, seizing the opportunity, dug one iron hard elbow with devastating force into his opponent's stomach.

Even when turning his head to obtain a better position for the second attack he saw that the man he had knocked unconscious was very ill with a kind of *mal de mer,* and that Dugdale and his partner were giving an exhibition of the fistic art before the interested Watts family and two station hands. What he failed to see was that, no longer able to resist the temptation, Henry McIntosh, reared in the rough-and-tumble atmosphere of the wharves, handed Tiger into the care of one of the hands and proceeded to take his part in the war. The time arrived when the leader, holding Blair in his powerful arms, suddenly saw a maze of shooting stars, followed by a great light which preceded a greater darkness. The contact of a bootheel—removed from the foot for the purpose—with a man's unprotected head is liable to cause such effects.

The leader sagged at the knees, and Blair, discovering himself a free man, turned to observe the hugger collapse with 'Enery beyond, the boot upraised for a second blow.

"I ain't got no time just now, 'Enery," Blair snarled, "but when I 'ave I'll do you up, boots and all, for trying to spoil this scrap. No one told you to interfere."

Dugdale was still engaged in a heart-to-heart argument, and the policeman, recovering from his sickness, lurched to his feet to continue the combat. He was mightily sick, but very game.

"Take yer time now, Giles, me lad," Blair counselled pleasantly. "I don't forget how you made me whitewash the jail, but I bear no malice, I don't. Take yer time—take yer time!"

Giles took his time. His introduction to Fred Blair had taken place some two years earlier, and consequently he knew precisely the little man's prowess. Swaying for a moment or two, he wiped away the imaginary lights dancing before his eyes, and then called on Mr Watts in the King's name.

"Better do a bunk, Mister Watts," Blair advised.

Waiting, the little terror saw Dugdale floored by a straight left which produced generous admiration for the giver of it. He saw, too, the sunlight glint on handcuffs and waited no more. The policeman was caught bending. Also he was caught unawares, and the impact of Blair's boot sent him sprawling on his face for a yard or two beyond the gasping, prostrate Dugdale.

"Git away, Dug—I'll manage 'em," Blair roared. "'Enery, Mister Dugdale's 'orse."

The tumbled one was rising, but received a swinging blow against his ear which sent him down again. The second man was tripped and flung with amazing rapidity into the arms of the anxious, uncertain Mr Watts. The two station hands cheered. Then Dugdale was lifted on Tiger and the reins thrust into his hands. He was feeling giddy and sick, and almost without sense; almost but not quite, for he had sense enough to urge the grey into a smart canter along the track to the Washaways.

The leader now returned to active service. The three policemen were mad, fighting angry, for their horses had been freed from the stockyards and the prisoner was speeding away on the only horse then at the homestead.

They pummelled and fought the little bullocky till blood flowed in streams from all combatants, and till eventually superior force and superior weight bore Blair to the earth; whereupon, at long last, he was handcuffed in no gentle fashion. One eye closed, the other was closing. A broad grin developed in spite of his awful face. He said:

"For that, gentlemen all, I'll whitewash yer blasted jail three times. It's a nice day, isn't it?"

Chapter Thirty-Six

Flash Harry Deals the Cards

FROM THURLOW LAKE to the Washaways was twenty six miles. Six miles west of the Washaways was One Tree Tank and a hut where lived a rider named Flash Harry. It was from Flash Harry that Dugdale hoped to secure a fresh mount.

Now, while the rider of Tiger still felt a little dazed—while his jaw ached and bore the mark, rapidly colouring, of the policeman's fist—there was no real excuse for Dugdale's forgetting the telephone wire. Not being an habitual criminal, the cutting or breaking of the single wire between Thurlow Lake and Barrakee never entered his mind. It is probable, too, as he himself admits, that if he had thought of the telephone he still would have felt secure, since the possibility of further troopers barring his way was remote. But the fact was that the country was alive with policemen, all engaged, or till just then engaged, in closing in upon Sinclair before he met Knowles and his death.

Henry Lockyer was about thirty years old, tall, lank, and dark, with a hint of China in his make up. He wore brown elastic-sided riding boots, kept always in the highest condition of polish, white moleskin trousers, ever white, a black silk shirt, a sky blue kerchief, and a wide brimmed felt hat which he only removed when he went to bed.

Flash Harry was eating a late lunch—he had been out all day—and a police trooper was sitting down to a pannikin of tea and a slice of brownie, his tunic removed for ease, his peaked cap on the table beside him.

"What beats me is all this hullabaloo about a bloke who knocks a nig," Flash Harry was saying. "Why, when I was over in West Australia a few years ago, me an' a feller called

Purple Joe shot seventeen of 'em afore breakfast one morning."

"But New South Wales is not West Australia," the trooper observed with a grin. "And King Henry wasn't a wild nigger exactly."

"Aw well, I suppose a bloke—"

Flash Harry paused in the supposition he was intending to put forward. The telephone bell rang four times, which was the ring for him; for all the huts were on the single line and each hut had its own particular ring. Languidly he got to his spurred feet and stalked to the instrument. A moment later, turning to the trooper, he said:

"One of your blokes at Thurlow Lake wanting to talk to you."

For several minutes the trooper was engaged at the phone. Flash Harry heard references to Dugdale and Blair and McIntosh, and became interested; so, when the other resumed his seat, he inquired:

"What's gone wrong now?"

"Seems to have been a brawl at Thurlow Lake," the trooper told him. "Some of our fellows were instructed to arrest Dugdale, the late sub-overseer, but Blair and McIntosh barged in and Dugdale got away. He's heading here, and I've to arrest him."

"What for? What's he done?"

"Dunno properly. Appears Dugdale has a wallet belonging to Clair. Clair and Sergeant Knowles met beyond the Paroo and Clair is dead—shot."

"Humph!" Flash Harry regarded the youthful trooper thoughtfully. Then: "Well, you won't have much difficulty in collaring Dugdale. He can't cross the Washaways now—they're running a banker."

"Still, orders is orders, and Dugdale's got to be apprehended. I am just going to sit here and arrest him when he walks in."

"Humph!" Again Flash Harry looked thoughtfully at his visitor. A silence fell between them: the trooper looking forward to making an easy arrest when three of his mates had failed; Flash Harry devising ways and means of outwitting the trooper and conveying a warning to the man from whom he had invariably received courtesy and kindness. And Dugdale's attitude to him had been the more appreciated because Flash Harry was very selfconscious about his mixed ancestry.

The talk during the next hour was desultory. The second hour's waiting found the trooper tunicked and hatted, his horse saddled and waiting for emergencies out of sight behind the chaff-house. From where they sat they could see along the straight open track for some three miles, and dusk was falling before they espied the white gelding coming at a slow, tired walk.

"He'll be here in ten minutes," estimated the trooper.

"Yes—in ten minutes," Flash Harry agreed. "I'll put on the billy. He'll want a drink of tea."

The trooper continued to watch the coming horseman. He heard the rider fill the billy from the petrol-tin bucket, heard, too, more wood being put on the glowing coals of the fire. Firelight flickered on the interior walls of the hut. No one saw Flash Harry get something hard and sinister looking from a small tin trunk.

So they sat, one on each side of the table, and waited. The minutes passed slowly, till eventually they could hear the grey gelding's hoofs softly thudding. Whilst they could plainly see Dugdale dismount, he could not see them distinctly within the hut. He walked stiffly towards them. The trooper silently rose to his feet, handcuffs ready, anticipating easy victory. And then came Flash Harry's drawling voice:

"Better sit down, old boy, or you'll flop down."

The trooper looked sideways at the owner of the drawling voice, and stared with dazed wonder right into the barrel of a revolver. Dugdale entered the hut. Again Flash Harry spoke, saying something about tea being made shortly.

"Oh!"

At the threshold Dugdale paused, taking in the scene with narrowed eyes and quickly taut muscles. The trooper was fascinated by the intimidating barrel, which never wavered. Flash Harry's eyes gleamed beyond the small black circle, and in them the trooper saw deadly determination. The newcomer walked across to the fireplace which was behind Flash Harry.

"What's the great scheme, Harry?" he asked.

"Oh, some feller rang up from Thurlow Lake giving orders that you were to be arrested," Flash Harry replied evenly. "This is my hut, and there is no arrests going to be made inside it. It follows that, as I am king within these four walls, things go as I want 'em to go. Where are you heading for?"

"The river," came from Dugdale, making tea in the now boiling billy. "That is, when I've had a drink of tea and a bite to eat. I'm dog tired."

"Righto! Have a feed. The trooper an' me will give each other the glad eye."

"Then you want to mind your step," the uniformed man informed Flash Harry. As a policeman he was very much annoyed, but as a sportsman he was optimistic. "When my chance comes, as it will do, things will happen. They'll happen all right in any case."

"I wouldn't be surprised," Flash Harry remarked calmly. "Somehow things are always happening to me. In my time I've whitewashed more jails than I have fingers and toes. In fact, me and Blair are tradesmen."

"Are your horses in the night paddock?" Dugdale asked.

"Yaas, Mister Dugdale. You'll have to run 'em in if you want a fresh hack. Better take 'The Devil'—he's lively, but he's a great swimmer, and it's a lot o' swimming you'll have to do if you want to get to the 'Gutter'."

"Why, is the flood down the Washaways already?"

"If the water rises another foot, orl them creeks will become a single river. Me and the trooper are going to bet a level pound that both you and The Devil gits drownded: at least, I'm going to bet you do, and he is going to bet you don't."

"I'm not going to bet he doesn't get drowned," the trooper cut in emphatically. "I was down along the Washaways this morning, and they are not to be crossed without wings. You haven't got a chance in the world, Dugdale, so you may as well tell this idiot to lower his fool gun and you come quietly with me. You'll be making more rods for your back by carrying on."

Dugdale sighed. He was cold, stiff, and weary. Whilst still determined to carry out Sinclair's request, he was heartily sorry that he had ever undertaken it. It seemed preposterous that such a to-do should be made over his possession of a wallet explicitly confided to him by the dying Sinclair; but, having accepted the commission, he was not going to be daunted by the difficulties ahead of him, or the consequences of his defiance of the police.

Whilst he ate and drank, Flash Harry and the trooper maintained the tableau that might well have been labelled "Stalemate". Never for an instant did either man's eyes wander nor did the revolver waver. It was a pose trying enough for the stoutest nerves.

"I'll be getting along, Harry," Dugdale said at last. "I'm grateful for your assistance, which you might extend long enough for me to catch and saddle The Devil."

"Well, don't be too long," came the drawling voice. "I always have one cigarette every half hour, and I'm sure our friend is dying for a draw, too. This 'ere act finishes directly you're mounted, 'cos we must give the trooper a sporting chance. Now, about that there bet, it's a level chance—"

Dugdale was compelled to smile on hearing the half sentence when crossing to the night paddock gate. Yet he wasted no time. Knowing that the paddock in area was only about three hundred acres, he started to cross it quickly with the intention of getting beyond the rider's mounts and driving them into the catching yards. But luck favoured him for once. The two loose horses were not fifty yards beyond the hut, being attracted to that part of the paddock by the stranger horse ridden by the trooper.

The Devil was a gigantic black gelding, of uncertain temper but of unquestionable courage; and it was almost dark when Dugdale had him saddled and led him towards the hut door after allowing Tiger to go in search of grass.

Flash Harry was as good as his word. Immediately Dugdale was astride The Devil, his gun dropped and the trooper rushed out and dashed for his horse. Out upon the track the black stretched his glossy neck and laid himself out into a hard gallop.

It can be truthfully said that most men are but indifferent bushmen on a dark night. Some there are, however, who can ride a straight course home when caught out in their paddocks after daylight has gone; but one bushman here and there is no less efficient on the blackest night than under the brightest sun. Dugdale was one of these latter, and an added advantage to his keen night vision was absolute knowledge of every single acre of the Barrakee run.

Knowing that the Washaways were aflood, he realized that the point of his attempted crossing would best be about a mile below the main track, where many of the interwoven creeks formed but three separate channels. The flood having risen to the level of the creek banks, there would be no possibility of fording them, and, whilst the width of the streams was no more than sixty yards, the danger would lie in even a good horse being unable to land on the precipitous banks.

He could hear the trooper's horse thundering along behind him, and found that he could maintain the distance between them without allowing The Devil a slack rein. That was all to the good, because the fresher in wind and muscle The Devil was when they reached the creeks the greater the chances of safely crossing them.

Five miles along the track they came to a wire fence and a gate. Dugdale saw no necessity for putting his horse at either fence or gate, and, with a quiet smile, he dismounted and opened wide the two gates. He was through them and in his saddle when the trooper swept up.

"Now, Dugdale, stop the foolery and submit," ordered the trooper, bringing out his heavy calibre revolver and kneeing his horse towards The Devil who, under pressure, sidled away.

"Be a sport, Smithy!" coaxed Dugdale. "I opened the gate for you, and I want to shut the gate because the sheep in the two paddocks will get boxed, and Mr Thornton has enough on his hands already without having to draft about nine thousand sheep. Let one of us dismount and shut the gates while the other stands by. Once both are mounted again we stand a level chance."

"Darn it!" the trooper cried. Being a true sportsman he should never have been a policeman. It was he who dismounted and closed the gates, and not a second before he was comfortably in the saddle did Dugdale spurt The Devil into a lightning getaway. The trooper, however, was determined. He had his duty to perform, and his revolver cracked three times in rapid succession. The first bullet flicked The Devil along his rump; the second tore a strip of trousers and strip of skin across Dugdale's body just above his belt. The owner of Eucla Station felt as though a crowbar had struck him; The Devil "went to market".

He screamed and then squealed with pain and outraged dignity; he almost unseated the nauseated Dugdale in a series of evil bucks that so delayed progress that the trooper was almost upon them before Dugdale could master him.

At that point, but a quarter of a mile from the first creek, The Devil was reined off the track into the soft black soil of the flood areas. Only the darkness prevented the determined Smith from again using his weapon, because a mere ten yards separated the two men during the one mile to the chosen crossing.

Praying that The Devil would avoid the box trees, the holes in the ground, and fallen branches, Dugdale suddenly swerved at a left hand angle towards the creek rushing with menacing roar between its tree lined banks. He heard the trooper shouting behind him, but caught not the words. Is it not faith that can move mountains? With such a faith did the young man urge his powerful mount in one gigantic leap far out into the racing water.

With a mighty splash The Devil sank. With his feet free from the stirrups yet clinging to the saddle, a task demanding all his strength, Dugdale's body went under, but not his head. He was forced upward by the horse beneath him till only the lower half of his body was submerged whilst The Devil struck out with fearless energy for the farther bank.

The dim mass of bordering trees rushed past them as soon as they were gripped by the current. By a foot only did they miss a mass of partly submerged tree snags amongst which the water roared, snags set thick with disembowelling points up and down and out. Dugdale heard a shout, half exultant, half defiant, followed by a splash, which told him that the trooper, determined and dauntless, had sent his horse into the creek after him.

And a moment later he heard the trooper's horse scream in pain when the cruel snags caught it upon their spikes—heard the trooper yell once, and only once—and then he and The Devil were swept round a bend into a temporarily quiet backwater.

Chapter Thirty-Seven

Duty—and Common-Sense

THE BACKWATER into which Dugdale was swept was on that side of the creek nearer to Barrakee. The rushing waters of the main stream were invisible to horse and man, and a point of terror to the former. Hemmed in on all sides by the trees, it was impossible to see anything other than the brilliant stars; but Dugdale knew that the jutting point of ground that caused the backwater was a kind of sand bar and the only place where a horse would find a footing.

The Devil, fearful of the roaring stream, hugged the curving bank where its steepness gave him no possible chance of getting out. The man could have managed it, because the water was almost level with the bank lip; but the horse was much like a mouse in a bucket of water. Even when Dugdale got him at last on the inner side of the jutting sand bank, The Devil was forced to use all his tremendous strength to clamber up on dry land.

On the creek bank Dugdale dismounted, his mind centred upon the probable fate of Trooper Smith. That the rash policeman was drowned he thought more than probable; and, knowing of the mass of snags he and his horse had barely missed, Sinclair's messenger estimated that nowhere else would it be possible to find Smith or his horse. If the snags had not caught their bodies, it would be useless to search for them till daylight came.

In the darkness, too, it was more than likely that he would pass the snags on his search upstream. Slowly and with great care he led the fidgeting Devil along the bank almost awash with the swirling, hissing torrent, and had proceeded a quarter of a mile before he heard Smith call within a dozen yards distance. Although the voice was so near, Dugdale could not see the owner of it; but he did see where the water was lashed with foam among the branches and snags of the fallen tree. And where the water was whitened, there was Smith.

"If you're not drowned, you ought to be," Dugdale shouted at him.

"What was good enough for you was good enough for me," came the voice. "I suppose you'll lend a hand to help me out?"

"What! For you to arrest me?" Dugdale inquired.

"You bet!" came the prompt reply. "But I've lost my gun and my horse; so you should not find it difficult to avoid arrest, should you?"

"I shall certainly object to your trying to arrest me till I've done a little job I promised I would do. Can't you work your way to me along those snags?"

"No. Between you and me there is a three foot gap. If I let go I'll be swept away—and I can't swim."

"You idiot! Do you mean to say you put your horse into the creek and can't swim? Smithy! you're game, but you're mentally deficient. Hang on awhile."

Dugdale fastened the reins of his horse to a tree trunk. Taking off his coat, he made sure of Sinclair's wallet and the sodden letter in one of its pockets, and placed it at the foot of the tree to which The Devil was secured. Returning then to that point on the bank opposite the mass of snags, he examined the water very carefully. The tree that now formed the mass had been growing at the edge of the creek before a storm had uprooted it. Its roots were still high and dry, the trunk slanting downward into the foaming tide. Dugdale removed his boots.

"What are you doing, Dug?"

"I am coming in after you, Smithy," the policeman was informed. "I am a fool to give you a chance to collar me, and you are a bigger fool to have taken that header."

Dugdale worked his way along the tree trunk into the water, and when the tree disappeared he slipped down into it and, reaching for a footing of some sort, found none. His legs were swept up and outward by the strength of the rushing water, and only with his hand could he hold on and work farther out from the bank till he came to a branch lying about a foot above the surface and stretching horizontally.

At that time some dozen feet separated the two men.

"How are you enjoying yourself, Smithy?" Dugdale asked caustically.

"Goodo! Water's a bit wet, though," came the quiet but grim response.

"Ah, well! Let's be thankful for small mercies. A man won't die of thirst. Sure you can get no nearer to me?"

"Quite sure."

Halfway along the branch Dugdale found another with his swinging body below the surface. It helped to steady him; helped him, too, to edge a further yard outward. A jagged point of wood jarred his kneecap, causing his teeth to clench with the numbing pain. The temperature of the water was equally numbing. Both men began to feel that all the world's wealth would be well spent on a fire.

After much manoeuvring, Dugdale decreased the distance between them to three feet, having come to that space where there were no supporting branches.

"Can you get your belt off?" asked Dugdale.

"I don't know. I'll try."

"Well, don't try so much as to let go of that branch." Dugdale saw the dark head and shoulders of the policeman twist and turn, rise and sink, accompanying much hard breathing and chattering of teeth.

"Got it. What now?"

"Throw the buckle end over to me. Right! Now your only chance is to take a good hold of your end, and when you leave go the branch you are hanging to the force of the stream will sweep you down below me and over to my side, where there is a good snag sticking up out of the water. Perhaps you can see it?"

"Yes, I can."

"Right. Well, let go and hang on."

Trooper Smith let go. Unable to swim, he was facing the ordeal with extraordinary courage. To them both was need of coolness and calculating judgement, for a blow from one of the hideous unseen snags, or a failure of strength at a critical moment, meant certain death for Smith at least. The weight of the trooper's body on the belt was terrific, and had not the strain been over quickly it would have been impossible for Dugdale to have maintained his one handed hold. Smith, as Dugdale foresaw, was swept down and against the upflung branch, to which he clung desperately. Their hands were blue and numbed with cold, and their bodies were reaching the state in which pain is not felt.

To Smith the five minutes which followed were a pro-longed nightmare, full of noise, full of water demons clutch-ing his limbs to destroy him. The tree branches tore his hands, and pointed sticks prodded his body and his face in a thousand places. Above the noise he heard Dugdale's com-mands and forced himself to obey them with mechanical promptness. The noise, the demons, the reaching snags, came to be enemies attacking his body, which appeared to have been detached from his tired brain; so that the last half dozen yards were accomplished in a semi-conscious state, and the final struggle to the bank was a matter of unreality.

"What is it going to be? Peace or war?" he heard Dugdale ask.

"Peace for five minutes at least," he managed to gasp. "God! I'm frozen."

"Maybe. But you're alive, which is something," Dugdale pointed out. "Luckily, I've a watertight box of wax matches, so we'll get a fire going. There's a quart pot on my saddle, so we'll get a drink of hot water, which, my dear Smithy, is a great luxury compared with cold."

Five minutes later, two half naked men stood close to a roaring pillar of fire, taking turns in sipping from the quart pot. The heat stung their flesh, and from their clothes rose clouds of steam, and eventually, when Smith's tobacco and papers were dried, they smoked cigarettes and talked about the future.

"Tell me—during the armistice—what your idea was to pinch Clair's wallet," inquired the policeman, breaking a long silence. "Duty and all that aside, Dugdale, you're getting yourself into a dickens of a mess over it."

Dugdale related the coming of Sinclair to his hut and the events leading up to and following his death. "You see," he pointed out, "Clair particularly asked me to take and deliver his wallet to a certain person. In fact, he got my promise to do it, and, having promised to deliver the wallet, deliver it I must. Now, I am scared by the flood and the attitude of Knowles and you fellows towards me, and damned sorry I did promise. But all that can't be helped now."

"But did Clair, or Sinclair, say why the unnamed person has to have his wallet?" Smith pressed.

"No, he did not. Aside from that, I consider that he had a perfect right to dispose of his wallet as he liked, and I had no justification for refusing to take and do with it as he directed."

"Humph! In one way you are right. You are wrong, however, legally, because Sinclair was a man wanted for murder. He was killed in escaping the law, and what property he possessed, as Sergeant Knowles said, belongs to the State till his assigns are established. Anyway, it's a knotty point; too difficult for me. I'm only a policeman. I've got to obey orders, which are to arrest you and convey you to Wilcannia."

"And you will, I suppose, carry out your orders?" asked Dugdale with his quiet smile.

"I shall."

"You will, I should say, find it a little difficult, especially as you cannot swim."

238

"I shall hold you here till they come with a boat or something."

"And where do you suppose they are going to get the boat?"

"Oh, I don't know. It's up to them."

"Of course—if they know we're here. But by the time they find out we shall be fairly hungry."

"That, of course, cannot be helped."

"In fact, we shall become so hungry that we shall never want any food again—unless, of course, we are fed in the next world."

The two men looked keenly at each other. Suddenly Smith grinned and burst into a guffaw of laughter. Dugdale laughed at, and with him. He looked so absurd in his underclothes, and he himself felt he must appear no less absurd. The Devil pawed the ground impatiently and attracted their attention.

"I am going to put on my clothes, as it is useless drying them," Dugdale explained with the placidity of determination. "You see, I have to swim The Devil across two more creeks before I can get clear of the Washaways and send help to you."

"But what about my orders?"

"You were not ordered to starve me to death, or yourself either," Dugdale observed whilst dressing. "When I pulled you out of the water you were unconscious, and when you came to you found yourself against a nice warm fire, with a quart pot of hot water beside you and no sign, absolutely no sign, of Frank Dugdale. Now isn't that right?"

Trooper Smith, of the New South Wales Mounted Police, closed one eye.

"Now you recall it, Dugdale, I think it is about correct," he said, adding, with sudden gravity: "But you are not going to attempt those two creeks, are you?"

"Of course. There is no other way of getting to the Darling, but across them, and the water won't go down for a month."

"Well, even at school you were an ass," Smith reminded his prisoner.

"Better a live ass than a starved corpse. However, I would prefer not going till day comes. What about promising not to relieve me of the wallet, so that we could get a good warm and enjoy a sleep?"

"My dear chap, there is no wallet!" Smith rejoined cheerfully. "As a personality you don't exist. I neither know nor see you. You have vanished, and I regain consciousness alone between these creeks. Let us camp. Let us heat more water and talk of the last dinner we had in the city."

"Yes, let's," agreed Dugdale.

Chapter Thirty-Eight

Bony Takes Command

Napoleon Bonaparte, Australia's brilliant but little-known bush detective, was walking down the river. His walk would have been more direct had the volume of water in the great channel been normal. Now the channel was marked only by the bordering gum-trees, for on both sides the river overflowed its banks in places many miles out over the flats. Water was sent out into the meandering creeks, it crossed the established tracks and cut off direct communication with the towns of Bourke and Wilcannia.

To walk down the river meant, therefore, wide detours round billabongs, gutters, and creeks. Where Bony walked was about four miles west of the Darling proper, and had he wanted to cross the flooded river he would have been obliged to swim some eight or nine miles.

So great was the volume of water that the station of Barrakee, standing on high ground, was surrounded by water, except for a ramp or causeway, sufficiently wide to allow a car to drive along it, which connected the island with the dry land. It proved to be the second great flood which the Western Division of New South Wales had experienced and on the crest of the flood there appeared myriads of wild fowl, water-hens, ducks, geese, and members of the vast crane family.

It was the birds rather than the volume of water which fascinated the detective, but even the fascination of the birds paled before the events of that morning in mid-August. On the disappearance of Ralph Thornton from Barrakee and Nellie Wanting from Three Corner Station, the river from Barrakee downward had been carefully watched at more than one point.

A peculiar feature of the disappearance became intelligible to Bony when it was known that the girl left her employment three days before the departure of the young man. On the face of it it appeared that Ralph had hidden a boat a mile below Barrakee, and had gone down river to Three Corner Station to pick up the gin. On account of the wide detours made by the river it would take him all of three days to get to Three Corner Station, precisely as long as it would take a person to walk the same distance by the track which ran from bend to bend.

These distances and times Bony had quickly learned from two old pensioners camped on the side of the river, who were now sheltering, on account of the flood, in the Barrakee woolshed. It appeared, therefore, that the girl had walked up river to Ralph and his boat; and, since it was not likely that she would do that only to go down river again in the boat, it became obvious that the pair had gone up river past Barrakee.

For two days the half-caste had been searching for indications of the missing couple. The first day he drew a blank, but on the afternoon of the second he saw drifting down a small creek the empty shell of a duck's egg, and on securing this, found that it had been recently cooked. Even whilst examining the shell the faint report of a shotgun came floating to the boxtrees, and thirty minutes later Bony found a native humpy constructed of green boughs and leaves, half way up a sand ridge at the foot of which lapped the flood-water. Precisely six seconds were spent in discovering that the inhabitants were away, and a further three in reading their tracks. Positive proof lay over the ground that dainty Nellie Wanting and slim, small-footed Ralph were the occupants.

A second report of the gun told that they were away hunting ducks for food, and in retiring Bony threw sand over his own tracks to obliterate them, knowing full well that otherwise the girl would see them, whereupon they would fly in terror of discovery and pursuit. And it was Bony's wish that they should remain where he could find them for a further forty eight hours at least.

At the homestead end of the causeway one of the men told him that he was urgently wanted at the office; and, arriving there, he was informed by Mortimore that the police at Wilcannia had been ringing for him that morning, as well as the preceding day. He got Sergeant Knowles.

"Ah! I've been wanting you badly, Bony," the sergeant said rapidly. "I found Clair on Dugdale's block, and, like a raw recruit, allowed Clair to best me. Anyway, I winged him, and came on him again in Dugdale's hut just as he died. He left a confession."

"Ah! Read it."

The sergeant did so, adding: "You will note that Clair calls himself Sinclair."

"Exactly. That is his name."

"You know that?"

"I've known it for some little time. Anything else?"

"Yes. I found Dugdale, later, with Clair-Sinclair's pocket-book in his hands, and when I demanded it in the name of the State he refused to hand it over, saying that Sinclair had made him promise to deliver it to some person, whose name he wouldn't tell me. We had a tussle, and for the second time I was bested. I'm getting old, Bony, and if I'm not dismissed the service I shall retire."

"Go on! What more?" asked Bony.

"Dugdale left the hut at daybreak yesterday morning. From his tracks I saw that he was making for Thurlow Lake; and, as I was a sick man, I rode to a hut on Yamdan Run and telephoned to our fellows at Thurlow Lake to apprehend Dugdale and relieve him of that wallet. I am sure, Bony, that in that wallet is something of great importance in connexion with the case. Anyway, Blair and his mate happened to be at Thurlow Lake, and they, with Dugdale—chiefly Blair on his own—bested three of our fellows. Dugdale escaped and the senior trooper there phoned to Smith, stationed at One Tree

Hut, six miles west of the Washaways. This morning the boundary rider there says that Smith did not arrest Dugdale, who arrived at sundown. Somehow Dugdale discovered Smith there, and bolted towards the Washaways, pursued by Smith.

"This morning the rider tracked them to the first creek of the Washaways, where he saw both men had simply ridden straight into the creek that was running a banker. And on the farther side of the creek, on a sort of island, was Smith, horseless and marooned, because he cannot swim. The creek being too wide for the rider to do anything, he returned to his hut for a wire well rope to get across to Smith with a lighter hemp rope.

"But, before he got back, Dugdale himself rang up Thurlow Lake from Cattle Tank Hut, ten miles this side of the Washaways, having, of course, swum his horse over the remaining creeks, to tell them of Smith's situation and urge immediate relief. It seems obvious, Bony, that Dugdale is bringing Sinclair's wallet to someone on the river—it might be someone at Barrakee; and, as all our fellows are west of the Washaways and it is impossible for me to reach Barrakee in time, you'll have to arrest him when he reaches Barrakee and secure that wallet."

Bony was silent for a little while. Then:

"I don't think it will be necessary to arrest Dugdale yet," he said. "You see, Sergeant Knowles, he is bringing that wallet to me. I expected Sinclair would send it if anything happened to him."

"Oh! Well, anyhow, Dugdale will have to be arrested for assaulting me, a police-sergeant, and resisting arrest at Thurlow Lake. Blair and McIntosh are under arrest now."

"Pardon my mentioning the matter, Sergeant," Bony cut in silkily, "but I must point out that I am the officer in charge of this case. The recent circumstances are peculiar, I know, but I do not advise, and probably shall not advise, Dugdale's arrest. And, for one or two reasons, which I shall explain later, I think it expedient that Blair and his offsider be released for the time being."

"Very well," snapped the sergeant.

"Now, please don't get angry," Bony exhorted. "Anger upsetteth judgement. The Emperor knew that, which was why he seldom indulged in the delightful emotion. I can assure you that, as far as the law is concerned, the case ends with the death of Sinclair. His confession rounds it off. Let those extraneous happenings drop; for to do so lets you out from the misfortune which has dogged you, and will save the force from the slight discredit it has incurred. You will agree, I think, that that will be the best way."

"All right, Bony. Perhaps it will," Knowles agreed, with less rancour. "Still, if the fool Dugdale had told me to whom Sinclair was sending his wallet, all this hullabaloo would not have happened, and I wouldn't be here with a splitting headache."

"Take some aspirin," Bony advised.

"Darn it! That's what Dugdale said."

"Take it, anyway. I'll ring you up later. Now I'll get you through to Thurlow Lake, when you can order Blair and Co's release."

When he left the office Bony was smiling. While not positively certain, he was almost sure that Dugdale was bringing the wallet to Mrs Thornton. Had the intended recipient been a person of lesser importance, Bony considered that the young man would not have risked so much, and would have been less hurried.

The men's lunch gong sounded, but Bony ignored it and decided to wait for Dugdale on the sunny side of the blacksmith's shop, which was close to the stockyards; and he had been there barely an hour when Dugdale, riding The Devil, came in sight over the causeway.

Bony waited till the young man was dismounting. Then, slowly, he walked over the short distance to him, and said:

"Why, Mr Dugdale, I didn't expect to see you here today! I quite thought you were settling down on Eucla."

"I have a little business to transact with Mr Thornton," Dugdale replied stiffly.

"Well, well! That is none of my affair, I suppose," Bony said easily, drawing close. "Horse appears done up. Wonder you crossed the Washaways, for I hear they are in full flood."

The two men stood against the horse, Dugdale with his back to Bony, removing the saddle. Both his hands were engaged, and both his arms were raised. Bony's hands, however, flickered with movement truly astounding. It was a superb conjuring act; for, with the lightness of butterfly wings, the half-caste's arms slid round Dugdale's body and Bony's fingers found and abstracted from one of Dugdale's inner pockets Sinclair's wallet with Sinclair's letter still inside.

"Yes, I had to swim him," Dugdale admitted.

"He must be a good horse, indeed. Alas! I am getting too old to enjoy a good gallop," Bony sighed, drawing away.

"Mr Thornton about?" Dugdale asked, when the freed horse was rolling in the sandy stockyard.

"I saw him half an hour ago. It must be lunch time. In fact, the gong has just sounded."

Bony sauntered off towards the men's quarters. Dugdale walked along to the homestead, where at the double gates Mr Thornton met him.

"Dugdale!" he exclaimed. "Why are you here? Have you brought news of Ralph?"

"Ralph! No. What has happened to Ralph?"

Chapter Thirty-Nine

'Judge Not'

"Dug, the flood has brought material disaster to many people on the river; it seems to have brought disaster of another kind to my wife and me."

The two men were seated in the station office. Mr Thornton had suddenly become aged. His mouth drooped at the corners, his hair was greyer, his eyes were full, and beneath them were small puffy swellings. Dugdale was shocked by the change in him: he felt stunned by the story of Ralph's infatuation with Nellie Wanting, which he had thought to be only a passing flirtation.

"Mrs Thornton—how does she take it?" he asked.

"I am afraid, Dug, terribly afraid. My wife has turned into a block of stone, like the block of salt which held Lot's wife. She hardly ever speaks, but the look in her eyes makes me afraid. Sometimes I think, after all these years, she is still a stranger to me."

"And Kate?" The young man's eyes were riveted on the saddened face of the squatter. There was a spice of sharpness in his voice, for at that moment Dugdale hated Ralph for preferring a black tulip to so fair a rose.

"Kate, of course, is greatly upset," Thornton said slowly. "About her, I think, I have found out a surprising thing. She seems more concerned for my wife and me than for herself, as though she grieves because of our grief and not because of the wrong she has received. I have come to think that Kate did not love Ralph as a prospective husband."

"That she feels relief at being justified in breaking the engagement?" demanded Dugdale swiftly.

"It appears that way. Matters being as they are, I am thankful for that."

"And no one has any idea where he is now?"

"That is so."

A long silence fell between them, a silence throughout which the squatter's mind wandered aimlessly, deadened to lethargy, whilst the thoughts of the younger raced at lightning speed. Smitten though he was by the calamity which had fallen on the people dearest to him, yet he could not help feeling a sense of elation that Kate was not wholeheartedly in love with the fallen Ralph, a gladness that her hurt was not so very acute, a hope newly born when hope had been dead. He was about to speak when the office door opened and admitted Bony, who, seeing them seated at the broad writing table, came over and occupied a spare chair. Without preamble, he said:

"My work here is accomplished, Mr Thornton. Never yet have I failed in a case, and this one is no exception. I came to find the murderer of King Henry. I found him. I stayed on to discover the motive actuating the murder. I have found it. But at the end, at the moment when every clue, every proof, every motive, was in my hands, I found that I had a duty to perform—a duty not to the State, not to the Law, but to a woman. I would consider myself dishonoured if I evaded that duty, much as I could wish to; for I fear that, in doing that duty, I shall both shock and grieve you. I want you to request Mrs Thornton and Miss Flinders to meet both you and Mr Dugdale and myself in a place where we can talk in private. May I suggest your sitting room?"

"My wife is ill," objected the squatter.

"She is ill because she has a millstone weighing her down," Bony announced quietly. "At least I shall remove the mill-stone."

For fully half a minute the station-owner gazed searchingly at the detective.

"I have a mind to refuse you," he said. "Tell me what you have to say, and I will tell my wife."

"Permit me to do my duty in the manner I think best."

"I cannot agree."

"I am sorry." Bony regarded Thornton a little sternly. He went on: "In case you are unaware of it, I will tell you that I am a detective-inspector of the Queensland Police. I was sent here expressly to investigate the murder of King Henry. It was I who advised the arrest of Sinclair, alias Clair, the brother of Mary Sinclair, one time your wife's cook and the mother of your adopted son, Ralph. If you refuse to allow me to speak to your wife in your presence, you will compel me to advise the arrest of Mrs Thornton."

"For God's sake, why?"

"For complicity in the murder. Come, let us go to your sitting room and hold a conference. It will be so much better for all of us, even better for me, for I should find the arrest of your wife a matter of lasting regret."

Bony met Thornton's blazing eyes with steady calmness. He saw the fierce light die out of them, fade and become dull with the tiredness of despair which no further shock could lift. A chair scraped, and Thornton got to his feet. The others rose and followed him silently from the office, through the gates, to the house veranda, to the sitting room. Bony and Dugdale remained standing while Thornton went in search of his wife and niece. A clock ticked with startling loudness, ticking away the seconds of fate.

The door opened again to admit the Little Lady. When she saw Bony her eyes showed no recognition, but surprise flickered in them for a moment at sight of Dugdale. Behind her came Kate, and into her eyes leapt a light that blinded the eyes of Dugdale's soul. The young man smiled at her, and moved forward to escort Mrs Thornton to a seat. It was Kate, however, for whom he performed this courtesy. Bony, having reached the Little Lady first, with ineffable gallantry led her to a great lounge chair.

"Mr Bonaparte wishes to speak with us all, dear," Thornton explained, seating himself near his wife. Kate sat on the other side, Dugdale stood behind them. Bony's eyes were half shut, as though he wished to conceal emotion or experienced pain. His voice reached the Little Lady faintly, as coming from a great way off. The startling scene in the office was burned into Dugdale's brain. The possibility of the Little Lady's arrest was balanced by the amazing revelation that Bony, the half-caste painter of boats, was a detective-inspector; whilst above and beyond that was Bony's statement that Ralph was not Mr Thornton's son, but the son of some woman named Sinclair, a cook.

"I fear that in order to make matters quite clear it will be necessary to go back to the year 1908," Bony was saying. "It was a mere coincidence that Mrs Thornton and Mary Sinclair gave birth to boy babies within forty eight hours of each other. The records show that the baby born to Mary Sinclair died and the one born to Mrs Thornton lived. Whether the doctor attending the two patients was aware whose baby died and whose baby lives it is impossible to discover, as the doctor is dead and his case books are destroyed.

"In any case, Mary Sinclair died shortly after Mrs Thornton's baby died, and Mrs Thornton took Mary's child, reared it, loved it, and called it Ralph Thornton. But before Mary died she confided to Mrs Thornton the name of her betrayer."

Bony saw the squatter's eyes narrow and turn upon his wife, whose face was an alabaster mask. Bony went on:

"I think, and the philosophers agree with me, that the most wonderful thing in the world is a woman's love for a baby. Mrs Thornton, saddened and heartbroken at the loss of her own child, took and cherished Mary's child; but when Mary whispered the name of her paramour, the father of her child, Mrs Thornton deliberately took to her bosom a living asp. The laws of heredity are immutable, and it is a very great pity that she did not recognize this.

"The father, moreover, was unprincipled, or perhaps proud of his paternity. We will credit him with the latter motive when he interviewed Mrs Thornton a few weeks later and demanded his child. Apparently he was refused and offered payment, which he took; but, being dissatisfied, he came again to Mrs Thornton, who again paid and eventually wrote an appealing letter to Mary Sinclair's brother, whom we knew till recently as William Clair. That letter I found in Sinclair's pocket wallet."

Dugdale's hand went convulsively to his inside pocket. For a second or two he stared into the half closed eyes of the detective-inspector, then took a stride forward:

"You have no right to that wallet," he said fiercely. "I don't know how you came by it, but it was given me by Sinclair before he died to deliver to a particular person."

"Exactly, Mr Dugdale," Bony murmured. "He gave it to you to bring to Mrs Thornton. As the contents of the wallet bore upon the case under discussion, I relieved you of it. It is fortunate indeed that Knowles, or his juniors, did not do so. I will now read Mrs Thornton's letter to William Sinclair. It is dated April 1908, and reads:

Dear Mr Sinclair,

Thank you for your letter written from White Cliffs. Your thanks for what I did for your poor sister are appreciated, as is your assurance that never will you speak of the fact that I have adopted her child or claim relationship to it. I did all I could for Mary, and now you must do all you can for me and the child.

I have paid King Henry over £20, and now he is demanding more. I have thought and thought about this menace till my head aches. What can I do? Can you do something to seal his lips and stop his demands? It would be no crime to slay a black—would it?

Ann Thornton."

"Am I to understand that King Henry was Ralph's father?" exclaimed the squatter; and, not waiting for Bony to reply, turned to the Little Lady: "Tell me, Ann, is that so?"

In reply she nodded, but kept her eyes unseeingly upon her shoe. Thornton's breath hissed between his teeth. He would have spoken, had not his wife said very softly:

"Let Mr Bonaparte go on. This is my Waterloo."

"We know how Sinclair, calling himself Clair, replied to that letter," Bony continued. "Somehow King Henry learned of Clair's determination to kill him, and fled. Clair tracked him for more than nineteen years. A report being circulated that Sinclair was dead, King Henry returned to his people. As he himself said to Mr Dugdale, he made an appointment with somebody at Barrakee—we will presume with Martha—and Sinclair, hearing of this, as we will again presume, waited in the dark for the black fellow to come down the river.

"We know, or rather the police know, that Sinclair spent many years in North Queensland and there learned the art of throwing a boomerang. In his confession, written an hour or two before his death in Mr Dugdale's hut, he describes how he missed his throw, how the boomerang returned, how they both stooped for the weapon. Sinclair got it and struck King Henry whilst the latter was still stooping forward.

"There is one point which still remains unexplained. It happened that one day a gentleman named Pincher Joe ransacked Mrs Thornton's boudoir, and among other things he stole a boomerang. Without any shadow of doubt it was the boomerang which killed King Henry, because it was made by a member of the tribe with which Sinclair sojourned. It bears the marks of the tribe on it, and it left an outline of those marks when it struck a gum-tree instead of King Henry when thrown. Either Martha was at the meeting place and handed the weapon to Mrs Thornton, or Mrs Thornton herself was present and picked it up.

"Parallel with this story, we have the parentage of Ralph and its effect upon him. Like many half-caste children—even like myself—the baby was white of skin. For years the black strain in his blood was held in abeyance by his upbringing and education; for years the pigmentation of his skin remained

252

white. But the inevitable change of colour began much earlier than the heredity of character. The cessation of college life, the return to the native bush of his father, hastened the hereditary urge, so that Ralph's reversion to ancestral blackness was accelerated.

"In no case does a half-caste rise to the status of his superior parent. In this case we have the mother possessing, as all white people possess, a veneer of what we call civilization; and the father full-blooded and wild, able to speak the white man's language, but without the mother's veneer of civilization.

"I watched the growing change in the lad, and for a long time it puzzled me. I saw the growing love of colour in his clothes, I noted how quickly his college accent dropped from him. For many years at school, and only for short periods in the bush when on holidays, the young man picked up the art of tracking with remarkable ease. You will remember how he tracked the dingo and slew it. You will remember how he caught the outlaw horse at Thurlow Lake and rode it. He took to the bush as a duck takes to water, he who most of his life was away at school.

"The lure of the bush gripped him. I could see it in his face, and I marvelled. He felt the lure and could not explain it even to himself. And then came this last, this fatal yet inevitable surrender. He fell in love with a black gin. He was betrothed to a beautiful white girl, he was heir to a great estate, yet he fell in love with a gin. Mr Dugdale reasoned with him. I discovered the affair and pleaded with the girl. She went away, persuaded by me, but the youth learned of her whereabouts and wrote passionate letters, and she, being a woman, and a poor ignorant black woman, too, could not resist.

"Blame not the boy, Little Lady. You could not wipe from his heart the lure of the bush planted by his black father, not with all your forethought, all your love. Do not blame nor cherish anger against him, Mr Thornton. Would you be happy in the city now? Would you not long for the bush? You are wholly white, but the lad was half black, half wild, half of the bush. And you, Miss Flinders, bear no rancour for the wrong done you. Crimson lips and black velvet cheeks were a greater magnet than your lily complexion and azure eyes. For countless ages his ancestors found beauty in large black eyes and black velvet cheeks.

"The boy fought his battle, the battle which could end only in his defeat. I watched and wondered. I saw a headstone in the cemetery bearing the name of Mary Sinclair. I knew Clair's name was Sinclair, from a friend in North Queensland who remembered him. And at last I saw the light. I saw clearly how Mrs Thornton's maternal desires overwhelmed her judgement, her prudence, even her morality. As I have said, she took to her bosom an asp.

"I knew what she knew. I knew that Ralph Thornton was to marry Miss Flinders, that Miss Flinders, unknowingly, would marry a half-caste Australian aboriginal. The wonder of it was that neither she nor Mr Thornton guessed. Even during the few months I have been at Barrakee, I have seen Ralph's skin slowly darkening, as my skin slowly darkened when I was his age. Five or six more years at the outside, and the colour of his skin will be as mine is.

"My duty, then, was clear. Sinclair, in his letter to Mrs Thornton, written just before he died—for even the water has not obliterated the drops of blood which I assume fell from his lips—rings clear the call of Duty. This is what it says:

Dear Mrs Thornton,

I am dying, and have but a few hours at most to live. Friends have been supplying me with tucker, but Knowles got me. If he hadn't, some other policeman would. Only yesterday I heard that your adopted son is betrothed to the Darling of the Darling, and that is not right. You must not let that be: you must not wrong a white woman. Let her be told, and then if she wishes they can marry.

You know me for a poor man, my sister for a poor working woman. Yet our people were high, and always did we keep our colour. Keep yours. Do not let your love of Mary's child blind your eyes to facts.

You are safe, Little Lady. I am about to pay the price for all you did for Mary. When I die, I die free of debt to you. And dead, I demand of you that this marriage does not take place.

Till the end,
Your obedient servant,
William Sinclair."

Bony refolded the letter and put it back in the envelope. In the same envelope he put Mrs Thornton's letter to Sinclair, and then for a while regarded her and her husband and niece with curious intensity.

Memory of a Sydney waxwork exhibition occurred to him in gazing at the Little Lady. The waxen pallor of her face, the expressionless immobility of her features, the absolute stillness of her body, caused her to resemble nothing so much as a dainty doll. What she was thinking or what she felt was hidden by a deathlike mask. Her husband, seated at her side, appeared shrunken in stature, hardly recognizable for the hale, bluff, and genial squatter of Barrakee. Kate, only Kate, retained her vividness, but down her cheeks Bony observed that now and then ran unheeded a tear.

"It is not for me, or for any man, to judge you, Mrs Thornton," he said very softly. "Only a woman could understand a woman's craving for a baby to love, a woman's determination to fight for a baby she has come to love. Throughout your actions there is, I think, only one point to censure, and that was in not telling your husband that King Henry was Ralph's father. Had you confided in him, you both would have been better able to meet the inevitable event of his return to his native wilds, whilst the betrothal doubtless would never have been permitted.

"My duty, as I saw it, is finished. I am a stickler for duty, as was that illustrious man whose name I bear. These letters are now yours. Destroy them. I shall forget their existence. The case of King Henry will end with the death of Sinclair, who has paid the price that the law would have exacted.

"As for the young man, you will never get him wholly back. The chains forged by countless nomadic ancestors are too strong. I know, for I am bound by the same chains. Probably he will tire of the gin and return to you for a few weeks, but the bush will draw him back for ever longer periods. I will send him to you this evening, after I have told him everything. Judge him not; for you cannot judge him, as I, Bony, cannot judge you."

Chapter Forty

Maternal Love

WITH QUITE startling suddenness Mrs Thornton came to life. Her eyes, flashing upward, met those of the detective, in them a blazing white light of hope and joy. Yet, if her eyes became alive, her body for a few seconds longer remained immobile. Instinctively the half-caste rose to his feet, whereupon the Little Lady rose, too, and almost ran to him.

"Bony, did I hear you say that you would send him to me presently?" she cried appealingly, placing both her hands on his shoulders and searching his face with eyes that were astoundingly brilliant.

"I did so, madam," he said gently. "This morning I discovered their camp. I shall now return to it, where I shall explain everything to the lad. I cannot promise that he will remain with you; in fact, I know he will be unable to do so, but I can promise that he will come to you this day."

And then Mrs Thornton did a very strange thing for a woman so proud, so self-contained, so strong of will. She sank on her knees and took his hands in hers whilst looking up into his red-black, downcast face.

"Oh, Bony!" she cried softly, "I am a wicked woman. I have been a wicked woman for years and years, and now when I should be scourged with scorpions you whip me with a feather. You say you cannot judge me, but I know you understand how I loved Mary's baby, how I thought ahead for it, how always my mind dwelt upon its future and my heart lay down for its little feet to tread upon. If God had only let my real baby live!"

Slowly her head fell forward on their closed hands. For a moment Bony kept still. His usually impassive features were softened to an almost beautiful expression of tenderness. Gently he raised the Little Lady to her feet, when she regarded him once more, but with eyes no longer wide and appealing, her face showing again its habitual firmness. Into her eyes came suddenly a cloudiness, and her body drooped.

"Take me to a seat—I am tired," she gasped. "Bring me a little water, please."

Her husband instantly was at her side, and almost carried her to a sofa, where Kate Flinders was arranging the cushions. A glass of water was offered, and she drank as though exceedingly thirsty.

"Sit down, please; I have something to say," she said painfully at last. "Just a moment—my heart is beating—too fast. Better presently."

It was Kate who ministered to her aunt, wetting her fingers and soothing the Little Lady's forehead, while one round arm was about her shoulders. The others one by one sat down, and after a while Mrs Thornton spoke with her eyes closed:

"I have fought many battles and won them all, but this is my Waterloo," she said haltingly. "Like the great Emperor, I have risen to great heights and tasted the joy of life; and like him, too, when the pinnacle was reached, I fell. His enemy was Man; my enemy is Nature.

"I remember as though it were yesterday when Ralph came," she went on slowly, dreamily. "My baby lay dead in the cot beside my bed. Mary's I heard crying in her room. For years, and during the waiting period especially, I dreamed of my baby, planned for him, schemed to protect him, and ensure his love. And he for whom I had planned, and dreamed, and hoped, and felt, lay dead in the tiny cot I had created myself.

"It was a warm afternoon. My husband was engaged with the carpenter making the coffin. The windows were wide open, and above the cries of the sleepy birds and the droning of the insects there came the regular chug-chug of the steam-engine. And there upon my bed, my empty bed, I writhed in the agony of my grief and the torturing pains of my body, which screamed for the feel of tiny pulling hands and gentle working lips.

"Then Martha came in to me. She told me that Mary was very still. Martha was frightened, and I made her lift me up and carry me to Mary's bedroom, where she put me down beside her.

"'Mary, are you worse?' I asked her. But she was silent. If she heard, she could not or would not speak, and while I lay on my side looking at her white rugged face the baby between us clutched my nightdress with his little hands and cried out again. And then—I don't know how it happened—I took the baby in my arms and suckled it.

"Oh, the glory of that moment, the sweetness of it! The relief from the torturing pains, the satiation of awful hunger! What kisses I showered upon the dark little head and the little pink shoulder! And, whilst thus I held Mary's baby in my arms, Mary opened her eyes and smiled at us.

"'Will you take him, Ma'am?' she whispered eagerly.

"'Oh, Mary, if only you knew how much I want him you would not ask,' I said weakly.

"'Make him yours, Ma'am! Oh, Ma'am! I am dying because of my sin. Never let him know of it, or who his father is.' For a little while she lay so still that I thought her dead, and then quite distinctly she said: 'I don't know why—perhaps it was because he was so magnificent a man that I became as putty in his hands. When he put out his arms I was compelled into them; when he touched me he lifted me off the earth. Oh, Ma'am! he is King Henry.'

"I looked at Mary with amazement. Then I looked down into the child's face and gazed long at the child's body. I saw the tender flesh was as white as my own, and I could not believe it. It was incredible, impossible; and when again I turned to Mary I saw that she was dead.

"Martha carried Mary's baby and me back to my room. I made her take the dead baby and lay it beside the dead Mary. John came, and I told him what had happened, everything but the name of the man Mary had mentioned. The doctor came, and I persuaded him to shut his eyes to the exchange, and when he signed the certificates the living baby was my own, my very own.

"Very quickly I grew strong again. I lived in paradise with the baby, whom we had christened Ralph. Three weeks, deliriously happy weeks, sped by, and then one early evening, whilst baby and I were in the garden, King Henry came and demanded the baby. He knew, and I could not deny it, that my baby had died, and that Ralph was Mary's child and his own.

"When I refused to surrender it, he said he would sell it to me for ten pounds. I went into the house and brought out the money, and paid him. A week after that he came again, saying that ten pounds was not enough. I gave him another ten pounds, and when he took it I saw in his eyes the determination to batten upon me for ever.

"For long days and longer nights my mind dwelt upon the problem of Ralph's father. It came to me that I must kill him. Then came the idea of getting Mary's brother to kill him. I had seen William Sinclair several times when he came to Barrakee to visit Mary; the last time he came was the day before Mary died, and I did not see him. I wrote to him the letter you read out, Mr Bonaparte, and three days afterwards I learned from Martha that King Henry had fled from the vengeance of William Sinclair."

The Little Lady took a few sips from the glass held against her lips by the kneeling Kate, from whose white face slow tears fell on Mrs Thornton's dress. When the Little Lady again spoke, her voice was low and tired, so low that Bony drew his chair nearer her.

"The months and years passed quickly after that, and every day I felt more secure," she went on. "With indescribable happiness I watched my baby grow and heard him lisp his first words. I used to cry for very happiness. The years were just wonderful, and as he grew up into a splendid young man I came to believe that Mary was mistaken, that she had named the wrong man, or made some mistake when her mind was clouded by the approach of death.

"And then one day I saw a man working in the garden. It was just after Martha told me that King Henry had come back to the Darling and was coming to Barrakee. Imagine my relief when I was told that the new man's name was Clair, and instantly guessed that he was Sinclair. There he was working in the garden, my protector, my son's guardian.

"King Henry came back. He sent word through Martha that he wanted to see me, that I was to meet him near the station boats after dark that evening. I made Martha go and tell Sinclair that, and he sent her back to say that I must not be there.

"But at half past eight Martha and I went and waited between the boats and the billabong. It was very dark. Sinclair joined us. He told us to get on the house side of a gum, and keep still. He was angry at our presence, and would have sent us away had not it been too late. We could hear someone coming along the riverbank.

"Indistinctly, I saw Sinclair throw the boomerang. It hit something, and I heard it fall between where he was and us. King Henry sprang upon Sinclair and bore him to the ground. Now, though Sinclair was a heavy man, King Henry was much the stronger. How it happened I don't know, but I found myself beside them as they fought on the ground, the heavy boomerang in my hands.

"In spite of the darkness I saw that King Henry had both his hands about Sinclair's throat. I saw with horror my protector's face grow ghastly and horrible. I was shocked by the knowledge that Sinclair was being killed, that when he was dead there would be no one to stand between my Ralph and his terrible father. I saw my love destroyed, my hopes, all my care, my plans.

"Upon the level of my waist I saw King Henry's white head, and with such strength as I have never felt before, I struck it with the weapon in my hands."

The tired voice suddenly ceased. A stupendous silence fell upon the room, unbroken by a breath. Then:

"It was Martha who helped Sinclair to his feet. The man fought for air and staggered, but, recovering, bent over the black fellow and felt his heart. Then he took me by the arm and, with the trembling Martha on my other side, he led us quickly to the garden gate.

"'Remember,' he said, 'whatever happens, remember that it was I who killed King Henry. You must live free to love your son. You are free now.'

"I remember the lightning. It flared as Martha and I stood before the gate. I almost ran to my room, and when there I found the boomerang still in my hands."

"It was you, then, who warned Sinclair at the Basin?" Thornton put in quietly.

"Yes. I went into the office on my way to the store that morning," Mrs Thornton said softly, her voice hardly a whisper. "I could not have Sinclair caught. He might, I considered, tell the truth at the last; but I misjudged him. Sinclair was a gentleman. I wish you—I am feeling ill. Please—please, take me—to my room. Tell Ralph—to—come quickly."

Chapter Forty-One

The Midnight Visit

THE BRILLIANT sun hung over the western sand-hills and already the air had become appreciably colder. To the east a vast sheet of water shimmered under the gentle south wind, and reflected dully the foliage of the box trees growing on the submerged flats. The flood was at its highest point and about four miles north-west of Barrakee it lapped against the foot of a steep clean hill of sand.

Midway up the hillock the wind had scooped out a wide ledge, and upon this was built a circular humpy of tobacco-bush. Smoke rose slanting northward from a small fire of boxwood, and about this fire Nellie Wanting was busy preparing the evening meal. Occasionally she stood to her slender height and gazed steadily out among the box trees, through which she knew Ralph Thornton would row the boat back from a fishing expedition.

He came presently, sitting in the stern and propelling the boat forward with one oar; and she waved a scarlet handkerchief in greeting, and showed her pearly teeth in a smile of welcome.

From the summit of the sand-hill Bony waited, hidden by a clump of tobacco-bush. He had been waiting there for an hour or more, and he waited yet while Ralph backed the boat and climbed to the ledge with a string of fish and a tin of swans' eggs in his hands. The half-caste saw the youth lay his catch beside the fire and then, turning, hold out his arms and take Nellie Wanting within them; and whilst they stood toe to toe, he slid quietly down the hillock to them.

"Bony! What do you want?" was Ralph's challenge, even before he released the girl. Instinct prompted her to hide within the whirlie, leaving the two facing each other: anger on the face of the younger, genial friendliness on that of the older.

Ralph was dressed in plain tweed trousers and blue shirt open at the neck. He wore neither boots nor hat. Even during the short time Ralph had been away from Barrakee, Bony saw how much darker had become his complexion.

"I have come to speak to you on a matter of importance to yourself," Bony said in his graceful manner. "I have been waiting for you for some time. Could not your wife provide us with a pannikin of tea whilst we talk?"

Ralph hesitated, then nodded and called to Nellie. They seated themselves near the fire, and Bony rolled himself a cigarette. Not until the cigarette was made and he was inhaling the smoke did he speak. Gently and slowly he told the story of King Henry's murder, and then revealed the motive of it. He explained with wonderful tact how Ralph was not Mrs Thornton's son, but the son of King Henry and Mary Sinclair. And when he had finished the young man sat with his face hidden upon his arms, resting upon his hunched knees.

Bony expected a wild outburst against the fate of his birth, and a feeling of remorse for having deserted the Little Lady, and for having broken his troth to Kate Flinders. When, however, Ralph did raise his head, his face was quite calm and his eyes, if a little misty, quite steady. He said:

"Then that accounts for my being here. I have been wondering why I am here. I am glad you have told me, for now that I know my mind is at rest. How does the Little Lady feel about it?"

"Badly, Ralph, badly," Bony murmured, rolling his fourth cigarette. "In spite of it all she still loves you, still wants you with her. She is expecting you. I told her she might expect you."

Again the young man's head sank to his knees. "You have told me," he said, "how when a young man you were white of skin. I suppose I shall not remain white much longer?"

"A few years at the longest, Ralph."

"A few years! Somehow I am not greatly sorry for myself. My thoughts now are of Mrs Thornton, to whom I was and am so necessary. You would think, wouldn't you, that such a love would keep a fellow back from this—this— And yet what you find here is irresistible to me."

"Of course it is," Bony agreed. "But it seems no reason why you should wholly desert Mrs Thornton."

"It is an all-sufficing reason. I could never look into the eyes of anyone at Barrakee again. I would see shame in those of my foster-father, contempt in those of Dugdale; in Katie's eyes I would find horror and loathing."

"I don't believe it," protested Bony vigorously. "Even should you find what you expect, you will see in the Little Lady's eyes only a hungry love, a mother's love. She is ill, Ralph, very ill. Won't you come back with me now?"

For a little while Ralph was silent. Then:

"No, not now. I will go to Barrakee when it is dark, when no one sees me. I want to see only my mother." And then, after another pause, he said, looking up again: "Leave us now, Bony, please. I want to think. I must think."

So it was that the detective went back to Barrakee, leaving Ralph with his face resting upon his knees. Nellie came out of the whirlie and stood near him, wanting to comfort him, yet afraid. The sun went down, and when it was almost dark he said to her:

"I'm goin' alonga Barrakee tonight. You will stay here and if by sun-up I am not back, you will take the boat and go find Pontius Pilate."

"Oh Ralphie," she murmured softly.

"You will do as I have said," he commanded, more than a hint of the buck speaking to his gin in his voice.

Nellie went into the humpy and cried noiselessly. The youth sat where he was, hour after hour, till by the stars he decided it was midnight. Then, rising he crept into the humpy, and with his hands found the sleeping Nellie. He kissed her without awaking her, and so left her, and walked down beside the floodwaters to the causeway and to Barrakee.

He was aware that Mr and Mrs Thornton occupied rooms separated by the squatter's dressing room. He knew, too, that the Little Lady's bedroom was between the dressing room and another she used as her boudoir. There was some doubt in his mind whether he would rejoin Nellie immediately for he foresaw the possibility that the woman who loved him might temporarily overcome his determination never again to resume his former status.

His mind, whilst he followed the causeway, was troubled by the old battle which he had considered lost, and well lost, in favour of Nellie's embraces. No man can forget his mother; exceptionally few look back upon their mothers with no one tender memory.

The whole of his life formed a chain of tender memories of a loving woman, whom he had cherished as his mother. He felt ungrateful, ashamed, not a little frightened; yet he knew that his severance from white people was dictated by a power which only that afternoon he recognized as the power of his ancestry. Realizing that he had brought pain and anguish to the woman who had given him her all, he blamed himself less than he blamed his fate. What he did not realize was that this midnight visit represented the last link binding him to her, that when it had been strained and broken the forces of heredity would become for ever victorious.

Noiseless as a shadow he entered the garden. He moved across the lawn and round to Mrs Thornton's rooms as lightly as a stalking cat, the inherent tracker in him enabling him unconsciously to avoid fallen leaves and obstacles the touching of which would make a sound.

He came to the boudoir door and, opening it an inch, listened. There was no sound within. Familiar with the arrangement of the furniture, he crossed silently to the bed-room door, which he found open. Still no sound reached him. As silently as he had come he crossed the Little Lady's bedroom and closed the dressing room door, whereupon he stole to the dressing table on which invariably stood a candlestick, for he knew that the electric current would have been shut off by Mr Thornton at eleven o'clock.

Having matches with him he struck one and lit the candle. He turned then towards the bed—to see no one lying upon it. Yet there was something strange about that bed, not wholly revealed by the dim candlelight. Picking up the light, he stole towards the bed, and by it stood looking down upon the sheet that was spread over a distinctly outlined form.

Even in that terrible moment, when his limbs were shocked into paralysed inactivity, Ralph felt no fear, nor any desire to cry out or run. For a full minute he stood as a statue of marble, and during that minute the world appeared to die and become a whited grave. And then, very gently, he took a corner of the sheet in his free hand and pulled it down from the face of the dead.

The candle became slightly tilted, and drop by drop the grease fell on the sheet. And drop by drop there fell on the sheet, near the grease marks, great globes of tears from his wide eyes.

He set the candle on a bracket at the head of the bed, and very slowly bent forward and touched the Little Lady's cold lips that would meet his never again. And then gently he lowered his head and pressed his lips to the granite cold brow and icy lips of the dead. Gently, soundlessly, he laid himself down beside the body, his brain numbed by the shock, his limbs strangely heavy. He felt inexpressibly tired. And there, with his head resting on a bent arm, he silently studied every beloved feature, whilst the large tears continued to fall.

There was something tremendous in that soundless grief, far more poignant than if it had been accompanied by breath-catching sobs. The lad, during those terrible minutes, saw himself exactly as God had made him, and the sight brought about the revelation of all that he had meant to the dead woman, especially when nineteen years before she had made him her own. She had given him a great maternal love, she had surrounded him with that guarding love, yet a love not potent enough to keep him safe from the power, the unseen power, of his ancestors of the bush. No power was adequate to deal with that inherent, compelling impulse.

The candle on the bed bracket burned steadily down to half its length before he moved. No man might know all that passed through his mind, wearied by the struggle of the last few months, stunned by the disclosure of his origin, shocked by the discovery that the Little Lady, his mother in all but birth, lay dead with a broken heart.

And she had sent Bony for him, and he had not come till it was too late!

He kissed her once, and after a little while kissed her again. One long look, his face saddened by tragic grief, he gave to her to whom he had belonged.

One agonized sob burst from him just before he extinguished the candle; and slowly, very slowly, he drew away from the bed which had become a bier, and passed out of the homestead of Barrakee for ever.

Chapter Forty-Two

Flood-Waters Subside

TOGETHER WITH Mr Thornton, Bony walked down the veranda steps to the garden. They walked slowly, Bony with bent head, the squatter with head held high, unashamed of the sorrow that welled from his heart and shadowed his fine face. Coming to a garden seat, the half-caste caught his companion by the sleeve and urged him to be seated.

He spoke softly, a world of sympathy in his voice, and told the story he had read from the closed dressing room door, the half-burned candle, the grease spots on the sheet, and beside them the marks of Ralph's tears ... For a while, when he ceased speaking, there was silence. Then:

"What do you intend doing regarding my wife's confession that she killed King Henry?" inquired Thornton with forced calmness.

"Nothing—nothing whatever," Bony replied. "As I have said before, I think, I am a detective, not a policeman. Sinclair willingly paid the price. The law is satisfied. The police are satisfied. Knowles will take no action against Dugdale or Blair and McIntosh. The case is finished. Besides, I would find it utterly impossible to tarnish the character of so great a woman as was the Little Lady. If she, and not the poor Empress Josephine, had been the beloved of the Emperor Napoleon, today the nations of the earth would be a peaceful and prosperous World Federation.

"You are a fortunate man in having been her husband. Remember that. It will ease your load. I myself have been fortunate in having known her. I leave Barrakee less vain, less sure of myself, a better man than when I came. Good-bye! My car is coming."

The two rose to their feet and shook hands. Thornton tried to smile and, unsuccessful, sank down on the seat. Bony looked back once when crossing the lawn, and then, seeing Kate descending the veranda steps, swept off his hat and said gravely:

"I leave your uncle on the seat yonder, Miss Flinders. He needs your consolation and sympathy—he needs your love. Presently, when this tragedy has been dimmed by time, remember that you and he have now and always the respectful regard and sympathy of—Bony."

She stood watching him pass out of the garden and climb into the car that waited to take him to the train at Bourke. At that moment she almost loved this strange being, with his understanding, gentle smile. And then, forgetting him, she ran to her uncle, and, seating herself beside him, slipped an arm about the broad shoulders, drew the greying head down to hers, and whispered:

"Uncle dear, do not grieve so much. We have lost them, but we still have sweet memories of them to cherish always."

*

It was the first Tuesday in October, and the shearing had cut out very early that morning. The company that had contracted to shear Mr Thornton's sheep was well satisfied, as it usually was with the Barrakee operations; for there was not and never had been any labour trouble. The last of the men had been paid off, the last lorry had gone with its load of men, and because the day was warm Kate and the squatter were lunching on the veranda of the homestead.

Time, the healer of all sorrow, was at work on these two whom the falling flood had left high and dry upon the hill of Eternal Hope. The girl noted with joy that the lines of grief on the rugged face of her uncle were disappearing one by one, and sometimes he laughed gently in the old amused way, thereby brightening her eyes and swelling her heart.

"We shall be hard at work for another fortnight getting the sheep settled into their summer paddocks," he was telling her.

270

"Now that the water is falling rapidly the river paddocks are becoming very dangerous, there are so many places where the sheep can get bogged. But when the work is finished, dear, we'll take a long holiday to Sydney, and a trip to New Zealand thrown in. How will that do?"

Looking into her glorious eyes, he was not surprised to see the coming and going of a shadow. It was momentary, and was followed by a gleam of happy expectation.

"Wouldn't you like that?" he asked.

"Why, of course, Uncle. It will be lovely."

Leaning across the small table he took her hands affectionately in his, saying:

"No secrets, now! You would like to go on that holiday, and yet you wouldn't. Why? You have been a rock to which I have clung, let me now be a rock to which you can cling."

He saw her eyes grow misty, and then her head drooped, and on his hand splashed a large tear.

"Do you love Frank very, very much?" he asked her softly.

A moment passed before she raised her face and regarded him with brimming eyes.

"How did you come to find out?" she whispered.

"Because the flood left me with a keener vision to see the troubles of others. Don't be downcast, Katie. I have seen the trouble lying behind your eyes, lying behind his eyes, too. We will talk of this again. Will you have afternoon tea ready at three o'clock? I have an important business visitor calling this afternoon."

"Why, of course," she agreed, smiling bravely. "I hope he will be nice."

"M'yes. Not a bad sort of a fellow. In fact, when I met him a few weeks ago, he impressed me very much. Well, I must get along to the office. There is a tremendous amount of work waiting for me."

They left the lunch table together, and arm in arm strolled to the garden gates, where he embraced her with gallant tenderness before going on to the office. There he seated himself at his table and wrote letters for an hour.

"Find out if Blair has come in, will you, Mortimore?" he said over his shoulder to the bookkeeper.

"Certainly, Mr Thornton," replied the old man, who then, taking a pith helmet from a peg, went out. The squatter smiled softly, and turning to the telephone, rang up Thurlow Lake and was answered by Mrs Watts.

"Has Dugdale left yet, Mrs Watts?" he asked.

"Yes. Oh yes! He had a cup of tea about eight o'clock," she said. "Told us he had a rough crossing of the Paroo, on account of the mud."

"What time did he leave?"

"About half past eight. Certainly not later than a quarter to nine."

"Very well. Thanks! I'll ring up Cattle Tank."

A minute later he was speaking to Flash Harry.

"Seen Mr Dugdale today, Harry?"

"I'm seeing him now, Mr Thornton. He's coming along the track from the Washaways," replied the man who only took off his hat when he went to bed.

"Then ask him to wait till I get there with the car, will you?"

"Righto!"

The station-owner put down the receiver and turned to Fred Blair, who had just come in.

"Good day, Fred. How's the Three Mile Creek?"

"Better. Only three sheep bogged," Blair reported.

"Ah! Then I suppose you'll be wanting to go for a walk-about and spend that sweep money, eh?"

The little man's blue eyes danced. "Yaas," he drawled. "But not all of it. Not by a long shot. I'm thinking of gitting married and buying a fruit farm down near Adelaide."

"A fruit farm?"

"A fruit farm. It's a sin for a man like me wot knows all about sheep bein' obliged to go in for fruit wot I don't know nothing about."

"Humph! Would your wife be prepared to live in the bush, say at Eucla Station, where Dugdale now is?"

272

"Of course," Blair said simply.

"Well, I don't know for sure, Blair, but I think Dugdale will be taking a job here that I am offering him. Only last week I saw the chairman of the Land Board and asked him if he would consent to Dugdale giving up the lease of Eucla in your favour, and he said that he would."

Blair gazed at the squatter with growing wonder in his blue eyes.

"I like you, Fred," Thornton admitted frankly. "You've stuck by me when the flood pushed me hard, and every man was urgently needed, and when you had plenty of money. I shall be seeing Dugdale this afternoon, and I will inform you about the transfer for certain this evening. I thought that you could take over Dugdale's sheep and improvements, for which I shall pay him cash. You can pay me how you like."

Blair found a speck of dust in his right eye which he removed by the simple method of drawing a bony, hairy forearm across the optic. Yet his voice was quite steady when he said:

"Excuse me bolting, but I've got to write a letter to me tart."

And Blair bolted, because he felt another speck of dust in his other eye.

At half past two the same afternoon Dugdale sat beside Thornton, whilst the car hurtled towards Barrakee over country covered with waving grasses a yard high. They had been discussing sheep and wool, when the squatter said abruptly:

"I have asked you to Barrakee to put to you a certain question, Dug. It is this. Do you love my niece?"

Although he kept his eyes on the track, Mr Thornton knew that Dugdale looked at him for one second with strained intensity. Then, very softly, came the answer:

"God alone knows how much, and for how long."

A minute passed in silence. Then, from Thornton:

"I am glad of that, Dug. You will find her waiting for you. I believe you will make her a good husband, and because of my loss I don't want to lose her altogether. Would you stay at Barrakee if I made you my partner?"

"Yes." Dugdale's voice was very low.

"Thank you," Thornton said as though the younger man were conferring a favour. "I thought, perhaps, you would be willing to give up Eucla. I could buy your stock and improvements and sell them on terms to Fred Blair. The Land Board agrees to the transfer of the lease."

"I am quite agreeable, Mr Thornton."

"Would you object greatly to calling me Father or Dad?"

"No. I've been wanting to do it for years, Dad."

And then the squatter's eyes were lifted from the track and looked into Dugdale's face with genuine affection.

*

Martha, wearing a pink blouse and sky-blue print dress, her feet unencumbered by hateful, unnatural footwear, rolled ponderously along the veranda, and set upon the small table the afternoon tea-tray. Kate Flinders smiled into the ugly yet lovable old face, and helped the gin to move the table a little way along the veranda to where the vines cast a heavy shade.

"Visitor come tree minutes ago, Missy Katie," Martha informed the Darling of the Darling. "Mine tinkit him plurry nice man. Lor—here he come!"

The huge woman rolled off towards her kitchen, and turning, Kate saw Dugdale through the vine leaves nearly running towards the veranda steps. Her heart almost stopped its beating, then raced with sledgehammer strokes.

And when he stood before her, when his eyes became accustomed to the shadows, he saw her lovely-face lit with wonder, with yearning, with love unmasked. And without a word between them, he took her in his trembling arms, and heard her sigh rapturously before his lips found hers.

Glossary

Billabong—*Inland pool*
Billy, Billycan—*Bush teapot*
Bonzer—*Splendid*
Boxed—*Mixed*
Brownie—*Bush cake, no eggs or butter*
Buck—*Aboriginal man*
Bushed—*Lost in the bush*
Clay-pan—*Hollow in clay soil, sometimes holding water*
Damper—*Bush bread*
Dingo—*Wild bush dog*
Dinkum—*Honest, proper, correct*
Galah—*Rose-breasted cockatoo*
Gin—*Aboriginal woman, lubra*
Goodo—*All right*
Humpy—*Bush hut, whirlie*
Jackeroo—*Station apprentice*
John—*Policeman*
Kirras—*Boomerang for throwing*
Kookaburra—*'Laughing jackass', bird whose cry resembles laughter*
Lubra—*Aboriginal woman, young gin*
Murrawirrie—*Boomerang for striking*
Outlaw—*Unbroken or vicious horse*
Planted—*Buried*
Plurry—*Very*
Snifter—*A drink (Alcoholic)*
Squatter—*Station owner*
Station—*Large cattle or sheep farm, ranch*
Sundowner—*Tramp*
Swag—*Bushman's roll, bundle, or pack, containing necessaries*
Tart—*Girl, sweetheart*
Tucker—*Food*
Waddy—*War-club, walking stick*
Walkabout—*To go walkabout is to go on tramp, holiday, etc.*
Whirlie—*Bush hut, humpy*
Wongium—*Throwing boomerang that returns to the Thrower*
Wowzer—*Religious fanatic, killjoy*

CPSIA information can be obtained
at www.ICGtesting.com
Printed in the USA
BVHW04s1651220418
513848BV00004B/220/P